UNJUST DESERTS

Also by Gar Alperovitz

America Beyond Capitalism: Reclaiming Our Wealth,
Our Liberty, and Our Democracy

Atomic Diplomacy: Hiroshima and Potsdam

Cold War Essays

The Decision to Use the Atomic Bomb and
the Architecture of an American Myth

Making a Place for Community
(with David Imbroscio and Thad Williamson)

Rebuilding America (with Jeff Faux)

Strategy and Program (with Staughton Lynd)

American Economic Policy (edited with Roger Skurski)

Also by Lew Daly

God and the Welfare State

UNJUST DESERTS

HOW THE RICH ARE TAKING OUR

COMMON INHERITANCE

Gar Alperovitz and Lew Daly

THE NEW PRESS

NEW YORK
LONDON

For Ben, Nate, and Cora

Requests for permission to reproduce selections
from this book should be mailed to:
Permissions Department, The New Press, 38 Greene Street,
New York, NY 10013.

Published in the United States by The New Press, New York, 2008
Distributed by W. W. Norton & Company, Inc., New York

LIBRARY OF CONGRESS CATALOGING-IN-PUBLICATION DATA

Alperovitz, Gar.
Unjust deserts : how the rich are taking our common inheritance /
Gar Alperovitz and Lew Daly.
p. cm.
Includes bibliographical references and index.
ISBN 978-1-59558-402-1 (hc.)
1. Wealth—United States. 2. Inheritance and succession—
United States. 3. Technological innovations—Economic aspects.
4. Income distribution—United States. 5. Industrial productivity—
United States. I. Daly, Lew. II. Title.
HC110.W4A47 2008
339.2'20973—dc22 2008014417

The New Press was established in 1990 as a not-for-profit alternative to the large, commercial publishing houses currently dominating the book publishing industry. The New Press operates in the public interest rather than for private gain, and is committed to publishing, in innovative ways, works of educational, cultural, and community value that are often deemed insufficiently profitable.

www.thenewpress.com

Composition by dix!
This book was set in Walbaum

Printed in the United States of America

2   4   6   8   10   9   7   5   3   1

What do you have that you did not receive? And if you received it, why do you boast as if it were not a gift?

—1 Corinthians 4:7

CONTENTS

ACKNOWLEDGMENTS

This book had its origins in a 1994 essay by Gar Alperovitz written for MIT's *Technology Review*. He would like to express special appreciation to Thad Williamson and to Sandra Hackman, then an editor of *Technology Review*, for their help in developing an early form of the book's argument, and to Ian Murray for further important contributions along the way. As always, the support of friends and colleagues has been critical. Warmest thanks for their ongoing friendship and help especially to Patricia Bauman and John Bryant; Ron Goldfarb; Seymour Hersh; Ted Howard; Marc Raskin; to my children and their partners, Kari, David, Jamie, and Joanna; and above all, to my best friend and wife, Sharon Alperovitz, for her love, her continuing and unflagging support, and for all that truly matters in life. Lew Daly wishes to thank Bill Moyers for his support, guidance, and example. He is also grateful to colleagues and friends who first listened to the ideas of this book at an early stage, especially Neil Glazer, David Callahan, and Ross Zucker—and to his wife of seventeen years, Pam Rehm, poet, mother, moral compass, and maker of ways; heartfelt thanks for all that you do. Both authors wish to express their thanks to Anne Hale Johnson for her financial and moral support at a critical time, to Richard Leone and the Century Foundation, and to Lance Lindblom and the Nathan Cummings Foundation, for timely research grants. Deepest thanks also to the many experts who gave their valuable time to read chapters in draft and to provide written comments: Kenneth Arrow, Dean Baker, Andy Clark, Richard Freeman, William Galston, Robin Hahnel, Andrew Levine, Richard R. Nelson, Martin O'Neill, Robert Pollin, and John Shea. Our appreciation also to University of Maryland colleagues who gave important feedback at an early point: Steve Elkin, Mark Lichbach, Joe Oppenheimer, and Karol Soltan—and to all those who participated in an early Century Foundation discussion of the core ideas. Special thanks to Thad Williamson for critical help on philosophical questions and ongoing feedback throughout the long gestation of this book, to Judith Lichtenberg for her review of the entire manuscript and detailed comments, to Steve Dubb for invaluable research support throughout, and to Laura Gilliam, David Ferris, and especially to Katie Nelson for research and administrative help over the course of this work.

Introduction

The Gift of the Past

Technological progress . . . has provided society with what economists call a "free lunch," that is, an increase in output that is not commensurate with the increase in effort and cost necessary to bring it about.

—Joel Mokyr, *Lever of Riches:
Technological Creativity and Economic Progress* (1990)[1]

Warren Buffett, one of the wealthiest men in the nation, is worth over $60 billion. Does he "deserve" all this money? Why? Did he work so much harder than everyone else? Did he create something so extraordinary that no one else could have created? Ask Buffett himself and he will tell you that personally he thinks that "society is responsible for a very significant percentage of what I've earned."[2] But if this is true, doesn't society deserve a very significant share of what he has received?

Buffett may not know it, but he has put his finger on one of the most explosive issues developing just beneath the surface of public awareness. In recent decades researchers working in a broad range of economic, technological, and other fields have clarified much more precisely than in the past the many ways "society" contributes to the creation of "wealth"—and, accordingly, how relatively little any one individual can be said to have earned and "deserved." Their research, in turn, raises profound moral—and ultimately political—questions that are becoming increasingly difficult to avoid.

At the heart of this revolution in understanding is a fundamental reconsideration of the extraordinary role of knowledge in economic growth—and of how ever-increasing knowledge, accumulating across the generations, is central to the creation of all wealth.

The distribution of income and wealth in the United States is more unequal today than at any time since the 1920s. The following study shares with Buffett a fundamental skepticism toward the belief that the nation's extraordinary inequalities are simply a natural outgrowth of differences in individual effort, skills, and intelligence. "We didn't rely on somebody else to build what we built," banking titan Sanford Weill tells us in a *New York Times* front-page story on the "New Gilded Age." "I think there are people," insists another executive, "who because of their uniqueness warrant whatever the market will bear."[3] The new research findings suggest that such views are profoundly wrong—but for reasons that go well beyond Buffett's general view and, indeed, beyond the understandings that until recently have been common among specialists concerned with these matters.

Often in history something dramatic is brewing in the quiet work of scholars—something the public doesn't know about or understand until much, much later. Einstein's famous $E = mc^2$ equation meant absolutely nothing to most people when it was first published in 1905—but it hit the world literally as a bombshell when atomic weapons exploded in 1945. The sophisticated mathematics Claude Shannon worked out in the 1940s laid theoretical groundwork for the digital communication that today ramifies into every corner of domestic and global life. The structure of DNA was deciphered by scientists in 1953, but the public is only now beginning to realize just how radically genetic engineering may revolutionize medicine, food production, and many other important fields.

Unjust Deserts suggests that something at least as portentous as these extraordinary developments is silently emerging among scholars studying the sources of wealth, and that once the implications are fully grasped, it too is likely to have dramatic implications—in this case for the distribution of income, wealth, and power throughout society. It suggests, moreover, that this new understanding and the steady evolution of the knowledge economy, combined with growing social and economic pain and set against a backdrop of ever-worsening inequality, are likely to contribute to potentially massive political change as the twenty-first century unfolds.

Consider the following truth: a person working today the same number of hours as a similar person in 1800—and working just as hard (and no harder)—can obviously produce many, many times the economic output. Recent estimates suggest that national output per capita has increased more than twenty fold since 1800.[4] Output *per hour worked* has increased an estimated fifteenfold since 1870 alone.[5] Consider further that the modern person on average is likely to work with no greater commitment, risk, or intelligence than his counterpart from the past.

What is the primary cause of such vast gains if individuals do not really "improve"? The answer is obviously more productivity—more output from the same level of input. And self-evidently what this means is that we are more productive *as a society*. But how does a society become more productive if individual effort and intelligence remain relatively constant? Clearly, it is largely because on the whole the scientific, technical, and cultural knowledge available to us, and the efficiency of our means of storing and retrieving this knowledge, have grown at a scale and pace that far outstrip any other factor in the nation's economic achievement. "The central phenomenon of the modern age," economic historian Joel Mokyr observes, is quite simply "that as an aggregate we know more."[6]

A half century ago, in 1957, the future Nobel Prize–winning economist Robert Solow calculated that nearly 90 percent of productivity growth in the first half of the twentieth century (from 1909 to 1949) could only be attributed to "technical change in the broadest sense."[7] The supply of labor and capital—what workers and employers contribute—appeared almost incidental to this massive technological "residual." Subsequent research inspired by Solow has continued to put a spotlight on "advances in knowledge" as the main source of growth. Another highly respected economist, William Baumol, argues that "nearly 90 percent . . . of current GDP was contributed by innovation carried out since 1870." Baumol judges that his estimate, in fact, understates the cumulative influence of past advances: even "the steam engine, the railroad, and many other inventions of an earlier era still add to today's GDP."[8]

Looked at another way, if today's high earners are typically highly educated, this is clearly not primarily because they are more intelligent or work harder, and it is not mainly because they were lucky in the "birth lottery," as some argue. Above all, they are highly educated because there is more knowledge for them to obtain and more opportunity to do so. "A college-educated engineer working today and one working 100 years ago have the same human capital," Stanford economist Paul Romer observes. But the engineer working today is far, far more productive. The reason, again, is self-evident: "He or she can take advantage of all the additional knowledge accumulated as design problems were solved during the last 100 years."[9]

Today a society's "stock of knowledge" and its "technological state" are the subject of intense discussion by scholars and policy makers. An obvious truth that emerges from their work is also clear and lies at the foundation of the following study: *All of this knowledge—the overwhelming source of all modern wealth—comes to us today through no effort of our own.* It is the generous and unearned gift of the past. In the words of Mokyr, it is a "free lunch."[10]

An obvious question arises from these facts: if most of what we have today is attributable to advances we inherit in common—what another economic historian, Nathan Rosenberg, has termed a "huge overhang of technological inheritance"[11]—why, specifically, should this gift of our collective history not more generously and broadly benefit all members of society? Once the modern understandings are fully grasped, today's distributive realities become much harder to ignore: the top 1 percent of U.S. households now receives more income than the bottom 120 million Amercans combined.[12] The richest 1 percent of households owns nearly half of all individually owned investment assets (stocks and mutual funds, financial securities, business equity, trusts, non-home real estate). The bottom 90 percent of the population owns less than 15 percent; the bottom half of the population—150 million Americans—own less than 1 percent.[13] If America's vast wealth is mainly a gift of our common past, how, specifically, can such disparities be justified?

Although a great deal of research has been done on knowledge and economic growth—and although one can find related moral reflections scattered throughout the work of many writers—very few have dealt directly with the equity issues posed by our scientific and technological knowledge inheritance. We seek to remedy this large-order gap in public understanding. We hope thereby also to contribute to shaping new policies appropriate to the era of the knowledge economy.

A fundamental implication of modern research on economic growth is that past advances contribute far more to today's economy than current activities. Following Solow, the aggregate effects of this historical process are now generally termed the technological "residual"—a word that usually means something left over or unaccounted for in an economic calculation, but that also suggests a kind of general buildup over time. It is perhaps surprising that modern economics largely ignored the central role of knowledge and technology until the mid-twentieth century. In a sense, the discovery of the residual was really the "discovery of the obvious." Philosophers, historians, and social thinkers discussed and understood the economic importance of knowledge long before economists began to take it seriously in the 1950s.

Solow is said to have "discovered" the residual because prior to his work in the 1950s economic growth was considered mainly a matter of changes in the supply of labor and capital, on the "classical" model of production reaching back to Adam Smith. Although its precise magnitude and methods of estimation are the focus of ongoing academic discussion, today the existence of a very significant technological residual is widely recognized in mainstream economics. In general, most economists now agree that a very large share of economic growth over much of the last century—one leading expert suggests roughly 80 percent—was created not by the labor and capital inputs of workers and employers, but by technological progress broadly understood.[14] And many economic historians—pointing to generation upon generation of earlier scientific, technological, and cultural development—might attribute even more of modern wealth to inherited knowledge.

In Part I of the following work we examine research in several areas that has contributed to our understanding of the various ways inherited knowledge contributes to what we have today. Chapter 1 begins with an overview of the pioneering work of Solow, Edward Denison, and Moses Abramovitz, among others. After World War II, these economists helped develop a method known as "growth accounting" to gain a better understanding of the process of growth. In examining this work, we find a new way of thinking about the role of knowledge and what it means for society. Related research by economic historians then allows us to peer deeper into the longer trajectories of development that preceded—and laid the foundations for—the modern era. Research by Mokyr, for instance, has focused attention on the eighteenth-century "industrial enlightenment" as a critical turning point that allowed the principles of isolated discoveries to be understood and then exploited in a wide range of applications. Numerous detailed historical studies have demonstrated how knowledge increased productivity and quality in industries ranging from agriculture and cloth production to steelmaking and shipbuilding. Research by Nathan Rosenberg, David Noble, and other scholars has illuminated how government and other agencies have facilitated the transfer of technological innovation to real-world economic applications. Such work has been supplemented by still broader cultural studies that trace the growth of knowledge back to the evolution of basic cognitive tools such as alphabets, writing, mathematics, and scientific method.

In the remaining chapters of Part I the focus shifts to the work of scholars in other fields concerned with the evolution and growth of knowledge and the process of invention. A wide range of psychological, cultural, and historical studies converges with the technical work on the residual to create a broader understanding of the central role of knowledge in economic growth. The conception outlined in chapter 2, for instance, is complex and dynamic: briefly, the development of knowledge does not simply involve learning one thing and then another about how the world works. The process is neither simple nor linear, but cumulative and highly networked across society. It depends upon layered historical change and on how the social networks that produce unexpected creative insights evolve, steadily becoming more methodical in how they share and preserve what they learn. Nobel laureate Douglass North characterizes cumulative knowledge as the "scaffolding" of economic growth. Many, many contributions taken together over time, science historian Derek de Solla Price notes, form an "intellectual edifice" reaching from "primitive foundations . . . to the upper limits of the growing research front of knowledge."[15] Furthermore, the intellectual edifice itself does not simply float in thin air. *How* knowledge is passed on—by what methods it accumulates across generations to become a general inheritance—has also been the subject of deep study.

Chapter 2 also reports on research in cognitive psychology that explores the processes, devices, and systems that allow knowledge to expand across communities and to be passed on and built up through time. Merlin Donald's work, for instance, demonstrates the myriad ways a society's growing stock of knowledge increasingly "leverages" human intelligence itself. The fact is, only limited prosperity was possible until scientific and technical knowledge began to accumulate "outside of biological memory," as Donald describes it— in books, journals, libraries, and now databases. Since the seventeenth century the growth in these "symbolic storage devices" has exploded. Before 1650 there were fewer than ten scientific journals published in the West. By the mid-twentieth century, some fifty thousand scientific journals had been founded; approximately 6 million scientific papers had been published during the previous three centuries. In 2000, college and university libraries in the United States held over 900 million items.[16] Add to this the transmission and circulation of knowledge facilitated by public library systems, universities, and now the Internet, and the central importance of specific ways to communicate—and then to transmit knowledge from one generation to another—becomes obvious.

In chapter 3 we explore the history of invention and technological change, a field of scholarship that came to the fore after World War I. Historians of technology were among the first to apply Darwinian perspectives to human developments. What stands out here is their powerful challenge to conventional "heroic" views of technology in which progress is defined as a sequence of extraordinary contributions by "great men" (occasionally "great women") and their "great inventions." In contrast to this popular view, historians of technology have carefully delineated the incremental and cumulative realities of how most technologies actually develop. In general, a specific field of knowledge builds up slowly through diverse contributions over time until—at a particular moment when enough has been established—the next so-called "breakthrough" becomes all but inevitable.

Often many intelligent people reach the same point at virtually the same time, for the simple reason that they all are working from the same developing information and research base. The next step commonly becomes obvious (or if not obvious, very likely to be taken within a few months or years). We tend to give credit to the person who gets there first—or rather, who gets the first public attention, since often the "real" first person is not as good at public relations as the one who jumps to the front of the line and claims credit. Thus we remember Alexander Graham Bell as the inventor of the telephone even though, among others, Elisha Gray and Antonio Meucci got there at the same time or even before him. Less important than who got the credit, from our point of view, is the simple fact that most "breakthroughs" occur not so much because one "genius" makes an extraordinary contribution, but because of the longer historical unfolding of knowledge.

Collective knowledge is also often created by public efforts, the subject of chapter 4. Many of the advances that propelled our high-tech economy in the early 1990s grew directly out of research programs and technical systems financed and often collaboratively developed by the federal government. The Internet, to take the most obvious example, began as a government defense project, the ARPANET, in the early 1960s. Up through the 1980s there was little private investment or interest in developing computer networks. Today's vast software industry also rests on a foundation of computer language and operating hardware developed in large part with public support. The Bill Gateses of the world—the media heroes of today's "New Economy"—might still be working with vacuum tubes and punch cards were it not for critical research and technology programs created or financed by the federal government after World War II. Other illustrations from the modern era range from jet airplanes and radar to the financing of basic research undergirding many pharmaceutical industry advances. Nor is this simply a recent phenomenon. The Morrill Act of 1862 provided support for an agricultural college in each state, and in 1887 the Hatch Act institutionalized government funding for the agricultural research that helped make the American farmer the most productive in the world.

Taken together, the various perspectives explored in Part I document the quietly emerging new understanding of the centrality of our technological inheritance—and the breadth and depth of the "huge overhang" of knowledge created by hundreds of previous generations. This perspective, in turn, forces a confrontation with profound questions concerning the concept of inheritance itself. In Part II we ask: What is the *moral significance* of our technological inheritance? If so much of what we have is largely the product of knowledge that comes to us as the free gift of the past, who, precisely, deserves to benefit from it, and in what proportions, and why?

To clarify and then to attempt to answer this question, Part II traces certain developments in the history of philosophy and social thought, along with related contemporary explorations that converge with new understandings of the technological residual. One important and rich intellectual line age begins with the distinction between "earned" and "unearned" income. Today the basic distinction can be found in attacks on welfare cheats who refuse to work to earn their keep, as well as in calls even by Republican senators to tax the "windfall" or largely "unearned" profits of oil companies occasioned by the Iraq war and hurricane Katrina. An obvious question is the extent to which the distinction between "earned" and "unearned" might apply to that which comes to us as the free (hence unearned) gift of the past—the wealth that is generated by inherited technological capabilities and advances in knowledge, and by the culture, institutions, and infrastructure enjoyed by those born later rather than earlier in the development of society.

The concept of unearned income, chapter 5 shows, first came into clear focus during the era of rapidly rising land values caused by grain shortages in early nineteenth-century England. The underlying theory held that wealth derived *simply* from owning land was illegitimate because no individual truly "earned" such wealth. Land values—and especially explosively high values—were largely the product of "external" factors such as fertility, location, and population pressures. The huge profits (unearned "rents," in the technical language of economics) made when there were food shortages or other resource constraints were viewed as particularly egregious. David Ricardo's influential theory of "differential rent," along with religious perspectives reaching back to the Book of Genesis, played a central role in sharpening a critical point of ongoing importance.

John Stuart Mill, among others, developed the distinction between "earned" and "unearned" in the middle decades of the nineteenth century and applied it to other forms of "external wealth," or what he called "wealth created by circumstances." Mill's approach fed into a growing sense of the importance of societal "inputs" that produce economic gains beyond what can be ascribed to one person working alone in nature without benefit of civilization's many contributions. Here a second element of what appears, historically, as a slowly evolving understanding also becomes clear: if "contribution" is important in determining rewards, then it is also clear, Mill and others urged, that since society at large makes major contributions to economic achievement, it too has "earned" and deserves a share of what has been created. Mill believed strongly in personal contribution and rewards, but he also held that, in principle, wealth "created by circumstances" should be reclaimed for social purposes.

Chapter 6 carries the story forward by exploring a third element in the argument that builds upon judgments such as those offered by Ricardo and Mill. A number of writers in the United States and Britain accepted the distinction between earned and unearned gains, as well as the understanding that society as a whole contributes in numerous ways to economic growth. What they added, first, was an enriching of the notion of societal contribution, and second—and more important—a very general understanding that what society contributes is not simply "contemporary" in nature. Rather, it was emphasized that society's contribution must be understood as broadly historical as well. In short, what society contributes is both immediate and active, and also, at the same time, the product of a long buildup and accumulation of past contributions.

The American republican writer Thomas Paine was among the first to articulate a societal theory of wealth in this broader sense. Paine argued that everything "beyond what a man's own hands produce" was a gift that came to him simply by living in society, and hence "he owes on every principle of justice, of gratitude, and of civilization, a part of that accumulation back again to society from whence the whole came."[17] Another American reformer, Henry George, subsequently focused on urban land rather than the agricultural land at the heart of Ricardo's concern. George challenged what he called "the unearned increment" that is created when population growth and other societal factors increase land values. In Britain, J.A. Hobson argued that the portion of unearned value created by the industrial system was much larger than that which accrued to landowners, and that it should be treated in a similar (if not more radical and comprehensive) fashion. In a similar vein, Hobson's early-twentieth-century contemporary Leonard Trelawny Hobhouse declared that the "prosperous business man" should consider "what single step he could have taken" without the "sum of intelligence which civilization has placed at his disposal . . ."[18] Political figures on both sides of the Atlantic also took up such themes, among them Winston Churchill and both Theodore and Franklin Roosevelt.

Chapter 7, the culmination of Part II, reports on a very broad and eclectic group of modern writers—including a small galaxy of Nobel laureates—who, taken together, can be seen to define a developing line of thought that both builds on the earlier thinkers and converges with economic work on the residual. The distinction between earned and unearned gains remains central to most of these thinkers. So too does the notion that societal contributions are important (and need to be recognized and rewarded). The understanding that societal contributions are both contemporary and historical is also widely accepted. What is new and significant here is the further clarification that by far the most important element in all this is the *knowledge* that society contributes over time.

Among the diverse group of thinkers whose contributions are reviewed in chapter 7 are the iconoclastic American economist Thorstein Veblen and Fabian socialists such as G.D.H. Cole, on the left, and founding members of the conservative "Chicago School" of economics, such as Frank Knight, along with contemporary figures like Judge Richard Posner, on the right. The latter, for instance, reminds conservatives and others that the "long life, spacious liberties, and extensive property of the average American citizen are the creation not of that American alone but of society. . . ."[19] The late Herbert Simon, one of the many Nobel laureates whose ideas are canvassed in the chapter, judged that if "we are very generous with ourselves, I suppose we might claim that we 'earned' as much as one fifth of [our income]."[20]

The emerging logic sketched in chapter 7 is straightforward: if a very great deal of what we have today derives from inheritance, this portion of wealth (in the words of the political philosopher Brian Barry) "fall[s] outside any special claims based on the present generation's having done something to deserve [it] . . ."[21] After reading Edward Denison's pioneering work on growth accounting, Robert Dahl, one of America's leading political scientists, put it this way: "It is immediately obvious that little growth in the American economy can be attributed to the actions of particular individuals"—and went on to suggest that if so, logically "the control and ownership of the economy rightfully belongs to 'society.' " Dahl also suggested that "changes in the way the economy is likely to be perceived in the future would almost certainly help to make distributive issues more salient."[22] This judgment points to what is perhaps the most intriguing of the issues presented by the modern knowledge economy—namely, how real-world changes in the economy itself can often create new understandings in theory and even in politics. As the knowledge economy evolves and its collective and cumulative nature becomes increasingly obvious, these changes, chapter 7 argues, are likely to give rise to new debates about distributive realities, including new questions about what is earned and what is unearned, and who deserves what, and why.

The work ends with a consideration of political and economic issues raised by the foundational analysis presented in parts 1 and 2. The conclusion first briefly explores a range of new policy directions that extend the theoretical ideas into real-world practice. The ultimate "trump card" against all forms of redistributive justice is the so-called trade-off between equity and efficiency—the idea that any effort to alter market distributions through tax policy, labor policy, or other strategies must inevitably harm the economy and make everyone worse off. In particular, it is held that incentives and efficiency will be destroyed if we do not allow people to keep what the market gives them. A growing body of research challenges trade-off theory and in important ways shows the opposite often to be true. Thus, for instance, America's longest and most expansive period of modern economic growth—the post–World War II boom—was a time when marginal tax rates reached 91 percent and corporate taxes were a far larger share of federal revenues.

The conclusion also briefly reviews promising new policy ideas—in particular, so-called asset-based approaches and strategies related to what is now increasingly termed "the Commons."[23] Such strategies go well beyond tax-and-spend redistribution, and many do not pose conventional efficiency problems. Who "owns" the stock of a company, for instance, commonly has very little to do with the efficiency of its investments. Equitable changes in the ownership of productive assets are accordingly an area of special interest from the inheritance perspective of this work. Another obvious area of interest involves education and publicly funded research. One question is how to recapture portions of the wealth generated by collective knowledge and transmitted—passed on—by collectively built educational systems. Policies here range from equalizing educational opportunities to taxing the many implicit "knowledge rents" received by the private beneficiaries of technological inheritance. Such strategies, however, are only a small part of a growing body of new policy work on economic alternatives. Broadly, it is clear, both in terms of policy alternatives and economic concerns, that there are no fundamental reasons why the implications of the new understandings of the sources of modern prosperity in our commonly inherited knowledge cannot be openly faced, debated, and acted upon.

The momentum for a new moral approach, and for new efforts to promote more equitable distributions, is clearly growing in American society. It is being driven in part by economic and social pain; in part by the extravagant inequalities suggested by the lives of the very rich; and in part by the malfeasance of corporate elites and the lobbying scandals created by powerful economic interests. Set against this troubling backdrop, our expanding inheritance of technological and other knowledge is the elephant in the room—too obvious to ignore, yet too powerful to simply push to the side. It forces us to confront fundamental issues of deservingness—what philosophers call "just deserts." If most of what we have comes to us from those who came before, we quite literally owe it to ourselves to consider how we as a society wish to use and divide this great and generous gift of the past. When and as we do, we believe Americans are increasingly likely to demand answers to the question of why, specifically, any one person should receive more than any other from the gift of the past—from the large share of current wealth that no one living creates.

PART I

The Fruits of Knowledge

The present state of the nations is the result of the accumulation of all the discoveries, inventions, improvements, perfections and exertions of all generations which have lived before us.

—Friedrich List, *National System of Political Economy* (1841)[1]

1

Knowledge and Economic Growth

When one looks behind the rather unrevealing economic aggregates, one finds a stream of technological changes representing the applications of new inventions and new knowledge—and contributing, when applied, to further learning, discovery, and invention.

—Simon Kuznets, "Two Centuries of Economic Growth:
Reflections on U.S. Experience" (1977)[1]

Postmodern skepticism has taught us to be wary of grand narratives and "objective" claims. Modern economic growth, however, may be the one area where such skepticism simply does not apply. "Until at least the seventeenth century," William Baumol and colleagues remind us, "all of human history entailed an unending struggle with starvation."[2] The last two centuries, however, have experienced economic changes that have raised incomes and improved the living standards of a very significant portion of the world's population. It is against the backdrop of perpetual struggle for subsistence that growth has taken center stage in academia and public policy, with very un-economic talk of "miracles" and "manna" regularly intruding in the densest mathematical presentations. The basic trends in the United States are these[3]:

- The output of the American economy has grown exponentially since independence. Adjusted for inflation, U.S. gross domestic product (GDP) at the end of the twentieth century was nearly ten times larger than it was in 1940, more than a hundred times larger than it was in 1865, and more than a thousand times larger than it was in 1800. GDP has now surpassed $13 trillion. Cargill revenues alone in 2005 were substantially larger than the GDP of the entire country in 1850.[4] In the early nineteenth century the U.S. economy was smaller than the economies of England, France, and Germany. By World War I it was comparable to all three combined. By century's end the U.S. economy was larger than *all* European economies taken together.[5]

- Labor productivity, the central factor in the kind of economic growth the United States has experienced, has increased dramatically throughout our history. Between 1870 and 1913 the average annual growth of output per hour worked was approximately 1.92 percent. Between 1913 and 1950 it was 2.48 percent and between 1950 and 1973 it was 2.77 percent. After slowing down between 1973 and 1990 (1.41 percent), productivity growth resumed; between 1996 and 2005, annual productivity growth averaged 2.84 percent.[6] As noted in the introduction, the long trend is extraordinary: output for each hour worked increased an estimated fifteenfold since 1870.[7]

- One of the most commonly cited measures of economic prosperity, real per capita GDP—the amount of economic output per person, in constant dollars—has risen more than sevenfold since the beginning of the twentieth century and more than twentyfold since the beginning of the nineteenth century. Per capita income in 2006 was more than $42,000—the equivalent of almost $170,000 for every family of four.[8]

- The growth miracle of the last two centuries is not simply one of rising output, productivity, and incomes. Accompanying the larger changes there has been what Richard Easterlin calls a "mortality revolution." Average life expectancy in 1850 was thirty-eight years. In 2004 it was just under seventy-eight years.[9] Economic historian David Landes once opened his popular Economics 10 lecture class at Harvard University by asking students to turn to their neighbors and consider the fact that "if it were not for the Industrial Revolution, two out of every three of you would not be alive."[10]

Early in the nineteenth century John Stuart Mill suggested an illuminating distinction—relatively novel at the time—concerning the sources of economic change. Growth, he said, is the result of increasing either the "elements" of production, classically defined as "Labour, Capital, and Land," or the "productiveness" of these elements.[11] Economists Paul David and the late Moses Abramovitz have observed that the first and second hundred years of U.S. economic history can be broadly distinguished in these general terms: from the late nineteenth century forward, America's economy moved from a largely "extensive" to an "increasingly intensive" mode of growth. The latter term, "intensive," reflects advances in the productive quality of economic inputs rather than their sheer accumulation. Such quality improvements, in turn, depend "upon the acquisition and exploitation of technological and organizational knowledge."[12] Take the example of agriculture: adding more men, each working with one horse and one plow, can add more land to agricultural production. This *extends* production but does not change or improve its method—hence the term "extensive" growth. In the modern era, the tractor is substituted for the horse, and new forms of plowing are brought in as well. The use of sophisticated fertilizers and insecticides increases the productivity of these factors, intensifying what is done to, and what is produced on, the very same land: hence "intensive" growth.

There is no doubt that part of increased productivity derives from the addition of more capital per worker, or what is known as "capital deepening" (e.g. substituting a modern tractor for the farmer's horse-drawn plow). But capital deepening cannot account for most of the exponential growth of the modern period. Instead, what economists now realize is that other, less tangible factors play the central role in growth. At the heart of this understanding is knowledge— and more particularly, how the cumulative growth of knowledge gives us more and more power, as a society, to harness labor and resources for productive ends. Changes in farm technology leading from the horse and plow to the extremely sophisticated technical marvel of the modern (and often gigantic) agricultural tractor, for instance, involved advances in metallurgy and blade design as well as such entirely new fields as the development of the internal combustion engine. Similarly, modern fertilizers are the product of decades of research and experimentation.

What is particularly important about knowledge is that it allows us to create more output with less input. In traditional "extensive" growth sooner or later we run into less fertile land and it becomes less economical to continue adding men, horses, and plows. This is the classic law of diminishing returns. However, if new knowledge keeps developing— creating *new* fertilizers or *new* ways to genetically improve seeds—it is possible to keep going, perhaps forever, in effect "repealing" the law.

Although it seems remarkable today, the role of knowledge and technological change had no firm place in classical economic theory. Adam Smith's *Wealth of Nations*, for instance, works from a "cost of production" theory of value based on factor prices of land, labor, and capital. Although the first chapter of this famous work devotes several paragraphs to machinery, it is discussed largely as a beneficial secondary product of the division of labor, the main feature in his theory of development. The great political economists of the nineteenth century largely followed Smith in subordinating technology to other factors. David Ricardo, for example, focused mainly on trade restrictions, which he argued ran counter to British "comparative advantage" by propping up domestic agriculture (and landlords) at the expense of manufacturing.[13] Thomas Malthus thought growth would be undermined by population increases. These early economists were certainly aware of the benefits of technology, but the general view of the period was that economic expansion was essentially a natural phenomenon driven by population growth and thrift. In the main they did not focus on a type of growth generated by technological changes that made land, labor, and capital more productive (thus generating more output at much lower costs).

There were occasional exceptions to this rule. In 1921 American economist Thorstein Veblen observed that while it had been "usual, and indeed it still is not unusual, to speak of three coordinate 'factors of production': land, labor, and capital . . . this threefold plan of coordinate factors in production is notable for what it omits. It assigns no productive effect to the industrial arts . . . the indispensable foundation of all productive industry . . ."[14] Veblen thought the "unexampled advance of technology during the past one hundred and fifty years ha[d] . . . begun to call attention to its omission from the threefold plan of productive factors handed down from that earlier time," but the fact is writers like Veblen made almost no dent in the traditional argument.[15]

The first major break in conventional thinking on growth came about because of the work of an eminent conservative economist. Joseph Schumpeter's 1911 book *Theory of Economic Development* drew attention to factors that implicitly clarified the difference between extensive and intensive development—above all, the importance of entrepreneurial creativity and innovation in the development of new products and services. Economic development "in our sense," Schumpeter wrote, "is a distinct phenomenon, entirely foreign to what may be observed in the circular flow or in the tendency towards equilibrium." What matters most, he urged, was what he called "creative destruction" as *new* goods, *new* ideas, and *new* methods of production are introduced.[16]

Schumpeter emphasized a discontinuous form of innovation largely propelled by entrepreneurial competition. However, as growth expert Richard Nelson notes, he was "curiously uninterested" in where the basic ideas for innovations come from. "It is no part of [the entrepreneur's] function to 'find' or 'create' new possibilities," Schumpeter wrote. "They are always present, abundantly accumulated by all sorts of people."[17] Modern scholars accept the contribution of entrepreneurship and competition to economic growth. Increasingly, however, the deeper, more continuous "cultural" sources of knowledge-based innovation, acknowledged but not pursued by Schumpeter, have come into focus—including education systems, fundamental research, learning and cognition, beliefs and values, institutional "path-dependency," and other "external" factors such as war and military influence.

Serious theoretical work and empirical research on such issues took on new urgency in the 1950s when a group of younger economists, even less impressed with the "law of diminishing returns" than Schumpeter, began to study the basis of "real economic growth." These economists took their cue from the fact that a major recession did not follow World War II, as many had predicted. The economic recovery fueled by wartime spending continued through the 1940s, gaining a life of its own—and ongoing economic growth became a central focus of intense and concentrated study for perhaps the first time in history.

A critical turning point occurred in 1957 when Robert Solow, at the time a young MIT economist, published a brief but powerful article that applied a new growth model he had developed to measure the relative importance of various factors of production (labor, capital, etc.) as sources of economic growth.[18] To grasp the significance of Solow's contribution in this area—which earned him the Nobel Prize in 1987—it is important to understand that modern growth is commonly examined through what is known as a "production function," where what is produced (output) is viewed as a combination of many contributing inputs. Each specific combination of inputs is known as a production "technique," and firms generally choose different combinations of techniques based on factor prices to minimize total production costs.[19] By the mid-1950s the development of detailed aggregate data on inputs and outputs by such institutions as the National Bureau of Economic Research (NBER) made it possible for economists to examine the shares in national income of different inputs over time and to compare these to the outputs achieved over time.[20] What Solow found was that most productivity growth was due to a "shift" in the production function, a change in output *beyond what could be explained by changes in the supply of conventional inputs such as labor and capital.* The remainder, now commonly called the "Solow residual," essentially represents an increase in the efficiency—not an increase in the amount—of the combined conventional inputs.[21]

Specifically, the data indicated that between 1909 and 1949 the amount of output per hour worked roughly doubled in the United States. Solow calculated that nearly seven eighths of this increase, or about 88 percent, was attributable to the residual factor of "technical change." Strikingly, only one eighth could be attributed to increases in the supply of capi-

tal. Translated into monetary terms, Solow found that output
per hour (measured in 1939 dollars) increased from about 62
cents to $1.27 between 1909 and 1949, and only about 8 cents
of this increase could be attributed to increases in the amount
of capital. The remainder, or about 57 cents out of a total of
65 cents, came from increased productivity due to technical
change.[22] The diminished role of capital accumulation in
Solow's numbers attracted a very great deal of attention
among economists, because capital accumulation had been tra-
ditionally believed to "play a large part in explaining growth,
not just a small supporting role," as Moses Abramovitz later
wrote.[23] Clearly, a new type of progress was at work—one
based on improving the quality and efficiency of conventional
inputs. Such contributions to growth, Solow suggested, could
only be ascribed to "technical progress in the broadest sense."[24]

"Here was the answer to the question of why the economy
kept climbing the mountain of diminishing returns," economic journalist David Warsh has recently observed. "It had
relatively little to do with labor or capital accumulation.
'Technical progress,' the growth of knowledge as measured
by the Residual, was creating the new wealth."[25] Not surprisingly, Solow's breakthrough work inspired a stream of research that attempted to refine and explain his central
finding. Moses Abramovitz and Paul David, for instance, have
calculated that between 1929 and 1966 the share of productivity increase not attributable to increases in the supply of
capital was 84 percent.[26] Productivity growth, they find, was
mainly caused by changes in "labor quality," which in turn
were due to education and technological innovation. Another
respected economist, John Kendrick, has estimated that increases in "total factor productivity" (which became a common term for the Solow residual) accounted for more than 85
percent of real national income growth between 1929 and
1948, and more than 70 percent between 1948 and 1969.[27]

In his Brookings Institution series *Trends in American*

Economic Growth, Edward Denison also concluded that "advancing knowledge of ways to produce at low cost is the biggest and most basic reason for the persistent long-term growth of output per unit of input."[28] Denison developed a method of "growth accounting" that more precisely differentiated multiple aspects of the technological residual. For the period 1929–1982 he calculated that 72 percent of nonresidential business growth was not attributable to increases in the supply of labor and capital. He then estimated that "incorporation into the productive process of advances in knowledge of how to produce at low cost" accounted for 34 percent of such growth. Another 16 percent came from increases in the amount of education per worker. (Increases in the supply of capital accounted for a mere 12 percent.)[29] The impact of knowledge in its broader aspects was even more obvious when viewed in terms of labor productivity growth (output growth "per person employed"). Denison calculated that 64 percent of this growth derived from advances in knowledge—with another 30 percent traceable to increases in the amount of education per worker.[30]

The beginning of a productivity slowdown during the 1970s puzzled economists and raised questions concerning its causes. Evidence in support of technological theories of growth was nonetheless overwhelming, and the robust productivity gains that reemerged in the mid-1990s gave further support to technological understandings.[31] Today, few economists would dispute Simon Kuznets's overall judgment that "[increases] in the stock of useful knowledge and the extension of its application" are the "essence" of modern prosperity—and further, that intangible, knowledge-based increases in the quality and productive capabilities of goods and services are the keys to this transformation.[32]

A recent study of the period between World War I and World War II by Alexander Field illuminates the significance of knowledge-based growth and the technological residual.

Field discovered that total factor productivity rose faster in the 1930s, during the Great Depression, than in any other subsequent period in the twentieth century. Moreover, total factor productivity was responsible for "virtually all of the growth in output and output per hour between 1929 and 1941." Labor input remained basically unchanged and net capital stocks were actually lower in 1941 than they had been in 1929, yet output and productivity were both more than 30 percent higher.[33]

A reflection of the impact of knowledge-based growth can also be seen in the shift in capital stocks from tangible to intangible forms—from fixed physical inputs (such as raw materials, machinery, and physical labor) to knowledge embodied in new technologies or new human capacities, or both. Kendrick has estimated that by the early 1990s intangible capital (including education, training, health and safety improvements, and mobility) was on its way to surpassing conventional capital (structures, equipment, natural resources, etc.) as a share of the total U.S. capital stock.[34] Related to this, New York University professor Baruch Lev calculates that the ratio between market value and "balance sheet equity" (roughly the cost of replacing the entirety of a company's physical assets and inventory) was just under 1-to-1 in the late 1970s. By 2001, however, the ratio was 6-to-1.[35] Physical items were far less important and valuable than the knowledge content they embodied. The new pattern, in which much of the firm's value is intangible, has been dubbed the "weightless economy" by some writers.[36] Microsoft, with $1.9 billion in physical assets, yet nearly $330 billion in market capitalization in the year 2000, is illustrative.[37] Though semi-monopoly control of some markets accounts for a significant share of this difference, much of Microsoft's value is obviously due to the scientific and technological knowledge it controls. Bill Gates's huge fortune derives not from the sale of hardware but above all from the sale of the extremely valuable form of distilled productive knowledge we today call software.

The dawn of a vast historical domain of growth beyond the formal reach of traditional economic models—and outside of traditional ideas about the supply of land, labor, and capital—has haunted the economics profession and humbled its predictive power in several areas. The problem for economists is that technical progress appears in many ways to be exogenous to the economy—often arising broadly from society rather than narrowly from conventional economic behavior. Reflecting this uncomfortable fact, the residual of "technical progress in the broadest sense" has been variously termed "manna from heaven" and the "measure of our ignorance." Economic historian David Landes has wryly noted, however, that "science abhors residuals,"[38] and significant disputes concerning the size of the residual, how to measure its different specific dimensions, and what could be responsible for such large economic effects emerged after Solow's discovery.[39]

There is clearly room in all of this for considerable debate over statistics, methods, and analytical refinements. Importantly, some economists have attempted to demonstrate that technological progress is largely an embodied function of capital accumulation, not the result of broader forces.[40] Some theories of endogenous growth try to go "inside the black box" of technological change by assessing knowledge production within firms largely as a function of the input of business research or training investments.[41] Others focus on individual investments in education. These and other attempts to explain knowledge-based growth as a process driven by market incentives and investments may help us improve certain features of the economy, such as patent law, research subsidies, incentive policies, and training efforts. However, endogenous approaches inevitably need to be viewed alongside broader approaches that explain the ways private innovation feeds off sources of knowledge that clearly have much deeper roots in culture and history.[42]

In an important 1994 article, Solow acknowledged that while there was "some truth" to the concern that a residual approach to technological progress "leaves the main factor in economic growth unexplained," the new growth models face a "very hard problem" due to "irreducibly exogenous" elements in any research process. Growth in knowledge, Solow noted, has a logic that may be "orthogonal to the economic logic"—that is, immaterial or unrelated to many of the traditional factors related to investments, incentives, and the like. Indeed the work of historians and sociologists, he suggested, may be just as important as any economic model for understanding how and why economies grow.[43] More generally, it is obvious that private investment on its own cannot begin to account for the vast scientific advances of the modern era that contribute to economic growth—or, for instance, to the development of research and educational institutions that help create and convey knowledge of importance to economic growth.

At any point in time markets and incentives are certainly important drivers both of invention and of the risk-taking that moves research into the production process. From the perspective of the current study, however, the point of interest is that even those who stress market actors and investments agree that increases in knowledge (whether endogenous or not) are of central importance. And the larger truth that advances in knowledge are the main reason growth has so radically increased human well-being in the last two centuries, is, of course, all but self-evident to a wide range of other scholars—especially economic historians. Their research takes us well beyond what narrower economic studies and mathematical models can assess, dependent as they are on the kinds of proximate statistics that only crudely capture the process and impact of expanding human knowledge and, in any case, are only available for the modern era. In his book *The Gifts of Athena*, one of the leaders in the field, Joel Mokyr, bluntly observes, indeed, that the inherent relationship between the development of knowledge and economic performance is "obvious if not trite."[44] What must be explained is not the central importance of knowledge, but rather *how* knowledge "grows" in a society and how it leverages economic advance.

For Mokyr, the critical turning point is what he calls the "Industrial Enlightenment," which began in the seventeenth century and prepared the way for the better-known Industrial Revolution. It did so in two fundamental ways, Mokyr shows: first, by establishing a powerful new faith in the possibility and desirability of using knowledge for human progress; and second, by establishing common methods and standards for discovering, sharing, and applying knowledge of the physical world.[45] Although prior to the seventeenth century innovative developments generated by craftsmen, practical inventors, and experiments often increased production significantly, usually it was not clear *why* the innovations worked as they did. The scientific laws explaining new developments were simply not known and hence could not be systematically applied in other situations. In the Middle Ages, for example, more efficient waterwheel designs created through trial-and-error experimentation helped generate more power from the same amount of water flow. However, the new designs did not lead to further breakthroughs beyond this narrow application because no one understood the laws of hydraulics. Similarly, Edward Jenner discovered vaccination in 1796, but he did not understand why it worked, and widespread vaccination had to wait another century. Fertilizer has been used since antiquity, but farmers for most of history did not know that nitrogen was a critical element; nor did they know how to introduce it into the soil. Once nitrogen was understood by scientists, chemists could develop synthetic fertilizers. Mokyr emphasizes the importance of the radical shift that occurred between pre- and post-scientific culture: with the rise of scientific method it became possible to formulate and measure the underlying forces and principles that made technologies effective, thereby creating a common knowledge base for further improvements and innovations beyond one narrow application. The result was an expanding feedback process between practical inventions and scientific knowledge, greatly extending the range of technological problem-solving and accelerating the pace of change. The classic example is the steam engine, close observation of which by Sadi Carnot and others in the early nineteenth century laid the basis for the science of thermodynamics, which in turn helped open the way to internal combustion engines, refrigeration, and many other technologies.[46]

That it is "obvious if not trite" that knowledge is central to economic growth also becomes clear in studies of some of the major developments in mathematics and science. We often do not appreciate the role of basic mathematical tools and systems at the heart of virtually all modern technological development. Algebra is perhaps the most fundamental of such tools. The simplest branch of mathematics, arithmetic, is limited to using numbers and operations (addition, subtraction, multiplication, etc.). The ancient abacus was the greatest tool in this realm. But algebra took things to another level by introducing the substitution of symbols for numbers, greatly expanding the range of mathematical operations and reasoning. The term "algebra" comes from the Arabic word *al-jabr*, taken from the title of a book written by the Persian Muslim mathematician Al-Khwarizmi in the year 820. But long before this, as far back as 2000 B.C., the ancient Babylonians began using primitive algebraic methods to find unknown values and simplify arithmetical operations. Algebra made it possible to formulate general mathematical laws, the basis for the development of modern mathematical equations. It would be extremely difficult to calculate unknowns and complicated functional relationships between quantities or values without algebra. Indeed, without the powers of abstraction introduced by algebra, mathematics might never have evolved beyond a system of counting. Technological development would have remained a trial-and-error process dominated by uncertainty.[47]

Another example is geometry. The basic laws of geometry can be traced to discoveries by Greek mathematicians like Pythagoras and Euclid more than two thousand years ago. From this grew the axiomatic method and the first deductive proofs, in addition to practical tools for measuring length, angles, areas, and volumes. Architecture, civil engineering, navigation, aviation, astronomy, and many areas of physics (especially wave physics and, most importantly, the theory of relativity) are the modern progeny of these methods and tools. In fact, the first evidence of geometry (literally, "earth measuring") goes back to 3000 B.C. In the cities of ancient India streets were laid out at perfect right angles, and advanced brick technology, utilizing size ratios for optimal bonding, was already well established.[48]

Many other fundamental tools of modern scientific and technological knowledge are refinements of earlier discoveries and developments. Newton's work on the laws of physics dates from the late seventeenth century. The periodic table, at the heart of all work in chemistry, reaches back to the 1869 chart developed by Russian scientist Dmitri Mendeleyev. Movable type dates to the middle of the eleventh century in China. The invention of the Gutenberg printing press dates to 1440. All of these—and literally thousands of other specific contributions in mathematics, physics, chemistry, metallurgy, agronomy, navigation, biology, astronomy, and many other fields—contribute to the flow of information, knowledge, theory, and ultimately technologies that we draw upon today in the modern economy.[49]

The central role of long-term technological development is also obvious when specific areas of industrial change are studied. For instance, new knowledge in the form of a series of inventions—especially the flying shuttle, the spinning jenny, the spinning frame, and the power loom (along with numerous on-the-job contributions by craftsmen)—made Britain, once a net importer of cloth, the undisputed leader in worldwide textile production. As late as 1770 British factory production had been only two to three times as fast as hand weaving and spinning in India. By 1820, however, Britain could produce sixteen times as much cloth for the same labor effort,[50] and by 1850 Britain was responsible for more than 50 percent of worldwide commercial textile production.[51] Between 1800 and 1850 textile production increased by a factor of seven, while the price of textiles fell by three quarters relative to other goods.[52]

Modern iron and steel production—upon which all modern industry and transportation depend—evolved from many advances across two centuries, including the development of the coke blast furnace, the rolling (puddling) process for creating bar iron, and the Bessemer steel process. The coke blast furnace, developed in 1709, employed a new technique for smelting iron ore that was far more efficient and cheaper than the previously used charcoal method. These improvements helped increase iron-ore production more than thirty-fold between 1740 and 1835. Then, between 1783 and 1785, a technique for puddling and rolling was developed so that coke used to forge iron could also be used for the production of refined (i.e., malleable or shapeable) bar iron. Patented in 1855, the Bessemer steelmaking process (converting molten pig iron by using blown air to remove impurities by oxidation) generated massive productivity gains during the Gilded Age. By the late 1860s, the price of steel rails began to drop sharply; between 1867 and 1878 the price per long ton fell 400 percent, from $167 to $42.[53]

In agriculture—the very heart of the U.S. economy for much of the nineteenth century—the basic tasks of producing wheat and other grains were initially done by hand with the help of crude implements like the wooden plow and the forged-iron scythe. Plowing, planting, and harvesting (reaping, threshing, and winnowing) one acre of wheat took an estimated fifty-four labor-hours of work in 1829. By 1895, innovations reduced this figure to less than three hours.[54] Sulky-style and gang plows, with better-designed, more durable blades (made of cast iron and, later, steel), replaced the centuries-old one-furrow walk-behind plow, and steam and gas engines replaced animals to power the plow. Labor time for plowing was reduced from 6.67 hours per acre in 1829 to roughly one hour in 1895. Even more important were the mechanical reapers and threshers used to cut the crop and then separate the grain from the straw. Such innovations reduced harvesting man-hours by a factor of more than forty: harvesting one acre of wheat took approximately forty-three man-hours in 1829 but merely one hour in 1895.[55]

Collective advances do not come to us from the scientist and the engineer, the craftsman and the technician acting alone. Each, of course, has been supported by a vast number of other members of society at every stage of development. The miner and the farmer, the carpenter and the cleaning lady, the cook and the nurse and the ditchdigger as well—all contribute to establishing the conditions (especially time free from other obligations!) required to create and pass on productive knowledge.

Research on the basic and undeniable relationship of knowledge to economic growth, and detailed studies of the "residual" of a wide range of specific historical and industrial developments and of the productivity gains generated by technological innovation, have presented challenges that begin with economics but inevitably force us to consider questions of far broader societal importance. One of the most critical and obvious is the issue of distribution—how the "fruits of knowledge," as it were, are allocated to different groups and individuals in society as income and wealth. Conventionally, economists link what each factor of production (labor, capital, etc.) receives to what is called "marginal productivity" (a term that refers to the specific contribution each makes to a product or service). But as Nobel laureate George Akerlof observes, modern studies of growth and innovation make it obvious that "our marginal products are not ours alone"—meaning that what any one of us today *is able to contribute* is largely the result of a long, long historical process: the fruits of current labor and current savings "are due almost entirely to the cumulative process of learning that has taken us from stone age poverty to twenty-first century affluence." Accordingly, "our current standard of living," Akerlof adds, is clearly something we "owe" to the past.[56]

Such a judgment has far-reaching implications. Consider carefully William Baumol's estimate that nearly 90 percent of current U.S. GDP "was contributed by innovation carried out since 1870."[57] The implication of such an understanding is that our national output in any given year has much more to do with inherited productive capacity—the fruit of long-run technological change and other innovation—than with current contributions. Our inheritance, especially of what Abramovitz and David term "intangible, knowledge-intensive forms of wealth"—*not what "we" do today*—is chiefly responsible for the bulk of economic output at any given point in time.[58]

Even more striking, as time goes on the significance of contemporary contributions compared with those of the past regularly shifts increasingly toward the past: with only very rare exceptions, what each "new" year of effort adds becomes smaller and smaller, year by year, *relative to what the ever lengthening past has already contributed.* The denominator of this fraction (i.e., the contributions of the past) grows continuously through time, while the numerator (current contributions) is only what one year brings. The remarkable result is that we (today) contribute relatively less and less as time goes on, but obtain more and more. Most of what we produce is generated—*increasingly*—by what we inherit, not by what we add to the inheritance.

Understanding the overarching historical trend also has potentially important political implications. If "technological innovations . . . constitute the major permissive source of modern economic growth," as Kuznets wrote, it follows that bargaining between capital and labor—and arguments about which contributes more—is of reduced significance to many distributive questions.[59] Dividing the economic pie by even a rough approximation of contributions and rewards—as many other bargaining situations also attempt to do—also becomes extremely difficult when we understand the centrality of historical knowledge-based contributions to growth. Who or what generates growth—in any morally relevant sense—is, to say the least, a much more complicated question.

All of this, Daniel Bell has suggested, requires a new "knowledge theory of value"—especially as we move deeper into the era of high technology through computerization, the Internet, cybernetics, and cutting-edge fields such as gene therapy and nanotechnology.[60] One way to grasp what is at stake is to return to a point made at the very outset. We noted that a person today working the same number of hours as a similar person in 1870—and working just as hard (and no harder)—will produce perhaps fifteen times as much economic output.[61] It is clear that the contemporary person can hardly be said to have "earned" his much greater productivity. It is instead what Mokyr calls a "free lunch," an inheritance from the past. Consider further that if we project forward the past century's rate of growth, a person working a hundred years from now may be able to produce—and potentially receive as "income"—up to seven times today's average income.[62] By far the greatest part of this gain will also come to this person as a free gift of the past—the gift of the new knowledge created, passed on, and inherited from our own time forward. She and her descendants, in fact, will inevitably contribute less, relative to the huge and now expanded contribution of the past, than we contribute today. The obvious question, again, is simply this: to what degree is it meaningful to say that this person will have "earned" all that may come her way? These and other realities to which we now turn suggest that the quiet revolution in our understanding of how wealth is created is likely to have ramifications that may be difficult to contain behind the ivy-covered walls of academe from which it came.

2

Deep Knowledge and External Memory

The late twentieth century has witnessed an explosion in [our] ability to store knowledge in our culture rather than in our brains.

—Jack Cohen and Ian Stewart, *The Collapse of Chaos: Discovering Simplicity in a Complex World* (1994)[1]

Social knowledge, defined as the union of all pieces of individual knowledge, has expanded.

—Joel Mokyr, "The Intellectual Origins of Modern Economic Growth" (2005)[2]

It is important to understand just how deep, subtle, and far-reaching the modern understanding of "knowledge" has become—and why a profound discussion of its significance is now under way not only among economists and economic historians, but among cultural theorists, psychologists, and many other scholars. The emerging perspective emphasizes historical evolution and the ways in which the specific social interactions that produce creative breakthroughs occur (or do not occur). It is not simply learning one thing and then another about how the world works, nor is it mainly the process of one person adding a contribution to that of another and putting together a new combination or "aggregate." Rather, knowledge broadly understood emerges as a social product *greater* than the sum of specific contributions—the cumulative *union* of a vast array of insights and information in an interconnected and interdependent process of knowledge growth, of "knowing more" as a society.

Today's "open source" software offers us a glimpse of how this works, as hundreds and even thousands of minds working in diverse settings refine and reconfigure complex programs—in turn spurring others to do the same, and then others and still others again—in the process creating unexpected new forms. Nor do such interactions always take place at one moment in time or in a given period. Often certain creative breakthroughs can only take place after others have occurred—and sometimes there are long gaps in the developmental process because key interactions have not yet occurred and their contribution has not yet passed into the network of larger discourse and creativity.

This way of thinking about knowledge inevitably brings us to the question of how communication takes place—and the nature of the infrastructure of networks and "transmission belts," social and technical, needed to nurture the processes that produce what Nobel laureate Douglass North calls the "cumulative learning of a society."[3] Imagine, for instance, how difficult it would have been for scientists to communicate with each other had the printing press never been developed. Or the telephone and telegraph. Or the Internet. We take all these for granted and have a general sense that they help facilitate the flow of research, insights, and dialogue involved in the creation of knowledge. What we rarely consider is that such technical and symbolic capacities are not simply important; they are essential: without them certain things *cannot* happen.

We also rarely face the obvious fact that the fruits of the interactions and creations—including the transmission belts—also come to us free from the past, another huge element in our common inheritance.

•   •   •

A useful way to begin to grasp the deeper issues is to consider how the world of genetic research began—and why it did *not* develop for decades. The economic impact of what was to follow, needless to say, was to be extraordinary: had modern scientists not been able to perfect and build upon techniques of genetic selection, one recent estimate suggests that virtually all the arable land of the planet might today be required to feed the world's population.[4] The opening chapter of the story is well known: Gregor Mendel's 1860s experimentation with plants in his monastery garden led to the development of the genetic theory of inheritance of physical traits—a concept very different from the then dominant "pangenesis" understanding. The latter, associated with Lamarck, included the idea that characteristics and influences acquired during an organism's lifetime could be physically transmitted to subsequent generations. Even Darwin did not deny this at the time.[5] The striking fact, however, is that Mendel's genetic theory was ignored for more than a generation after his death. One reason was competition with popular but erroneous theories of the day. A more fundamental reason, however, involved Mendel's use of statistics, a method then in its infancy. It was only when a shift in what might be called "a way of knowing" had been achieved—when botanists and biologists had come to take for granted the use of statistical methods—that Mendel was rediscovered in the early twentieth century and became the "father of modern genetics."[6] Statistical ways of grasping large-order problems, and then developing practical applications, now inform many, many disciplines. But the point to note is that only after these ideas had become widespread, had been communicated and refined and digested, could their power reach beyond a tiny handful of people.

A similar story of how shifts in one realm of knowledge— *if communicated and distributed and refined*—can impact a broad range of fields involves another important branch of mathematics: calculus. This type of mathematical thinking, invented in the late seventeenth century amid the earliest stages of modern technological development (e.g., the development of steam power), began with the basic algebraic idea that symbolic systems, operated logically, were capable of expressing complex physical truths. The new language provided the symbolic tools for measuring material relationships and predicting outcomes under changing conditions. Everything from the theory of electrical circuits to most modern engineering achievements to the theory of relativity became possible only with the widespread understanding and use of calculus after the late seventeenth century. In turn, such developments impacted chemistry, physics, metallurgy, and many other fields of knowledge critical to modern economic growth.

We noted earlier that, relative to what is inherited from the past, each new generation contributes less and less to its own success. In contrast, the impact of certain kinds of knowledge, like innovations in mathematics, only grows over time. The scientific fields made possible by calculus generate more and more knowledge applicable to human problems as time goes on and as new specialized fields regularly continue to emerge. Calculus contributed a great deal to technological developments of the nineteenth and twentieth centuries. Today what it contributes includes everything that it made possible in the past—plus the many theoretical and practical refinements that mathematicians, physicists, and engineers continue, year by year, decade by decade, to develop out of existing knowledge in an ever-expanding process of improvement.

In the modern era, the development of quantum mechanics, the mathematical system used to measure and predict atomic-level behavior, has had a similar extraordinary impact. The classical Newtonian understanding of matter is based on such principles as the separability of objects in space and time, linear causality, continuity of motion, and the conservation of energy. With quantum mechanics, a whole new world of material behaviors—the energy exchanges between atoms—became accessible. This created a new starting point from which to think about how to harness or apply materials for technological uses. For instance, without quantum mechanics, semiconductors could not be used in microelectronics or in countless other technologies, such as magnetic resonance imaging or lasers. One recent estimate is that as much as 30 percent of GNP is based on inventions made possible by quantum mechanics, and many scientists believe that the current range of technologies is just the beginning.[7]

A truly profound change not only in ways of knowing but in what we even judge knowledge to be is commonly traced back to Francis Bacon's remarkable late works *The New Organon* and *The New Atlantis*, published in the 1620s. In a bold departure from medieval methods, Bacon divorced knowledge from its metaphysical moorings—above all theological doctrine. In *The New Organon* he argued that the church-approved science of his day was an "unhealthy mingling of divine and human," creating not only a "fanciful philosophy" but also a "heretical religion."[8] The most important contribution of Baconian philosophy was the inductive method. It is hard to imagine the weight of tradition and religious authority Bacon and his followers were throwing off in rejecting the deductive or "aprioristic" method of medieval science, which "leaps from sense and particulars to the most general axioms." Indeed, the deepest root of all science today is the opposite assumption, boldly outlined in *The New Organon*. Any "axioms" that may exist, Bacon argued, cannot be formed by "argumentation" but only by "duly and properly" abstracting from empirical observation.[9] Here, quite literally, are the beginnings of modern empiricism and ex-

perimental method, which freed knowledge from the theological and metaphysical constraints that had stunted its
growth in the medieval era.

Following Bacon, the inductive method took on ever-
expanding importance—but again, note carefully, only when
the new ideas were communicated, refined, and made more
widely available. As this happened, scientific and technical
authors began to develop a deeper sense of the collective and
highly distributed nature of knowledge—which in turn laid
the groundwork for ongoing collective efforts in general.
In contrast with the isolated "hermetic" approach of occult
philosophers and alchemists, Baconian knowledge was now
to be systematically shared and preserved so that it could be
tested and improved. Precisely *how* the sharing and commu-
nicating in this and other cases occurred is a question that
brings into focus the institutional and cultural developments that permit and nurture widespread and ongoing
interaction—and convey the knowledge produced by such interactions to those next in line . . . for them in turn to build
upon and pass on again.

Modern scholars have mapped many complex features of the
means by which ideas are communicated, added to, and then
transmitted and inherited in a culture. A leading figure is the
cognitive psychologist Merlin Donald, whose work can also
serve as an introduction to the key findings of this emerging
field of inquiry.[10] Donald is particularly interested in what
happens to the ways humans learn and think as knowledge
evolves, culturally and institutionally, over time. The capacity
of any one individual mind is very limited, he points out—
unless and until there are specific ways for it to interact with
other minds in the processing of complex data and ideas.
Such interaction ultimately depends upon "externalizing"
knowledge in durable symbolic forms that allow diverse indi-

viduals to have access to what others know. This requires
what he calls an "external memory system," a network of institutions, storage media, and symbolic codes and practices
that effectively preserves knowledge outside of individual
minds, allowing it to accumulate.[11]

Donald's theory involves three basic cognitive stages, each
of which corresponds to a particular type of memory system.
The lower threshold in this scheme is the "episodic" memory
of apes. Apes have the ability to mentally store perceptions of
specific episodes, but they have great difficulty accessing these
perceptions for intentional use without specific environmental cues. For example, apes will sometimes throw projectiles
during a fight, but—unlike young children—they commonly
do not rehearse throwing on their own to improve their skill
without external stimulation of one kind or another. Likewise, for the most part they do not build many things on their
own outside of a structured training environment, and their
range of expressive output is extremely narrow compared to
their intelligence in processing environmental input. Naming
responses and other communicative behaviors are possible,
but usually only under clinical training conditions governed
by direct stimuli. As Donald writes, this is a "reactive" type of
memory system, "designed to react to real-world situations as
they occur, [but] not to represent or reflect on them."[12] The result is a creature that, in its natural environment, normally
can improve its skills or its living situation only within very
narrow limits.[13]

The first development beyond the episodic memory of
higher mammals involves the skills used in mimicking and
copying, or "mimesis." This major step is associated with the
appearance of *Homo erectus* beginning about 1.5 million
years ago and lasting over a million years. Modeling power—
the ability to replicate what others do—is arguably the most
basic thought-skill. It is an arrangement in which a mem-

ory system enables rehearsal and refinement of movement for an intended effect. To mimic is to learn. In humans this cognitive capacity gave rise to individuals who hunted and systematically made tools, cooked food, and transmitted skills—acquired knowledge—across generations. From group hunting methods, to seasonal camp-making, to various social bonding behaviors and communicative techniques, mimesis was the key to developing regular, sustainable patterns of social coordination and decision-making, in many ways the precursor to all human cultures.[14]

Oral language, a critical breakthrough, emerged from within mimetic culture and allowed early human communication to develop in the direction of narrative, the first (and still prevalent) form of integrated thought. Oral culture also made possible effective representation and the first forms of integrated symbolism. The organized storytelling, ritualized recitation, mnemonic devices, and shamanic roles characteristic of pre-literate oral cultures were significant attempts to assist biological memory in the transmission and storage of knowledge—but, as Donald stresses, this system was still dependent on "biological working memory."[15] Isolated from other storage systems, biological memory is very limited, even when it possesses language and language cues that aid memory.

The move beyond biological memory and the ritualized storytelling and recitations of oral culture opened the way to a truly historic development: the externalization of memory. The transition to external memory can be dated from the emergence of graphic invention around forty thousand years ago, when engraved bones and carved ivory bearing animal representations proliferated in parts of Africa, Europe, and Asia. The most important symbolic shift, however, occurred with the development of formal writing systems in Mesopotamia in the fourth and third millennia B.C.—first appearing in cuneiform records of transactions. This profound transition, from pictorial representation to increasingly abstract script, is encapsulated in the Rosetta Stone, discovered by Napoleon in 1799 and dating back to 200 B.C.[16]

The development of graphical representation systems that could be displayed to others and expanded and refined was accompanied by two new dimensions of knowledge management that truly distinguish the modern human mind and its cognitive architecture from early human and primate predecessors. The first dimension is external symbolic storage, or external memory. The second is theoretic culture—the mind's integration at higher and higher levels of abstraction—which, Donald emphasizes, *could not be achieved until storage systems and external capacities had been developed.* The fundamental change occurred with the expansion of symbolic access across multiple external memory devices, beginning with written records and extending to today's vast library holdings and electronic databases. The invention of books, journals, libraries, databases, and other systems of symbolic storage constitutes an essential (and still expanding) "hardware" change in humanity's cognitive architecture. Essentially, knowledge now accumulates outside of the limits of biological memory. Although it developed only very slowly at first due to technological limitations, external memory grew exponentially with the invention of the printing press. It is ubiquitous today, and the vast portion of what humans know now resides in it.[17] Jacques Turgot's profound understanding more than two centuries ago is still a good description of external memory and how it works:

> The conventional signs of language and writing, affording men the means of assuring the possession of their ideas and of communicating them to others, have fashioned of all detailed forms of knowledge a common treasury, which one generation transmits to another like a legacy that is ever being augmented with the discoveries of each century.[18]

These changes in external memory—in our ways of assuring the ongoing possession and communication of knowledge—opened the way to further developments. Spoken words and images, Donald points out, can rarely be displayed in detail long enough in biological memory to allow extended reflection on them. But the external memory field that arose with writing, literacy, and symbolic storage devices provides us with sharp and *durable* representations. In turn, the ability to retrieve organized data at will (and at any time) from symbolic devices allows thinking to become a formal activity subject to standards of revision. As Donald writes, "each time the brain carries out an operation in concert with the external symbolic storage system"—say, by reading a book—"it becomes part of a network. Its memory structure is temporarily altered; and the locus of cognitive control changes."[19] This "results in a scaffolded cultural process that can accumulate and improve over time"—changing not only what we know in the present but how we think across generations.[20]

Books and other devices literally offload the knowledge-storage process from biological memory, allowing more knowledge to accumulate. At the same time external memory allows a freeing-up of cognitive resources for more refined or intentional operations, culminating in formal theory. External memory systems also radically reduce the "path dependency" of information and stories transmitted orally from one individual to another. "The path to a good idea can now criss-cross individual learning histories," Andy Clark adds, "so that one agent's local minima becomes another's potent building block."[21] By allowing knowledge to migrate between individuals more readily and through time, such "culturally scaffolded" reason is able to make connections that are simply unavailable to isolated individual memory. Donald shows how this has changed "the long-standing relationship of consciousness to its representations":

We can arrange ideas in the external memory field, where they can be examined and subjected to classification, comparison, and experimentation, just as physical objects can in a laboratory. . . . Thus the display characteristics of the external memory field expand the range of mental operations available to a conscious mind.[22]

The launch of the *Philosophical Transactions* of the Royal Society in 1665 marked an important stage in the longer-term shift. As Derek de Solla Price observes, the publication was conceived at the outset as a mechanism for "monitoring and digesting" publications and letters "that now were too much for one man to cope with in his daily reading and correspondence."[23] How to efficiently draw upon others' knowledge was the critical question. Today's search engine technology is a logical extension of the information-sharing principles behind the *Philosophical Transactions*.

The capacity of the external memory system is analogous to that of a computer network. The physical capabilities of a single computer (memory, processing speed, disk space, etc.) are extremely limited compared to those same capabilities when linked to a network. The human mind likewise has internal capacities—biological memory—but these are very limited in the absence of external systems that can hold knowledge and organize, preserve, and transmit it for repeated use. As Donald forcefully concludes, our "ideas are under constant revision by a collective process that often masquerades as a highly personal quest." Indeed,

Although we may have the feeling that we do our cognitive work in isolation, we do our most important intellectual work as connected members of cultural networks. . . . Individual minds are thus integrated into a corporate cognitive process, in which single individuals rarely play an indispensable role.[24]

While the devices in our work and home environments—maps, documents, books, periodicals, media products, computers connected to the Internet, etc.—seem quite ordinary in a highly literate society, the larger cultural system they create is an extraordinary historical achievement. External memory, as Douglass North observes, "extends our range of 'easy' decision making over space and time in ways that would be beyond the comprehension of our ancestors."[25]

Understanding how external memory helps build and convey knowledge—and then allows us, now, to think in ways that would not otherwise be possible—brings another fundamental dimension of technological inheritance into clear focus: there could be neither the widespread passing on of the many, many contributions that make up what we call knowledge, nor external memory itself, without the development of, *and our inheritance of*, very specific institutions that make this possible. Imagine a world in which there were simply no mechanisms with which to communicate and transmit scientific discoveries back and forth, and on through time. In such a world, there could be no common science or technology beyond tiny isolated circles. The platform of understanding upon which the next steps of development inevitably occur would not exist except in fragmentary, isolated realms. Even basic understandings—arithmetic, statistics, calculus, geometry—would not be passed on in ways that inform the next generation's potential contributions to human knowledge.

Before 1650 there were fewer than ten scientific journals published in the West.[26] Indeed, the publishing of discoveries was often actively avoided at the time. Newton's fundamental theorem of calculus looked like this when he first disclosed it (in a famous 1677 letter to Leibniz): "6accdae13eff7i319n4o4 qrr4s8t12ux." It was written as an anagram—possibly useful at the time for preventing ideas from being stolen, but completely counterproductive for practical purposes.[27] The occult culture of knowledge that still influenced even Newton and Leibniz was supplanted by a new "patrimonial" ethos of knowledge creation, transmission, and inheritance during the eighteenth century. A far-ranging network of institutions, professional bodies, publications, and patronage was created that served as the practical bridge between the scientific revolution of the seventeenth century and the industrial revolution that began in the late eighteenth century. By 1800 more than five hundred scientific journals had been launched, along with more than one hundred scientific societies.[28] The pace of expansion grew exponentially. As we noted earlier, by the mid-twentieth century some fifty thousand scientific journals added approximately 6 million scientific papers to the output of the previous two centuries.[29] In 2001 alone 650,000 papers in the physical, social, and behavioral sciences were published worldwide.[30] Derek de Solla Price, the founder of the field of scientometrics (the measuring of scientific development and growth) famously calculated the "exponential" growth rate of science in the modern era. As measured by scientific personnel, publications, and research spending, since the mid-eighteenth century the "size" of science essentially doubled every ten to fifteen years—far outstripping both population growth and economic expansion over the same period.[31] As a result, with each year and each decade there was literally more knowledge available *per person*—helping to accelerate the process of discovery and the development of new productive capabilities.

Other fundamental elements of the external memory system that help transmit knowledge include classification and cataloging technologies. From the earliest tax records, to the great royal libraries, to today's interconnected digital databases, a vast reference system has evolved to help us organize data and store and transmit information. As the amount of knowledge has expanded relative to the population, efficiency of access has also become a paramount need. It is one thing for other people's knowledge to be stored in a small number of books largely restricted to tiny groups of scholars. It is quite another to have vast numbers of books and journals organized and publicly available in libraries. College and university libraries in the United States held over 900 million items in the year 2000. In that year alone there were an estimated 194 million circulation transactions. In a typical week roughly 1.6 million reference transactions occurred.[32] The intentional, highly organized process of circulating knowledge is further supplemented by newspapers, radio, television, and other information-carrying media.

Educational institutions, particularly colleges and universities, bring enormous additional gains to the distribution, transmission, and inheritance of knowledge. The common use of canonical materials, teaching methods, curricula, and advisement systems in higher education facilitates knowledge acquisition and helps refine the learning process both for practical purposes and for transmission from one generation to the next. Modern economic growth in fact coincides with the spread of formal education. Only two centuries ago, there were barely more than a hundred universities in the entire Western world. In 2005–2006 the United States alone had just under 6,500 institutions of higher learning with a combined enrollment of approximately 18 million students.[33] In addition to the human capital (and related productivity gains) colleges and universities create by educating students and transmitting to them the received understandings of previous generations, such institutions create massive intellectual capital through dedicated research programs. Even today, in an age of growing corporate research investment, industry funds less than 20 percent of basic research and directly carries out even less, subcontracting a substantial amount to universities and other institutions.[34]

In 1930 the combined budgets of all accredited higher-education institutions in the U.S. totaled approximately $632

million. By 1958 the figure was nearly $5.7 billion, and dur
ing the 2003–2004 school year total spending by private and
public higher educational institutions in the United States
reached $826 billion.[35] Pioneering research by Fritz Machlup
in the early 1960s on knowledge production documented inti-
mately related developments. The number of scientists and
engineers in the United States, he showed, rose from 42,000
in 1900 to 691,000 in 1954, and the number of post-secondary
faculty rose fourfold over the same period. Since then the
numbers have grown exponentially: in 2001 there were
3,413,000 employed scientists and engineers, and in 2004
there were 1.6 million post-secondary teachers.[36]

Higher education, in turn, depends upon a system of
preparatory institutions—especially universal public education through high school, established in every state by 1940.
Even on its own terms public schooling had a significant impact: Harvard economists Lawrence Katz and Claudia Goldin
estimate that between 1915 and 1999, increasing educational
attainment in the U.S. labor force (public schooling most importantly) was responsible for at least 23 percent of national
productivity gains, or about 10 percent of the total growth in
gross domestic product.[37] Across the twentieth century, in
other words, a significant fraction of the total national wealth
was created not by firms and individuals (the basic units of
entitlement or reward in our society), but by school systems—
the collective institutional achievement of millions of tax-
payers, teachers, students, school boards, parent associations,
etc. Again, this is to say nothing of what they contribute in
preparing young people for college. In the absence of elemen-
tary and secondary public education, the entire edifice of
basic science and other forms of specialized knowledge and
expertise obtained, added to, and passed on in colleges and
universities would either collapse or would have to be developed (and paid for) in radically new public or private forms.

•　•　•

One way to grasp the significance of expanding knowledge is to consider a basic point well understood by historians and cognitive theorists: although we certainly "know more" than our ancestors, we cannot say that we are "smarter" then they were—more intelligent in any fundamental sense.[38] The average high-tech millionaire today has essentially the same basic mental capacities as his predecessors who made tools to improve the clan's living conditions at the very dawn of civilization. The real difference is that he (and his colleagues and rivals) *inherited much, much more knowledge, and much better-organized knowledge, with which to work.* And he also inherited (along with the rest of us) the cultural and technical transmission belts that carried the fruits of past creative developments to him through time. All the historically-evolved institutions of knowledge development and transmission—including those of printing, of information accumulation and storage, of electronic distribution, of education, research, and dissemination—all of this comes to each new generation as an inheritance from society.

The free-market economist Friedrich von Hayek shares an affinity with this view in his judgment that economic growth depends only "in part on the accumulation of capital"—that it is the growth and diffusion of knowledge that allows us to "use our resources more effectively and for new purposes." Hayek emphasized that knowledge contributes to growth as part of the broader cultural development of "tools of communication" evolving over centuries. "These tools which man has evolved consist in a large measure of forms of conduct which he habitually follows without knowing why; they consist of what we call 'traditions' and 'institutions.' " There also "always takes place an equally important accumulation of tools in this wider sense, of tested and generally adopted ways of doing things." Hayek's large-order generalization is apt: "civilization begins when the individual in the pursuit of

his ends can make use of more knowledge than he has himself acquired."[39]

In his 2005 presidential address to the Economic History
Association, Joel Mokyr put the central point this way: "The
short answer as to why the West is so much richer today than
it was two centuries ago is that collectively, these societies
'know' more." This does not mean "that each *individual* on
average knows more than his or her great-great-grandparent
. . . but that the social knowledge, defined as the union of all
pieces of individual knowledge, has expanded."[40] Even
though our "biological leash does not get longer," Richard
Nelson and Katherine Nelson add, humanity progresses because of "intergenerational cumulative learning." Compared
to our primate ancestors and even our nineteenth-century
human ancestors, "the contrast presented by progressive advances in know-how in many arenas of human activity is
staggering."[41]

Let us conclude by returning to Mendel and the development of genetics. When a modern seed-producing corporation like Monsanto makes an investment, its executives
consider many specific economic factors related to production
costs, market penetration, the availability of capital, etc. What
they do not have to consider—*ever*—is the huge collective investment that brought genetic science from its isolated beginnings to the point at which the company makes its decision.
All of the biological, statistical, and other knowledge without
which none of today's highly productive and disease-resistant
seeds could be developed—and all of the publication, research, education, training, and related technical devices
without which learning and knowledge could not have been
communicated and nurtured at each particular stage of development, and then passed on over time and embodied, too, in a
trained labor force of technicians and scientists—all of this
comes to the company free of charge, a gift of the past. The

residual of technological progress that Solow demonstrated explains that the greatest part of economic achievement ultimately encompasses things very far-reaching in the nature of knowledge itself, and in the deeper dimensions of how it is created, expanded, refined, and transmitted as an inheritance through decades and centuries to our own time in history.

3

How Does Technological Progress Occur?

Time is the greatest innovator.

—Francis Bacon, *Essays* (1597)

At the heart of modern understandings of how knowledge develops there has also been a profound revision of conventional ideas about invention and its relationship to technological change: heroic or lone genius theories have given way to deeper scientific and historical understandings.

Timelines are commonly used to illustrate technological progress and to mark off key dates when important inventions or discoveries were made by famous individuals. Often they convey a sequence of discoveries within one particular technological field. Here is how the popular online encyclopedia Wikipedia chronicles a "timeline of communication technology": The developmental trajectory begins in 3500 B.C.E. with the emergence of cuneiform writing in Sumeria and ends in 1991 with the invention of fiber optic transmission by Anders Olsson. In between, Johannes Gutenberg invents movable-type (1454), Joseph Henry invents the telegraph (1831), Claude Shannon creates the mathematical basis for electrical communication (1948), and so on.[1] The general impression is that of a series of heroic breakthroughs or "eureka" moments, located at fixed points in time and attributable to single individuals.[2]

Harold Evans's book *They Made America*, a major 2004 publishing event, captures this idea in its very title. The work includes a series of well-researched profiles of inventors and businessmen—people like Thomas Edison and Henry Ford. Evans does not ignore the role of luck, opportunism, and other less-than-heroic factors (as he especially emphasizes in his sympathetic profile of software pioneer Gary Kildall and his dealings with Bill Gates). However, the overall picture he gives is one of individual "genius." As *Publishers Weekly* put it, the book documents the "true American elite: the aristocracy of strategic visionaries, creative risk takers and entrepreneurial adventurers thriving in their natural environment, the free-market democracy of the United States."[3]

Although tenacious in popular publishing and school curricula, the "heroic" view of invention is viewed as simplistic by most historians and social scientists. Isolated "great men" and "eureka" moments do occur, but, for the most part, technological development occurs in a more continuous, evolutionary process of adapting and recombining existing elements—what the economic historian A.P. Usher describes as a process of "cumulative synthesis."[4] One of many reasons the special nature of specific genius figures is no longer emphasized has to do with the regular occurrence of simultaneous invention or simultaneous discovery of the same thing by two or more individuals. What commonly happens is that a field of research reaches a certain point in time when "the next step" is obvious to insiders—and because it is obvious, it is also inevitable that somebody, or more likely many somebodies, will take the step. Someone will connect the dots (but only, it is important to note, when the requisite dots have developed to the point where they can be connected). Something in the nature of knowledge also seems to create a kind of selection process that sweeps individuals along in the same direction. As the well-known sociologist of science Robert Merton put it, discoveries have tended to occur "as certain types of knowledge accumulated in the cultural heritage and as social needs directed attention to particular problems."[5]

Two famous examples of more than one person seeing the importance of the next step are quite typical: when Charles Darwin received a letter in 1858 that indicated that Alfred Russel Wallace was developing essentially the same argument as his own long-gestating theory of natural selection, he rushed to finish his great work, *The Origin of Species*, publishing it in 1859. Similarly, basic research had reached a point in 1953 where Francis Crick and James Watson knew they had to race to publish their "double helix" analysis of the structure of DNA or others—most likely Linus Pauling—might well do so in very short order. The cumulative buildup of knowledge that made the next step inevitable in this case included X-ray crystallographic photography by Maurice Wilkins and Rosalind Franklin, and Pauling's 1951 publication of the alpha helix structure of various proteins. Crick and Watson ultimately shared the Nobel Prize with Wilkins (Franklin died before the prize was awarded in 1962). The important deeper point is that the world would all but certainly have benefited from the key ideas at almost the same time even if the ones who got there first had never been involved.[6]

The early-twentieth-century economist Allyn Young once observed that "the fruits of progress" are not apportioned equally among "the cooperating producers" or given to those who "have made the largest effective contributions to the knowledge that makes progress possible." Rather, the fruits of progress go "to those who actively and successfully contend for them."[7] The patent disputes that have plagued many industries illustrate Young's point. Consider the case of the venerable "inventor of the telephone," Alexander Graham Bell: on February 14, 1876, Bell's lawyer filed a patent application for some advanced telegraphy ideas that suggested the possibility of the telephone.[8] On that very day, Elisha Gray arrived at the same patent office to secure a "caveat"—a statement of intent to patent—on his apparatus "for transmitting vocal sounds telegraphically." Bell was "no. 5" and Gray "no. 39" in the day's entries. Bell was awarded a patent three weeks later, but, in fact, while the device proposed in Gray's caveat would have worked, Bell's, as originally patented, would not have worked. Bell quickly secured a second patent that improved upon the first, however. He emerged the legal "inventor" of the telephone after years of litigation by Gray and many other claimants.[9]

Hundreds of claims, in fact, were ultimately filed against the original Bell patents. Moreover, five years before Bell took out his patent, an émigré Italian stage technician named Antonio Meucci secured a caveat on a voice telegraphy device he called the "teletrofono." Meucci, however, could not afford to file for a full patent and, three years later, let his caveat lapse for lack of the $10 fee. Meucci may have set up the first electronic voice transmitter in his Staten Island home in the 1850s, a communication link between his workshop and his wife's bedroom, where she was confined with crippling arthritis. Prototype materials he stored in a laboratory affiliated with Western Union, on promise of being allowed to do a demonstration, mysteriously disappeared in 1874 after two years of postponed appointments. A subsequent market-sharing settlement between American Bell and Western Union raised suspicions that Meucci's designs had not been lost but stolen.[10]

In 2002 the U.S. Congress recognized Meucci's contributions in House Resolution 269—more than a hundred and thirty years after the fact. Among its stipulations was a simple but startling point: "Whereas if Meucci had been able to pay the $10 fee to maintain the caveat after 1874, no patent could have been issued to Bell." That only $10 stood between Bell's and Meucci's comparable achievements is, at one level, extraordinarily poignant. Undoubtedly, other such random circumstances stood between Bell and his many other rivals as well. The important point, however, is that if Bell had not "invented" the telephone in the 1870s, someone else would have (and in fact somebody already did).[11]

Systematic research to document the phenomenon of simultaneous invention was first undertaken by sociologist William Fielding Ogburn and his student Dorothy Thomas in the early 1920s. The Ogburn-Thomas list, drawing on a broad review of then-available histories of science, mathematics, and mechanics, included 148 "inventions and discoveries made independently by two or more persons."[12] Building on the Ogburn-Thomas work, in the 1950s and 1960s Robert Merton published a series of well-known papers on simultaneous invention—"the multiple and independent appearance of the same scientific discovery"—placing this phenomenon at the center of the emerging field of the sociology of science. Indeed the "discovery" of simultaneous invention itself, he noted, was an example of the very same phenomenon—"an hypothesis confirmed by its own history"—since (among many others) Auguste Comte, Thomas Macaulay, Francis Galton, Friedrich Engels, and Albert Einstein had all themselves discovered simultaneous occurrence independently.[13]

The pattern is so obvious to modern scholars that it is no longer considered controversial.[14] Perhaps the most famous example is the invention of calculus. Both Isaac Newton and Gottfried Wilhelm von Leibniz are credited with inventing calculus in the 1670s (it should be added that, besides being simultaneous, "invention" here really means the development of the first *systematic formulations* of calculus, the basic ideas of which reach back to Archimedes in antiquity). Other simultaneous discoveries in mathematics, according to Ogburn and Thomas, include the law of inverse squares, logarithms, the decimal point, the principle of least squares, the method of indivisibles, and non-euclidean geometry (a cornerstone of Einstein's general theory of relativity).[15]

Many advances in chemistry have also occurred simultaneously, including the law of gases; the discovery of oxygen, boron, and other elements; the periodic law itself; molecular theory; and the hypothesis of the arrangement of atoms in space (leading to the study of molecular structure). Key developments in electrification such as the Leyden jar (the ancestor of today's capacitors), incandescent electric light, the induction coil, the self-exciting dynamo, electric motors, and electric trains were simultaneously discovered or invented, as were many other important instruments and devices, including the pendulum clock, telescope, thermometer, microscope, telegraph, typewriter, sewing machine, phonograph, microphone, and telephone. Also simultaneous in occurrence were any number of medical breakthroughs, including the germ theory of disease and anesthetics, as well as important scientific theories such as the theory of color, molecular theory, and the law of the conservation of energy—to say nothing, as we have noted, of the theory of natural selection and the discovery of DNA structure.[16] It is also a fact that, like Alexander Graham Bell, Thomas Edison had many rivals as "inventor of the lightbulb"—among them, Joseph Wilson Swan of Great Britain and Heinrich Göbel of Germany.

Scholars who study the development of technology also stress that most "inventions" mainly involve a combination of old and new contributions—and that most are very heavily tilted toward the former. The point where the title "inventor" truly applies in any such line of development, accordingly, is rarely clear-cut. Economist and patent law expert Alfred Kahn puts it this way:

> Strictly speaking, no individual makes an invention, in the usual sense or connotation of the term. For the ob-

ject which, for linguistic convenience, we call an automobile, a telephone, as if it were an entity, is, as a matter of fact, the aggregate of an almost infinite number of individual units of invention, each of them the contribution of a separate person. It is little short of absurdity to call any one of the interrelated units the invention, and its "creator" the inventor.[17]

In the fall of 2003, readers of the *New York Times* and the *Washington Post* were given front-row seats to a fascinating Nobel Prize dispute that illustrates this key point. Dr. Raymond Damadian took out several full-page ads claiming that the Nobel Assembly had overlooked his seminal contribution to magnetic resonance imaging (MRI) technology in giving its award to two scientists who later applied his ideas in developing effective scanning techniques. MRI technology, still in rapid development, was of course a major medical breakthrough in noninvasive diagnostic capability for many forms of cancer and other diseases. More than 60 million MRI investigations are performed every year.[18]

In making his case Damadian pointed to Alfred Nobel's personal specification that the prize in medicine be given for a "discovery" alone, rather than for a "discovery or improvement" (in chemistry), or a "discovery or invention" (in physics). Damadian claimed that his discovery of how normal and cancerous tissues react differently to a magnetic field was the foundation of MRI technology and thus qualified him by Alfred Nobel's own standards. The winners of the prize, Paul Lauterbur and Peter Mansfield, indisputably deserved credit for applying his ideas in the development of effective imaging technology, but Damadian urged that his underlying contribution deserved recognition as well.[19]

Damadian won a major patent infringement case against General Electric on the basis of such conceptual priority— and his company was awarded $128 million in a decision affirmed by the Supreme Court. Ironically, the legal system placed significant economic value on his prior conceptual contribution to the cumulative process of MRI development, while the Nobel Prize committee, in theory more attuned to the importance of ideas, ignored it.[20]

The classic case study in "cumulative invention" is S.C. Gilfillan's *Inventing the Ship*, a work that was to have a significant influence on a generation of economic historians and historians of technology.[21] In it Gilfillan traces the development of water-transport technology from antiquity to the modern ocean steamship. The earliest primitive boats, he suggests, may have been the reed boats of ancient Egypt (circa 4000 B.C.), derived from "the natural spectacle of a bundle of reeds floating on the water." Wooden dugouts—essentially hollowed-out logs—were also used at this very early stage of water transport technology. However, the contouring possibilities of the more flexible reed boats led to principles of hull design that had important subsequent, evolutionary application. Improvements in steerage and sail technology, he also demonstrates, rarely had discrete recognizable "origins" but rather emerged through trial-and-error experience in many settings, and through commercial diffusion.[22]

The subsequent evolution of shipbuilding occurred not in singular leaps but by the bringing together of existing elements and ideas in new ways. The steamboat, for example, mainly added existing engine technology to existing riverboat designs—and, specifically, integrated existing engine power with existing mechanical water-propulsion designs and equipment. Such development, Gilfillan observes, bears very little resemblance to the popular heroic tale headlined by lone genius Robert Fulton. ("Not one of the essential devices used by Fulton was new," Fulton's biographer R.H. Thurston adds; his was "a commercial success purely."[23]) The steamship, far from being what we commonly think of as an "invention," Gilfillan concludes, is "a museum of modern civilization, riveted together and called a ship."[24]

Like Alfred Kahn, Gilfillan discredits monumental approaches to invention that obscure the role of adaptation and combination in favor of a singular construction. Any great invention, he provocatively argues, "has no existence . . . outside of our habits of speech and thought, which group under a word like *steamship* or *telephone* or *railway* a certain very large and indefinite collection of all the achievements of men's minds since man began."[25] The same can be said of the gasoline engine or, say, the computer. Both are assemblages of components and knowledge taken from many, many independently evolving fields with long, long lines of development. Furthermore, *within* any particular component of a modern "invention," the past is also represented by a long lineage of numerous specific developments. This point can be illustrated almost at random. Commercial airplanes, for instance, are also a vast "aggregate," in Kahn's formulation, of many independent technological lineages—most importantly, metallurgy, aeronautics, and engine design. Each of these dimensions is highly complex in its own right, involving a long incremental history of advances in knowledge as well as numerous experimental legacies.

Take, for instance, the lightweight strength of the airframes surrounding us when we fly from New York to London. This incredible achievement—and it is only one element in the "invention" of the airplane—has many, many building blocks: the chief metal used in aircraft today is aluminum, but the quest for strong, lightweight metal is ancient. In fact, until the nineteenth century, such metals—combining light weight, durability, and efficiency—were more rare and valuable than precious metals like gold and silver. The isolation of aluminum is widely attributed to the Danish chemist Hans Christian Ørsted in 1825, but references to the metal arguably go back to the first century. Pliny the Elder's *Natural History* tells the story of a goldsmith who presented a light, dullish silver plate to Emperor Tiberius. He reported that the metal was extracted from clay (today aluminum is mainly extracted from the reddish sedimentary rock bauxite). Tiberius was allegedly so impressed that he had the goldsmith beheaded for fear that all his gold and silver would be worthless compared to the new lightweight metal.[26]

The modern "rediscovery" of aluminum (historian Joseph Needham argues that it was known in ancient China as well) took place over a period of eight decades during the nineteenth century. In 1808 Sir Humphry Davy first identified aluminum and named it. Then, in 1821, Pierre Berthier discovered bauxite containing 52 percent aluminum oxide in southern France. At the time, however, refining commercial quantities of aluminum from bauxite was impossible. Refined aluminum initially cost more than gold. In 1825 Ørsted successfully extracted tiny quantities of impure aluminum metal from bauxite using a new chemical process. But it took forty more years for an economically viable method of extracting aluminum to emerge. The key was using an electrolytic process—passing electricity through a substance to create a chemical change in its composition. In 1886 Charles Martin Hall, a recent Oberlin College graduate, and French experimenter Paul L.T. Héroult, working independently and simultaneously without knowledge of each other, developed such a process.[27] They found that if they dissolved aluminum oxide in a bath of molten cryolite and then passed a powerful electric current through the solution, molten aluminum would settle out at the bottom. This nineteenth-century process remains the basis of all aluminum production today.[28]

But Hall did not dream up the electrolytic method by himself. He, in turn, was mentored by legendary Oberlin chemistry professor Frank F. Jewett, who had studied at Göttingen in Germany, the leading center for scientific training at the time. Jewett's teacher at Göttingen, Friedrich Wohler, in turn, had begun experimenting with chemical refinement methods for aluminum in 1827.[29] From the electrolytic process to today's aluminum airframes, there were many further steps, particularly the development of aluminum alloys and "age hardening" (a type of heat treatment). Alfred Wilm's "Duralumin," patented in Germany in 1910, helped launch the modern age of metallic airships.[30] The pioneering German dirigibles (like the Hindenburg) and the Junkers F13 (the first all-metal aircraft), which first took flight in 1919, were built with Duralumin. However, it was not until the advent of electron microscopes in the 1930s (yet another long inheritance) that the age-hardening process was scientifically understood. Only then could alloys be efficiently improved. Today, scientific alloy development, spurred in part by advances in microscopy, remains a vital component of aircraft and other transport technologies requiring strong, lightweight metals.

When Boeing makes a new jetliner for a commercial airline, it benefits from a further vast inheritance—the knowledge of how to produce and modify metals strong enough to withstand the demanding conditions of high-temperature jet-propulsion engines. Among the most important developments were "superalloys" (nickel, iron, and cobalt based) used in aircraft turbines (as well as land-based gas turbines and rocket engines).[31] Needless to say, the beginning of all this—electrolytic treatment of aluminum—required yet another scientific inheritance: the discovery of electricity and the ability to generate and transmit high-voltage electrical current. Strong, lightweight metals for aircraft would have been impossible had we not developed a capacity to produce truly massive amounts of electricity. Public works, too, are part of the backdrop of this story: major hydroelectric projects like the Bonneville and Grand Coulee dams on the Columbia River were needed to bring aluminum production to industrial scale. World War II was the catalyst. From 1940 through 1945, these projects produced 47 billion kilowatt-hours of electricity, enough to build 69,000 military aircraft, 5,000 ships, 5,000 tanks, and 79,000 machine guns.[32]

When we turn from metallurgy to aircraft design, we confront the similarly long developmental story of aeronautics, or the science of flight. It would be possible to outline the long, cumulative history of flight as well, beginning, perhaps, with the Greek myth of Icarus or, more modestly, with Leonardo da Vinci's fifteenth-century flying-machine drawings. Although we cannot even begin such a review here, the essential point is clear: *most* of the knowledge that goes into building aircraft today comes from long, long streams of historic development that have been brought together in what we call the "invention" of the modern airplane.

Historians of technology have demonstrated similar lines of evolutionary development and combination in connection with virtually every form of significant technological development. The truly distinctive feature of invention, A.P. Usher observes, is "the constructive assimilation of preexisting elements into new syntheses, new patterns, or new configurations."[33] Accordingly, one further contemporary illustration: in a highly publicized 1994 *Playboy* interview, Bill Gates observed that one of the most important keys to Microsoft's success was "committing to the graphics interface." It was "a risk that's paid off."[34] Gates is referring to what is technically known as a graphical user interface (GUI)—the now widely used system of graphical tools (mouse, pointer, menus, hypertext, icons, etc.) that allows us to manage and operate computers. Before Windows, the basic Microsoft operating system, MS-DOS, ran by a "command-line interface," where computer operations are controlled by typing command words on a keyboard.

What Gates fails to mention is that "committing" to a

graphical interface involved very little at all that was new. Like its competitor Apple, Microsoft simply repackaged ideas and features that were previously developed by others over many decades—and long before Microsoft or even the personal computer was born. One important contributor, until recently largely forgotten, was Douglas Engelbart. In addition to developing the computer mouse, Engelbart developed prototypes of many of the features of today's GUIs as part of a research project he called "Augmenting Human Intellect," undertaken in the early 1960s under contract with the U.S. Air Force. Englebart's work, in turn, was itself in many ways derivative: GUI only became possible after decades of research and thought on human-machine interaction, including such advances as batch processing—i.e., using punch cards to enter programs into giant mainframe computers. This technology, in turn, originated more than a century earlier and in an entirely different field: the great Jacquard looms of early-nineteenth-century France first used punch cards to control thread placement, thereby automating fabric designs during weaving.[35]

A similar developmental history produced the modern transistor, the foundation of solid-state circuitry and of the exponential gains in computing power provided by today's high-speed microprocessors. Because of the transistor a musical greeting card one can buy at the drugstore today has more computing power than existed on the entire planet in 1945.[36] It is sometimes held that the transistor was born "fully formed" at AT&T's Bell Labs in December 1947.[37] Information theorist Brian Winston (among others), however, points out that accepting at face value the Bell Labs creation story comes at the cost of "profound amnesia" that clouds our understanding of how technological change actually occurs.[38] Materials were classified as conductors and insulators as early as 1729 by Stephen Gray, a cloth dyer and amateur astronomer. However, the first major step in the development of solid-state circuitry was the discovery of the element silicon by the Swede Jacob Berzelius in 1824. (Silicon, a "semiconductor"—a substance having conductivity between that of a conductor and an insulator—has critical properties for the kind of electrical control necessary for transmitting information.) Many other steps were taken after silicon was discovered. Michael Faraday's 1833 experiments with silver sulphide showed how conductivity varies with temperature, one of the crucial physical problems in computer processing. Then what came to be known as the Hall effect, discovered in 1879, showed that when a wire carrying electricity is placed in a magnetic field, a further electric force is produced. This inspired Julius Lilienfield to think about how semiconductors could be used for amplification, and in 1925 Lilienfield won a series of patents outlining a layered semiconductor structure that, although primitive, was arguably the first conceptualization of true solid-state circuitry.[39]

A crude type of solid-state technology was, in fact, already widely in use by the early twentieth century: the cat's-whiskers crystal radio, which relied on detectors using sand or silicon. Vacuum tubes enabled amplification of signals where crystal detectors did not, and were rapidly developed for commercial radios in the 1920s. During World War II, however, microwave technologies such as radar sparked renewed interest in crystal detectors, and a new breed of point-contact rectifiers made of germanium or silicon emerged. Wartime crystal-detector work on radar also played a role in advancing the state of the art in semiconductor applications. It was a radar and signal man, G.W.A. Dummer, who in 1952 first envisioned the development of integrated semiconductor circuitry—as he put it, "the electrical functions being connected directly by cutting out various layers" in a solid block.[40] Also important was government-sponsored research devoted to increasing the purity of semiconductors.[41]

Bill Gates himself implicitly underscored the deeper point in all of this concerning invention and inheritance. Responding to a question about why Microsoft chose to focus on software from the beginning, he observed: "When you have the microprocessor doubling in power every two years, in a sense you can think of computer power as almost free."[42] But the computer power that made Gates's fortune possible is "almost free" only because it reflects more than 150 years of extremely costly—yet freely inherited—developmental work embodied in knowledge received from the past.

It is worth stepping back from this focus on particular technologies to reflect upon the fact that easily available electricity is so ubiquitous it is often simply taken for granted. We turn on the kitchen light or power up a home computer without giving it a second thought. Yet our generalized system for producing and distributing power is perhaps what most distinguishes the nineteenth from the twentieth century— and the latter's great "inventions" and sustained economic growth from the marginal and often reversible gains of all previous periods. Without easily available electric current even the fastest solid-state computer architectures are as useless as raw silicon in a lump of clay. Here, too, a long, long trajectory of development is obvious: at the outset electricity was regarded as something of a toy, an interesting oddity noted as early as 600 B.C. Static electricity might make your hair stand on end, but no one took it seriously. Evolutionary stages in electricity's development include: a generator created by Otto von Guericke in 1660 that could produce static electricity; Robert Boyle's experiments on electric transmission in a vacuum; Benjamin Franklin's experiments demonstrating that lightning was a form of electricity; Henry Cavendish's experiments on conductivity; and Alessandro Volta's development of the first electric battery in 1800. It took another thirty years before British scientist Michael

Faraday, building on these achievements, developed the electric motor and the electric generator and transformer in the 1830s. The efforts of Charles Wheatstone, Wilhelm Siemens of Germany, and Zénobe Gramme of Belgium (among others) over the course of another four decades produced further improvements that allowed for larger-scale uses of electricity.[43]

Early technologies, however, made transmission of direct current (DC) efficient for only about a half mile. In 1888 a more efficient alternating current (AC) generator was developed by (again, among others) Nikola Tesla. In turn George Westinghouse obtained a contract to construct electric generators at Niagara, as well as another to design the lighting system for the 1893 Chicago World's Fair, attended by over 27 million fairgoers. The Niagara plant, which opened in 1896, demonstrated that large-scale generation and transmission of electricity was conceptually sound, technically feasible, and economically practical, and established the essential foundation for mass electrification in the twentieth century. The stage was finally set for everything from the production of aluminum to the creation of the computer—and many, many other inventions that were literally unthinkable (or wildly impractical) before modern electrical distribution emerged in the early decades of the twentieth century.[44]

So large is the elephant in the room we call electricity, it takes a conscious decision and a disciplined analytic stance to fully acknowledge the obvious further truth about the combinatory nature of invention: thousands upon thousands of what we call "inventions" are in fact *combinations* of specific developments *with electricity itself.*

Scholars working on the larger trajectory of evolving technological capability have taken both the historic and sociological understandings forward and have proposed systematic ways to trace and explain how invention builds upon what others do and upon multiple streams of knowledge inherited from the past. Another early study by S.C. Gilfillan, *The Sociology of Invention*, offers a comprehensive statement of the "social principles" of invention, most of which are now taken for granted by experts working in the field.[45] His reflections serve as a convenient summary.

What is called an "invention" is always a combination of diverse constituent elements, mostly drawn from existing technology. These elements, in turn, are often "separately variable" in their own right. The aggregative effect of "prior art" places invention in an evolutionary stream with "neither beginning, completion, nor definable limits."[46] Usually advances occur not in singular leaps but by bringing together existing elements in slightly new ways at a point in the developmental process when change is all but inevitable. Fortunes are made at various points in the process, and economic growth may occur as technological advances translate into higher productivity. The "geniuses" who get there first (or who, in rare cases, make singular discoveries) add creative energy and intelligence to this process—something very important, to be sure. But what the geniuses add is often, even mostly, quite modest compared with what they build upon. Moreover, it is all but certain that society would have enjoyed the benefit of the contribution in due course, and in most cases almost certainly in a very short time. Critically, inherited knowledge is the central element upon which all innovation builds.

A recent overview of contemporary research by Katherine Nelson and Richard R. Nelson does not equivocate on the central point. Although there was once a tendency for scholars "to see technological advance as occurring largely through the efforts of particularly creative inventors," they write, the cultural and collective nature of technological know-how and the process of technological advance are now clearly recognized. "There is no escaping the fact that, while particular individuals may know different things, what they know they have drawn largely from the culture in which they live." Powerful technologies, the Nelsons observe, "always are the result of the cumulative efforts of many participants, often made over a long period of time."[47] Put another way, there is no "cutting edge" without what Nathan Rosenberg terms the "huge overhang" of knowledge upon which it builds.[48] Or, as one of the greatest modern geniuses, Albert Einstein, put it: "Many times a day I realize how much my outer and inner life is built upon the labors of my fellow-men, both living and dead."[49]

4

Public Foundations of Private Wealth

Government has been a much more important and direct influence on the direction and rate of technological innovation than much of our national ideology and public rhetoric would lead us to suppose.

—Harvey Brooks, "National Science Policy and Technological Innovation" (1986)[1]

As it is usually recounted, the American business success story derives from a kind of dogged entrepreneurial spirit reaching back to the pioneer experience of those who settled the land and built the first farms and towns. Self-made prosperity is in our blood like the thirst for freedom itself. Horatio Alger and the lone genius inventor are parallel heroes. Rarely in this story is there anything close to a serious understanding of how the long history of public investment—and especially knowledge-producing investment—has helped the American economy develop over the past two and a quarter centuries.

In chapter 2 we noted the continuous and ongoing investment in public education at all levels. This, of course, is only one aspect of what government has contributed to the economy's achievements. Consider the following list of technologies recognized to be in many ways derivative of government military and space activities, as compiled by Harvey

Brooks, former president of the American Academy of Arts and Sciences:

> . . . semiconductors, solid-state electronic devices, and integrated circuits; computers; nuclear power; satellite communications; microwave telecommunications and radar applications, such as air traffic control; antibiotics; pesticides; new materials, such as high-strength steel alloys, titanium, high-temperature ceramics, fiber-reinforced plastics, and composites; and new methods of metal fabrication and processing, such as numerical-controlled machine tools or powder metallurgy.[2]

In 2004 federal government funding accounted for nearly two thirds of all basic research done in the United States. Federal obligations for research and development (R&D) and R&D plant and equipment topped $110 billion in 2005; included in this was more than $26 billion for basic research. Over the last decade and a half the federal government allocated more than $1.3 trillion to R&D and related R&D plant and equipment, and nearly $290 billion to basic research.[3]

One of the most important technologies on Brooks's list is the computer, which was heavily dependent on government investment. Federal support for computing research rose over the decades from less than $200 million in 1976 to $960 million in 1995 (in constant 1995 dollars).[4] During this period the federal government provided between 60 and 70 percent of university research funding in both computer science and electrical engineering.[5] By 2003 federal support for computer science totaled more than $2 billion.[6] An estimated eighteen of the twenty-five most important breakthroughs in computer technology between 1950 and 1962 were funded by the government, and in many cases the first buyer of the new technology was also the government.[7]

Biotechnology is also highly dependent on public research.

An influential 2000 study found that more than 70 percent of science citations in biotechnology patents were from papers originating in "public science institutions"—compared with 16.5 percent originating in the private sector (11.9 percent were joint public and private efforts).[8] Another study found that fully 73 percent of the scientific papers cited in U.S. industrial patents (for the 1993–94 period) derived from public science sources.[9] Nanotechnology—the latest "hot" field—is following a similar publicly supported path: in December 2003 President George W. Bush signed a bill providing $3.7 billion over four years for research in nanotechnology, the largest technology initiative since the space race. The federal government spent $1.2 billion in this area in 2005 and projects $1.3 billion in spending for each of the following two years.[10] The National Science Foundation estimates that by 2015 economic applications of nanotechnology could generate over $1 trillion annually.[11]

Public efforts do not involve money alone. Nor does money by itself account for the development of knowledge and innovation in connection with many new technologies. In numerous instances government contracts have given an essential boost to the innovation process by creating a market for new creations. The computer, again, is an obvious case in point. Yale president Richard Levin observes that the "articulated needs of the military provided strong inducement for two of the most important innovations in the evolution of semiconductor technology"—silicon transistors and integrated circuits.[12] President John F. Kennedy's 1961 call to put a man on the moon by the end of the decade played a major role in this: few integrated circuits were sold before Kennedy's speech; it was much cheaper to build circuits from individual components hardwired together. With the launch of the space race, however, it was quickly realized that the sophisticated computer controls needed for rocket guidance could not be achieved without integrated circuitry. Government demand,

John Orton observes, gave a "dramatic kick start to a technological revolution . . . No other country ever received a comparable boost."[13] Between 1963 and 1966 the number of
integrated circuits sold rose from 500,000 to 32 million. Another boost came from the air force, which elected to use integrated circuits for an improved version of its Minuteman
ICBM system beginning in 1962. That year, 100 percent of
total shipments of integrated circuits went to the federal
government.[14]

Government support also plays an important role in the
development of individual scientific research careers. An influential 1995 study of researchers with both government
and private funding found a clear sequential pattern in the
vast majority of cases, with government funding laying the
foundation for later work in private industry. In electronics 85
percent of researchers surveyed did government-funded
work prior to getting private funding. In chemicals the
rate was 86 percent, and in information processing it was 62
percent. In electronics 76 percent of researchers regarded
their government-funded work as "more fundamental" than
industry-funded work.[15]

The most well-known outgrowth of public investment in
technology is the Internet—the development of which
through the 1980s was largely funded and shaped by federal
initiatives. The first large-scale computer network, the
ARPANET, was launched in the late 1960s by the Advanced
Research Projects Agency (ARPA) of the Department of Defense; ARPA was established in 1958 in response to Sputnik to
promote defense-related technological advances. The original
purpose of ARPANET was to create a network linking several
computing research centers that had been established at
major universities such as Carnegie Mellon, MIT, and UCLA.
During the 1970s development remained under military control but expanded informally among nongovernment clients.
Significant "growth at the periphery" of the ARPANET was

further developed by a number of universities with the creation of the first local access networks (LANs) using small, locally controlled computers and commercial "ethernet" technology. Between 1985 and 1989 the number of computers connected to the ARPANET rose from 2,000 to 159,000.[16] The National Science Foundation also contributed to what ultimately became the Internet. Between the mid-1980s and the mid-1990s the NSF spent $200 million to build and operate a network of regional supercomputing hubs, the NSFNET. Connected to the ARPANET, this network established Internet access for nearly all U.S. universities, making it a civilian network in all but name.[17]

Strikingly, ARPA had sought as early as 1972 to persuade a commercial operator to take over the ARPANET.[18] However, the market in data services was deemed too small at the time. Although it is now difficult to imagine that this was ever in question, three basic changes subsequently paved the way for privatization of the Internet in the 1990s: the increase in network scale with the development of NSFNET in the late 1980s; the rise of personal computing, which created a vast new market for networking services; and the breakup of the AT&T telecommunications semi-cartel, which spurred greater flexibility and innovation in the computer networking marketplace.[19]

Although the economic impact of modern public investments like those that created the computer and Internet revolution is obvious, in fact, the story begins much, much earlier. It is so well documented that a few selected illustrations may serve as reminders of a vast array of diverse historical and current efforts. More than two hundred years ago (in 1798), for instance, the federal government helped launch the precision machine-tool industry with a $134,000 contract for ten thousand muskets given to Eli Whitney. To fulfill the contract Whitney proposed what was arguably the first machine-tool assembly line using mechanized, precision processes to create a uniform set of interchangeable parts. Whitney ended up delivering only five hundred muskets (a year past the deadline!) but his more important accomplishment was the introduction of machine-tool manufacturing. Whitney's production model had enormous influence on other industries in the decades that followed, and it might well be described as the original template for all modern manufacturing. Government demand for firearms was the catalyst.[20]

Several well-known nineteenth-century public initiatives helped make the American agricultural economy the most productive in world history. The Homestead Act, signed by President Lincoln in 1862, gave 160 acres of undeveloped land to any individual or family head who was at least twenty-one years old. The only stipulation was that the person build a house and live on the land for five years. Although beset by monopolistic speculators and railroad companies, the Homestead Act helped create 372,000 farms. By the end of the nineteenth century more than 80 million acres had been claimed under the law.[21]

Public land settlement was only one aspect of a much larger effort to promote agricultural development. Another effort, under the Morrill Act, signed by President Lincoln in 1862, provided land grants for an agricultural college in each Union state. (The legislation was extended to cover the former Confederacy in 1890.) Under the law every state received thirty thousand acres of public land for each member of its congressional delegation. States were then to establish colleges in agriculture, engineering, and military science with the proceeds they received from selling this land. Over seventy "land grant" colleges were established under the original Morrill Act, among them what are now some of the nation's leading universities—including the University of California, the University of Maryland, Texas A&M, the Massachusetts Institute of Technology, and Cornell University.[22]

The public system launched by the Morrill Act was expanded by further government investments made under the Hatch Act of 1887 and the Smith-Lever Act of 1914. The former authorized federal grants to establish an agricultural experimentation station in every state. For more than a century such centers have conducted scientific research to help farmers, ranchers, suppliers, and processors solve an extraordinary range of food supply problems. By 1988 the United States managed more than fifty stations overseeing the work of thousands of scientists. The government also invests in extension services to bring the knowledge created by public science directly to those who can put it to work. Supported by the Smith-Lever Act, the U.S. Department of Agriculture and the land-grant universities partnered to create a system of cooperative extension services in each state.[23]

Public research investments have been strongly linked to agricultural productivity and economic gain. Yield-increasing chemical and biological technologies, such as fertilizers, pesticides, and hybrid plant strains, were critical factors in the modern agricultural achievement. One of the most important of these is hybrid corn. During the 1930s New Deal secretary of agriculture Henry Wallace financed research and extension services that helped increase the share of hybrid corn planted in the Corn Belt from 1 percent to 78 percent.[24] Today 95 percent of U.S. corn acreage is devoted to hybrid corn. Accompanying these changes has been a revolution in average yields—from about 25 bushels per acre in 1930 to 130 bushels in the year 2000 (between 1860 and 1940 there was essentially no change in corn grain yields).[25] Another major USDA success story is citrus fruit. More than 70 percent of all citrus fruits currently grown in the United States are varieties developed by the Agricultural Research Service's citrus breeding program.[26]

Agricultural economist Vernon Ruttan attributes more than 50 percent of modern agricultural productivity growth to a combination of public-sector research and increased education in farm communities. The key to this growth was the transition from resource-based gains (using more and more land) to science-based gains, brought about by the "institutionalization of public sector research capacity designed to speed the advance of land-saving biological, chemical, and managerial capacity."[27] For the critical period from 1927 to 1950, R.E. Evenson calculates that for every $1,000 of added scientific research, $53,000 in additional farm production was generated.[28]

It is not difficult to catalog numerous other areas in which public support has been critical. Military and commercial aviation, for instance, were essentially launched on their modern paths by a government agency, the National Advisory Committee on Aeronautics (NACA), established in 1915 to "investigate the scientific problems involved in flight and to give advice to the military air services."[29] By the 1920s NACA was dealing with aeronautical and propulsion issues common to both military and commercial aviation. The committee built large wind tunnels to carry out extensive testing of airframe designs, accumulating the first reliable data in this field. The "NACA cowl," designed to reduce the wind resistance of air-cooled radial prop engines, had a major impact, cutting engine drag by nearly 75 percent.[30] NACA also did pioneering work on engine nacelle (enclosure) locations on the airframe, establishing design principles that changed military aviation tactics, made long-range bombers possible, and raised commercial cruising speeds by 50 percent.[31] The epochal Douglas DC-3, which first flew in 1935, incorporated these and other NACA discoveries, including retractable landing gear.[32]

During and after World War II, large-scale military investments propelled aviation into the modern jet age. The jet engine itself was originally developed for military purposes by

General Electric during the war.[33] The high-bypass-ratio engines that power today's wide-body commercial aircraft are also substantially an outgrowth of public investment. Nearly 70 percent of the research and development costs behind these engines was contributed by the Department of Defense and other government agencies. As late as 1969 more than 75 percent of basic research and development in aeronautics was financed by the federal government.[34] Here, too, the financial guarantee provided by military contracts was in many ways as important in nurturing and sustaining innovation as the underlying research. Through the 1960s military purchases represented a large share of the total sales of all the major commercial aircraft producers. The huge financial risks involved in developing safe, comfortable passenger planes were made possible for decades by a well-secured safety net of lucrative military and space-agency contracts.[35]

Many other technologies have been spearheaded in similar ways by government funding. Starting in 1955, for example, the National Science Foundation provided approximately $90 million to support research that contributed to the development of the commercial MRI technologies we discussed in chapter 3. Another important twentieth-century invention—the laser—grew out of research funded by the Office of Naval Research after World War II. Today lasers are in use everywhere: in consumer electronics, such as CD and DVD players; in many other data storage methods (beginning with barcode scanning, first released in 1974); in aircraft and missile guidance systems; in precision metal cutting; and in a variety of surgical techniques. More than 733 million diode lasers (the most common form) were sold in 2004. As was the case with the Internet, Charles Townes (who in 1964 shared the Nobel Prize for his work on masers and lasers) recalls that when he began his research, private industry had little interest in funding his efforts.[36]

The public's contribution to the development of important drugs is also well known. A 1995 MIT study found that eleven of the fourteen most medically significant new drugs developed over the previous quarter century originated with research financed by the government. Another federal study of thirty-two significant new drugs introduced before 1990 concluded that without government support 60 percent of the drugs would not have been discovered or would have been significantly delayed.[37] Many extremely profitable cancer drugs on the market today are products of government-funded research. A good example is Taxol: the General Accounting Office estimates that the National Institutes of Health spent a total of $484 million on the development of this drug between 1977 and 2002. Bristol-Myers Squibb—the firm that obtained the patent and marketing rights—achieved worldwide sales of $9 billion between 1993 and 2002, but the government received only $35 million in royalties from these earnings. In addition, the federal government is a major purchaser of Taxol. Medicare payments for the drug totaled $687 million from 1994 through 1999.[38] The story is similar for many other drugs—including Prozac (for depression), Xalatan (for glaucoma), and most of the leading HIV and AIDS drugs.[39]

U.S. life expectancy was roughly forty-seven years in 1900; it is currently more than seventy-seven years.[40] What Richard Easterlin has termed the "mortality revolution" was a triumph of both science and public policy. Along with supporting medical and pharmaceutical research, federal and state governments helped establish public health systems that brought fatal infectious diseases under control—especially diphtheria, typhoid fever, cholera, and scarlet fever. Of particular importance were investments in the construction of sewer and water treatment systems, as well as large-scale public immunization and vaccination programs.[41]

• • •

We may recall four further illustrations of less obvious but
equally powerful public contributions, the fruits of which we
also inherit with little thought. Two are large and well
known; one is subtle but of unusual significance, and one is
(seemingly) small but of great importance. Although our
central focus is knowledge and technological innovation,
these also illustrate and recall some of the many other ways
government has helped establish the context in which the
economic application and diffusion of knowledge occurs.

Consider first the most fundamental feature of American
development—westward expansion that produced the nation's
vast geographic scale and huge domestic market. The Louisiana Purchase was a public investment that paved the way for
what ultimately became the nation's commercial development west of the Mississippi. Costing $15 million in 1803
(the equivalent in 2005 of about $387 billion), the investment
added nearly 530 million acres to U.S. territory, almost doubling the size of the country.[42] Today, the thirteen states either
wholly or largely encompassed by the Louisiana Purchase
support a population of over 36 million people and generate
over $1.4 trillion in goods and services annually.[43]

The Louisiana investment also gave the U.S. substantial
dominion over the Mississippi River—which became the key
transportation system for the emerging regional economies
both east and west of the river. In 1815 Andrew Jackson and a
small army of state militiamen, Choctaw Indians, free black
battalions, and Caribbean pirates finalized U.S. control of the
river system by repelling an eleven-thousand-man British in-
vasion force in the Battle of New Orleans. With New Orleans
came the entire Mississippi Valley—and the commercial
awakening of the Mississippi River basin, the most important
transportation artery in America before the transcontinental
railroads were built. In the early decades of the nineteenth

century it was cheaper to ship goods from the Ohio Valley to the East Coast via New Orleans than by using ground transport over the Appalachian Mountains.

Additional public contributions were central to the development of the Mississippi and its tributaries. The Army Corps of Engineers excavated snags, rocks, and sandbars in the lower Mississippi. Later, two major engineering projects focused on the Des Moines Rapids and the Rock Island Rapids—long, shallow stretches with riverbeds of solid rock. The Corps built a canal around the Des Moines Rapids in 1877 and cut a channel through the Rock Island Rapids. Another Corps project, the Chicago Sanitary and Ship Canal, provided a link between the Mississippi and the Great Lakes.[44] During the 1930s, twenty-three new locks and dams were built on the upper Mississippi to accommodate larger transports and to extend navigation.[45] And this, of course, was only one element in a vast nationwide system. By the mid-1950s an estimated $4.5 billion had been spent on water navigation by the federal government. The work encompassed 286 coastal harbors, 131 Great Lakes harbors and channels, intracoastal canals, and numerous rivers.[46] By 2004 the Corps of Engineers operated and maintained 25,000 miles of navigable channels and 195 commercial lock and dam sites, and was responsible for ports and waterways in 41 states. An estimated 99 percent of the nation's international trade flows through the system that the Corps oversees.[47] These and other federal efforts generated huge transportation (and fuel!) efficiencies throughout the economy: estimated costs of shipping on navigation systems maintained by the Army Corps of Engineers in 1995 were less than one quarter of a cent per ton mile.[48] It is estimated that every dollar the government invests in navigation infrastructure returns three additional dollars of GDP.[49]

By the late nineteenth century, railroads became the main transportation system for the giant U.S. market, but these were no less dependent on public investment. In 1862 the Pacific Railway Act created large incentives for building the first transcontinental railroad. Financial aid in the form of government loans ranging from $16,000 to $48,000 per mile (depending on terrain) were provided to two railroad companies, Union Pacific and Central Pacific.[50] By 1872 Congress had given more than 100 million acres of public land to railroad companies and supplied over $64 million in loans and tax breaks.[51] Economic historian Albert Fishlow estimates the total value of railroad land grants at $400 million. Such land grants worked in significant part as a public financing system for the railroads, as land was sold to settlers and entrepreneurs seeking access to major transportation routes.[52] Railroad mileage increased from around 9,000 miles in 1850 to 123,000 by 1895. By 1900 it had risen to 193,000 miles. Land grants helped create most of the main lines of the Union Pacific, the Southern Pacific, the Santa Fe, the Burlington Northern, the Rock Island, the Northwestern, the Illinois Central, and the Missouri Pacific.[53]

"The cumulative contribution made by the transition from the common road through to the railroad," Fishlow observes, "is so large and so obvious as to defy accurate calculation."[54] In 1860 the cost of shipping corn exceeded 50 percent of its market price after traveling a mere ninety miles by road. Once both the water and rail systems had been established, the same shipment could be taken 660 miles by the New York Railroad, 1,370 miles by the Erie Canal, and 3,670 miles by the Mississippi River before shipping costs reached as high. Pig iron could go 3,310 miles by the Mississippi River for the same cost as taking it only 80 miles by road.[55]

Public investments in transportation helped integrate what became the world's largest internal market: measured by sales of goods and services, the U.S. market was twice as large as Great Britain's and four times as large as Germany's by the end of the nineteenth century.[56] This in turn was of central importance to further innovation: in small markets it is difficult to achieve the efficiencies of mass production so familiar to the modern world. Instead, individual artisans commonly undertake the handcrafting of goods. What came to be called the "American system of manufacture"—the production and assembly-line integration of parts created by different individuals and groups—developed in significant part because of the huge quantitative possibilities that America's scale and integrated transportation system offered.[57] Other innovations also flowed from the possibilities offered by the giant market: business historians have demonstrated that large-scale production helped create distinctly new techniques of efficient management.[58] New distribution techniques were also facilitated by a new communication infrastructure that developed in response to America's large market. By the 1830s countless newspapers and trade publications were circulating locally and regionally, and by the end of the nineteenth century an efficient postal system gave rise to national mail-order marketing (including the famous Sears, Roebuck catalog).[59] At the same time, 300,000 miles of telegraph lines had been built.[60] Because of "its domestic, one-language, tariff-free, continent-wide marketplace and the efficiency of its transportation and communications systems," Jeff Madrick writes, "the nation was raising mass production and distribution to technical heights that the Old World would not match until after World War II."[61]

America's impressive development is often ascribed to its extraordinary resource base—its land, timber, minerals, and other natural largesse. But natural resources have very little economic value without the capacity to transport them and the knowledge of how to develop them efficiently. Research by Stanford economist Gavin Wright has demonstrated that the exploitation of America's rich mineral base was centrally dependent on the creation of its water and rail transport system and on its technological development. Wright goes so far as to argue that resource abundance was not, in fact, a primary source of American industrial ascendancy. Rather, the opposite was the case: "The abundance of mineral resources ... was itself an outgrowth of American technological progress"—transportation efficiencies playing a critical role along with expanding knowledge of how to achieve the efficient extraction and refinement of natural resources.[62] The latter was facilitated by a high degree of integration between geological science, civil engineering, and mining enterprise encouraged by such organizations as the United States Geological Survey (founded in 1879) and the American Institute of Mining Engineers (founded in 1871).[63] Studies by the Geological Survey in particular helped reduce the risk and uncertainty of resource extraction: prospecting increasingly became a science rather than an adventurer's game.[64]

Another seemingly modest but important illustration of public effort involves the standardization of weights and measures. In 1901 the federal government established the National Bureau of Standards, now known as the National Institute of Standards and Technology (NIST). For large-scale production to be economical it has to be continuous, and this depends on the use of precision parts and a system of input and output governed by uniform weights, measures, and performance standards. The NIST standardized basic weights and measures and developed new standards for instruments and manufacturing operations. "Standardization," historian of science David Noble observes, was the "sine qua non of corporate prosperity." Standardization also laid the foundation for new approaches to accounting, distribution, marketing, and labor management.[65] The NIST also developed measurement and other standards in connection with time, electricity, temperature, light, sound, frequency, and radiation. Instruments used in medicine, environmental safety, weapons systems, information technology, and many other

areas would be of little use without the government's standardized measures. Of particular contemporary importance
are the NIST's manufacturing extension services, a network
of centers established in each of the states to help small manufacturers achieve improved productivity.[66]

Finally, something even more taken for granted is the role
of public administrative and legal systems in establishing
the market value of new technologies, thereby encouraging
further innovation. When Microsoft went public in 1986,
Fortune magazine published an article that began: "Going
public is one of capitalism's major sacraments"—a "rite of
passage."[67] The telling metaphor raises a basic question: if
the capitalized value generated by going public is "conferred" by the financial system (as *Fortune* put it), how much
of the value comes from the firm and how much from the system? The innovation cycle does not end with product development. Rather it ends with the gains made possible by the
secure regulatory environment created by public systems
such as the Securities and Exchange Commission, banking
law, property law, and trade policy. Without all these, the
motor that drives innovation in the private sector quickly
stalls.[68] Lucian Hughes, a leading Silicon Valley business and
technology specialist, adds that although the cycle of "invention to management" has been a major focus of economic
analysis in the high-tech world, no less important has been
the role played by public financial systems in taking innovations from the drawing board to production and beyond to the
market. The "invention to *public profit cycle*," as Hughes
terms it, is central to this.[69] His point is illuminated by
Google's much-discussed 2004 initial public stock offering,
which resulted in a market capitalization of nearly $29 bil-
lion when the dust settled (and far more now). The huge
sums involved stood in dramatic contrast to gross earnings of
only $1.47 billion the previous year.[70]

In their book *The Cost of Rights*, law professors Cass Sunstein and Stephen Holmes expand this argument to show the many other ways the market is interwoven with—*and cannot function without*—public systems at various other levels. The justice system protects property from crime and other infringements, resolves liability claims, and enforces contracts. Disaster relief and insurance, federal emergency management, patent and trademark protection—all protect private property or property claims. Food, animal, and plant inspections not only protect consumers but inspire confidence when goods come to market.[71] Understood in terms of institutions and institutional culture—what Douglass North terms "the scaffolds humans erect" against risk and uncertainty—these and many other governmental functions lie as quietly unnoticed but vitally important background to everyday life and to the functioning, productivity, and growth of the economic system.[72]

Discussions of the role of government commonly focus on specific contributions to the achievements of specific industries (e.g., computers, aviation, pharmaceuticals). Alternatively they focus on government's role in creating and sustaining the overall market economy. Both are important. Yet viewed in the broadest historical perspective, the illustrative contributions we have reviewed (and many others far too numerous to catalog) appear as of far greater significance when they are understood as year by year, decade by decade, century by century cumulative contributions to the development of the innovation and knowledge that are at the heart of the productivity of the economy as a whole. Along with the extended, often intersecting histories of particular inventions and entire technological fields, and the growing stock of knowledge accumulating in "external memory" systems, so too the long and ongoing contribution of public investments comes to us above all as an inheritance, still another gift of the past.

PART II

Just Deserts

[The] joint stock of technology is the substance of the community's civilization on the industrial side, and therefore it constitutes the substantial core of that civilization. Like any other phase or element of the cultural heritage, it is a joint possession of the community, so far as concerns its custody, exercise, increase and transmission; but it has turned out . . . that its ownership or usufruct has come to be effectually vested in a relatively small number of persons.

—Thorstein Veblen, *The Vested Interests and the Common Man* (1919)

Introduction to Part II

At the outset of this study we noted Warren Buffett's judgment, "Society is responsible for a very significant percentage of what I've earned." It is instructive to also note that when people ask Buffett why he is so successful, he commonly says that this is the wrong question. The more important question, he stresses, is why he has *so much to work with* compared to other people in the world, or compared to previous generations of Americans. How much money would he have if he "were born in Bangladesh," or if he "was born here in 1700," he asks.[1]

Buffett's explanation is in a sense self-evident—namely, the level of development is where most of the value seemingly "earned" by individuals really comes from. Differences between individuals are almost negligible compared to the influence of the resources, infrastructure, and, most important of all, the knowledge an individual has at his disposal—whether it be a computer program, a new algorithm, or a sophisticated theory of investment. As the Nobel laureate economist Kenneth Arrow puts it, technical progress is one area where nothing can "take the place of history." The "set of opportunities for innovation at any one moment is determined by what the physical laws of the world really are and how much has already been learned and is therefore 'accidental' from the viewpoint of economics."[2] Or to recall historian

Joel Mokyr's blunt formulation: most of what we have comes to us from the past through no effort of our own as a "free lunch."

It is admittedly a disturbing point. We are trained to view success as an individualistic process of some people achieving more than others because they work harder or are smarter. So, for example, we are naturally less impressed by the rich gadfly who lives off a trust fund than we are by someone who goes from rags to riches through hard work. But the evidence we have so far reviewed makes it clear that before anyone is a "talented" entrepreneur or a "menial" laborer, or anything in between, most of the economic gains that get distributed to individuals in a given year or period are derived from what is inherited from the past, not created by them in the present.

Profound moral questions arise once we confront such issues squarely. Nothing is more deeply held among ordinary people than the idea that a person is entitled to what he creates or his efforts produce. Most people believe, in other words, that fairness is essentially a measure of *deservingness*, or what philosophers call "desert." Further, when people are said to "get what they deserve," what the person receives is judged by the related actions of the person. It is wrong for someone who did not commit a crime to be put in jail for that crime. He does not deserve to be punished for something he did not do. The same moral logic applies to economic rewards. In the workplace, a person who shirks all day at his job will not be tolerated for long. His fellow employees, forced to work more to make up for his shirking, will say that he is "not earning his keep." The employer simply says "I am not paying you for nothing." Similarly, the conservative critique of welfare programs emphasizes the difference between the deserving poor who work and earn, and those who refuse to work and loaf. In the 1990s welfare was turned into "workfare" on the same principle of deservingness. We even have an "earned income tax credit" that subsidizes that which is earned by work (and therefore deserved) if it doesn't bring in enough to support a family. Paying corporate executives for "performance"—and not for vague, unspecified general reasons—now increasingly brings the same concept into play at the other end of the income scale.

There is a long history of philosophical thought and social criticism that focuses on the problem of "earned" and "unearned," "deserved" and "undeserved," in economic life. In Part II we review how several leading figures have understood various aspects of the fundamental question with a view to clarifying the moral and distributional issues involved. As we shall see, though numerous distinctions must be made, the central point cannot be avoided, and it has far-reaching implications: if much of what we have comes to us as the free gift of many generations of historical contribution, there is a profound question as to how much can reasonably be said to be "earned" by any one person, now or in the future. This is especially true in connection with inherited knowledge. Furthermore—as growing numbers of scholars are beginning to suggest—once we recognize that current wealth and income owe far, far more to past accumulations than to individual contributions, an equally profound question arises as to how to return to society a fair share of the gains that—over many generations—society as a whole has created.

As the "knowledge economy" continues to expand and the inherited sources of its enormous power become more widely understood, there are growing indications that the questions of earning and desert to which the new understandings point are likely to become ever more difficult to avoid.

5

Unearned Income

As soon as the land of any country has all become private property, the landlords, like all other men, love to reap where they never sowed, and demand a rent even for its natural produce.

> —Adam Smith, *An Inquiry into the Nature and Causes of the Wealth of Nations* (1776)[1]

The doctrine of the injustice of accumulated property has been the foundation of all religious morality.

> —William Godwin, *An Enquiry Concerning Political Justice* (1798)[2]

It would be possible to trace far back into antiquity the many thinkers who have focused on the difference between "earned" and "unearned" as a matter of fairness, justice, or moral concern. In his letter to the Galatians (6:7) Paul declares: "Whatever a man sows, that is what he shall reap." When God brings "new heavens and a new earth," the prophet Isaiah wrote, "no longer will they build houses and others live in them. . . . Or plant trees and others eat the fruit" (65:17, 22). The Roman emperor Justinian began his *Institutes* (535 A.D.) by defining justice as "the set and constant purpose which gives to every man his due."[3] Adam Smith later denounced the landlords who "love to reap where they never sowed."[4]

With the rise of classical political-economy in the nineteenth century, a more probing technical form of such thinking emerged, particularly in the writings of David Ricardo and John Stuart Mill. Both Ricardo and Mill developed their views in an era that largely accepted the standard argument of John Locke that an individual had a right to own or benefit from the products of his labor. In the largely agricultural economy of this period, the prototype of such "labor entitlement" was the farmer who converted untamed earth into a productive farm. As Locke put it in chapter 5 of his *Second Treatise*: "For 'tis *Labour* indeed that *puts the difference of value* on every thing."[5] When a person mixes his labor with nature, the result is something more valuable than nature alone. Locke held that a person's natural right to benefit from the value he creates with his labor is the fundamental moral basis of all private property.[6]

Ricardo, who preceded Mill both in time and in theoretical understanding, did not focus his work on issues of moral philosophy, but rather on how the political-economic system functioned. His foundational contribution to clarifying the concept of unearned income was anchored in his analysis of what is technically called "rent" in formal economic thought. Economic rent does not mean the payment a tenant makes to a landlord, as the term is commonly used by laymen. Rather, for economists rent is a particular category of income considered alongside wages and profits. In the classical economics of Ricardo and Mill, rent was defined as income derived from control of a resource—which, at the time, referred mainly to land. Unlike wages and profits, which are traceable to human labor and investment, rent is, as Mill put it, a "price paid for a natural agency."[7] The concept is still found in formal economic theory today in a variety of more technical forms, including "monopoly rent." Economic rent is generally defined as payment to a factor of production above what is necessary to keep that factor in its current use. As with the classical agrarian rent of Ricardo and Mill, this has the implication of being a type of unearned surplus.

Ricardo's view of what he called "differential rent" provided a way to understand more clearly how "natural agencies" fit into the economy. In particular, he drew attention to the importance of factors such as soil fertility, geographic location, and public policy in determining the value of land. Ricardo was writing at the time of the British "Corn Law" debates of 1814–1815.[8] In the years leading up to the debates, the Napoleonic Wars (1804–1815) reduced imports of grain dramatically.* As a consequence, the price of grains rose sharply, thereby creating huge windfall profits to landowners and spreading production to inferior lands.[9] When the military conflict ended, landed elites feared that cheap foreign grain "would pour into England at ruinous prices,"[10] and they succeeded in achieving passage of the Corn Law of 1815, which restricted importation of grain priced below the prevailing war-inflated rates. The Corn Law controversy pitted the landed gentry and some commercial farmers who did not want their war-inflated prices to subside against agricultural and factory workers, whose living standards depended significantly on the price of bread (at the time 40–60 percent of their weekly expenditures).[11] Angry mobs, aggrieved by high food prices, rioted at parliament during the initial passage of the Corn Laws—and Ricardo took the free-trade side of the argument, holding that the landlords' gains from protectionism were an unearned surplus that undermined the economic health of the nation.

In his *Principles of Political Economy* and his *Essay on the Influence of a Low Price of Corn on the Profits of Stock*, Ricardo attempted to work out a carefully defined theory of precisely why there were differences in rent and precisely

---

* "Corn" was shorthand for small grains in general, including rye, oats, barley, and especially wheat.

how differential rents arose. Following Adam Smith, Thomas Malthus, and others, he based his approach on the simple observation that different lands have different degrees of natural fertility, as well as different degrees of convenience relative to markets. Competition for the better lands of higher fertility and more convenient location produced higher rents on such lands. Critically, as the demand for food drove agriculture further and further onto more and more marginal lands, rents also rose on the intermediate lands, driving rents even higher on the most productive lands *even when there had been no change in their inherent capacities.* As Barbara Fried writes:

> [Each] time an increase in demand causes incrementally inferior land to be brought under cultivation, the price of wheat rises. . . . But that price will be obtained for wheat produced on more fertile land (and thus with less labor and capital) as well as for that produced on the marginal land. . . . The surplus, they concluded, will be paid as "rent" to the landlord holding inframarginal (that is, superior) land.[12]

Note carefully: nothing has changed from the input—work or capital investment—side of the equation for these lands. Their value goes up simply because an external factor changes dramatically. It was not difficult to see that this process was driven by increasing domestic food demand derived above all from import restrictions. Importantly, no one was doing anything new to "earn" the additional "rent."

It should be emphasized that for Ricardo "land" did not mean only soil or acreage, but any nonproducible, nonhuman resource used in the production of goods. As a further example, he explained how mines "generally pay a rent to their owner" because of natural variations in the quality and accessibility of the metals they contain.[13] The classification had an additional, deeper meaning as well: rent was also essentially a qualitative term, referring to the unique characteristics of that gain compared with other incomes. Set apart from wages and profits in Ricardo's distributive model, rent referred to a realm of intrinsic value, without human origins. He stressed that rent is often "confounded" (confused) with "the interest and profit of capital." It is qualitatively different, he held, and should be viewed as something taken out of the product of capital and labor—as "that portion of the produce of the earth, which is paid to the landlord for the use of the *original and indestructible powers* of the soil."[14]

Carefully defined, "rent" is thus not simply payment for this or that specific resource. Rather, it is payment for the use of the *inherent* productive capacities of the land, a "distinction," Ricardo stressed, "of great importance."[15] He criticized Adam Smith for sometimes confusing the concept of rent with payments for a commodity, as with fees paid for cutting timber on someone's land. A rent is not paid for "the liberty of removing and selling" timber, but only "for the liberty of growing it," Ricardo specified.[16] Understood in this light, "the laws which regulate the progress of rent, are widely different from those which regulate the progress of profits, and seldom operate in the same direction."[17] Ricardo's best known "slogan"—as his leading modern interpreter, Mark Blaug, observes—captures the parasitic essence of rent as a "nonfactor" in production, literally a deduction from both profits and wages: "Corn is not high because a rent is paid, but rent is paid because corn is high."[18]

By "getting rid of rent," Ricardo concluded, "the distribution between the capitalist and labourer becomes a much more simple consideration."[19] This view had the obvious political implication of making the landlord an exploiter of the community—and, it is again useful to note, the exploiter of *both* the productive capitalist and the productive laborer. Ricardo put it this way: "It follows, then, that the interest of the landlord is always opposed to the interest of every other class in the community."[20] At the most basic level, rent theory challenged any simple defense of unequal property. Although it was widely agreed that a person was entitled to what he created, by exposing the natural and institutional contingencies of landed wealth, rent theory created, in effect, a radical implicit corollary to the traditional view of labor entitlement: that a person has *no* moral right to wealth and resources that he *did not* create, whatever his legal status as owner, heir, etc.

These two closely related propositions are at the center of ongoing judgments about what is earned and deserved, and it is worth underscoring them: First, a person is entitled to what he actually creates. Second, he is not entitled to what he does not create. Not surprisingly, those who pressed these two simple arguments from the time of Ricardo on have not always been well received by those whose privileges depend upon ignoring or countering the logic of their dual claims. The chief economic apologist for the landowners Ricardo challenged was Richard Jones, a writer who characterized rent theory as "conjectural history" in his *Essay on the Distribution of Wealth* (1831).[21] While admitting that "there are cases in which the landlords *may* derive a limited advantage from circumstances which are diminishing the means of the body of people," it was unthinkable to Jones that "their permanent prosperity" does not "emanate from more wholesome and more abundant sources."[22] Another writer opposed to Ricardo, G.P. Scrope, argued that even if true, such opinions "amount to a crime" by "overthrowing . . . the fundamental principles of sympathy and common interest that knit society together."[23]

Other conservative writers also sensed that something well beyond the price of grain was ultimately at stake, and hostility to Ricardo's analysis of rent clearly arose from a much deeper problem than that associated with the corn laws and free trade. If it was clear, following Ricardo, that landownership was a kind of theft, it was also clear that land was not the only common resource wrongly captured by private accumulators. The transition from a topical resource economy, powered by wood and animals, to a stored-resource economy, based on fossil fuels and minerals, added new types of wealth to the land question and connected "land," by extension, to industrial development and capital goods.[24] Furthermore, those who urged repeal of the Corn Laws were joined by organized workers' movements that, building in part on Ricardo's ideas, challenged "capital" as merely "accumulated labor."[25] In his 1825 work *Labour Defended Against the Claims of Capital*, one well-known theorist, Thomas Hodgskin, drew on Ricardo's theory to argue that "the exactions of the capitalist cause the poverty of the labourer."[26] No democrat or socialist, Ricardo publicly supported laws to ban worker "combinations." However, he did not repudiate the underlying concept of rent and unearned income, nor the broad theoretical approach that others took in more radical directions.

The British political economist and philosopher John Stuart Mill was perhaps the most well-known nineteenth-century writer who extended rent theory and the theory of unearned income. Agreeing also with the fundamental Lockean proposition that a person has a natural right to what he creates in a state of nature, Mill nonetheless stressed that it was obviously society, not simply his own effort or intelligence, that enabled a person to produce so much more than he could if he were *alone* in nature—or, say, isolated on an island in the middle of an ocean. He urged that holdings not directly traceable to individual productive activities were, by definition, a kind of social wealth and should be treated as such. Hence, on the same "earned" contribution principle that would give to the person that which he creates, Mill argued that society, too, should receive its due—a rent, essentially, for the benefit it provided to individuals beyond what they could produce purely as individuals acting alone. Mill offered a nuanced argument that also extended the labor reward principle to capital by considering the supply of capital to be a type of individual contribution. He judged, however, that many conservative writers overreached by proposing blanket support for all accumulated wealth—including that which had no origins in individual productivity.

In 1870 Mill helped found the Land Tenure Reform Association, an important first step on the path toward modern welfare policy. As chairman of its provisional committee he had a significant hand in drafting its *Programme*, a classic statement of rent theory (and a further example of Locke's influence as well). The *Programme* declared: "The land is the original inheritance of all mankind." Private ownership may be necessary "for making the soil yield the greatest possible produce," but the right of appropriation

> is only valid for leaving to the owner the full enjoyment of whatever value he adds to the land by his own exertions and expenditure. There is no similar reason for allowing him to appropriate an increase of value to which he has contributed nothing, but which accrues to him from the general growth of society, that is to say, not from his own labour or expenditure, but from that of other people—of the community at large.[27]

The *Programme* proposed a national land-tax policy that would leave previously accumulated land values in private hands while reserving the "right of the State to all such accessions of income in the future."[28] It also offered landowners the option to escape future taxation by selling their claims outright back to the government. The twofold manner of obtaining revenue—from taxation of future unearned increments in the value of private land and from rents on repatriated public land—was designed to achieve major distributional changes over time. "That increase of wealth which now flows into the coffers of private persons from the mere progress of society, and not from their own merits or sacrifices," the *Programme* stated, "will be gradually, and in an increasing proportion, diverted from them to the nation as a whole, from whose collective exertions and sacrifices it really proceeds."[29]

In what today might be called political "reframing," Mill himself argued that "making the State a sharer in all future increase of rent from natural causes . . . ought not to be regarded as a tax, but as a rent-charge in favour of the public."[30] In contrast to landlords who contribute nothing in exchange for their rents, society had the legitimate moral right to obtain rent, given its vast contributions to wealth. At the same time, unearned wealth should be seen as a *private tax on society*, a point urged earlier and even more forcefully in France by Pierre-Joseph Proudhon. "By himself [the landlord's] property would bring him a product equal only to one," Proudhon wrote. And yet, without any effort or investment, merely through the scarcity caused by population growth,

> he demands of society no longer a right proportional to his productive capacity as proprietor, but a per capita tax. He taxes his fellows in proportion to their strength, their number, and their industry. A son is born to a farmer: "Good," says the proprietor; "one more chance for increase." How has this metamorphosis from farm-rent into a poll-tax been accomplished?[31]

Mill, like Proudhon, shared the view that some forms of legally sanctioned income were essentially an illegitimate capture of public wealth, a private tax on society at large.

Mill's broader influence hinged on the powerful moral connection he drew between natural and social forces. Societal development in general, he suggested, gave rise to other forms of wealth in a manner analogous to that which nature provides in its free gift of fertile land prior to any work done by individuals. That landlords grow rich "in their sleep," as he wrote, was emblematic of a more general contradiction in advanced economies.[32] As he explained in a famous passage in his *Principles*, ignoring societal contributions to the private economy permits a kind of legal plunder—a private "taking" of that which society, not the individual, creates and contributes:

> Suppose that there is a kind of income which constantly tends to increase, without any exertion or sacrifice on the part of the owners: those owners constituting a class in the community, whom the natural course of things progressively enriches, consistently with complete passiveness on their own part. In such a case it would be no violation of the principles on which private property is grounded, if the state should appropriate this increase of wealth, or part of it, as it arises. This would not properly be taking anything from anybody; it would merely be applying an accession of wealth, created by circumstances, to the benefit of society, instead of allowing it to become an unearned appendage to the riches of a particular class.[33]

By the same moral logic that would give both the worker and employer their productive "deserts," Mill held that wealth generated by social and natural forces should be treated as a type of common property: "[The laws of property] have made property of things which never ought to be property, and absolute property where only a qualified property ought to exist." When this happens, he urged, private property becomes incompatible with the democratic idea "that all should indeed start on perfectly equal terms."[34] Like

Ricardo, Mill nonetheless believed strongly in private property and fair incentives. But unearned wealth, he held, was subversive of the very institution of property:

> The guarantee to [individuals] of the fruits of the labour and abstinence of others, transmitted to them without any merit or exertion of their own, is not of the essence of the institution [of private property], but a mere incidental consequence, which, when it reaches a certain height, does not promote, but conflicts with, the ends which render private property legitimate.[35]

Where Ricardo had simply analyzed the natural origins of rent, Mill drew the normative conclusion that all such "natural" income—wealth "created by circumstances"—should be reclaimed for social purposes. He urged that corrective legislation should favor the "diffusion, instead of the concentration of wealth."[36] To achieve such diffusion, in addition to taxes on future land-value increases, Mill also supported a steeply progressive inheritance tax.[37]

Many other figures, of course, contributed variations of these foundational ideas—including, importantly, the American agrarian radical Thomas Skidmore, the young Herbert Spencer, and Charles Darwin's contemporary Alfred Russel Wallace. The essential points, however, are straightforward: from Locke at the outset, the argument that an individual is entitled to what he creates by his own contributions (but not more); from Ricardo, the insight that "rents" arise from natural and social circumstances, not from individual contributions on their own; and from Mill and others, the emerging understanding that society as a whole creates many unearned values, which, on implicit Lockean principles, should be treated as a type of social property and used for the common good.[38]

6

Unearned Income Extended

The ground problem in economics is not to destroy property, but to restore the social conception of property to its right place. . . . It is to be done by distinguishing the social from the individual factors in wealth.

—Leonard Trelawny Hobhouse, *Liberalism* (1911)[1]

Although various philosophers have offered challenges to theories concerned with unearned income, clearly there is a powerful resonance to the idea that what an individual receives should be related to what he contributes (and that those who contribute little do not deserve to be richly rewarded).[2] Not surprisingly, fundamental tenets of the basic argument appeared in diverse quarters throughout the nineteenth and early twentieth centuries—sometimes directly following and extending writers like Ricardo and Mill, sometimes quite independent of the analytical tradition they helped establish. Importantly, key thinkers on both sides of the Atlantic developed further sequences in the argument, and some began to bring critical questions of historical inheritance into much clearer focus.

Well before Ricardo's main works were published, similar arguments were in fact put forward with great moral force in the United States by Thomas Paine. In his late work *Agrarian Justice* (1796) Paine urged that if you separate an individual from society, and give him an island or a continent to possess . . . he cannot acquire personal property. He cannot be rich. So inseparably are the means connected with the end, in all cases, that where the former do not exist the latter cannot be obtained. All accumulation, therefore, of personal property, beyond what a man's own hands produce, is derived to him by living in society; and he owes on every principle of justice, of gratitude, and of civilization, a part of that accumulation back again to society from whence the whole came.[3]

Paine extended the argument beyond land to what he termed "personal property," a category that included machinery and what we would today call capital. "It is as impossible for an individual to acquire personal property without the aid of society," he stressed, "as it is for him to make land originally." From this understanding of the socially derived nature of property, Paine held that every member of society is due, by natural right, a certain amount of "indemnification" for losses that ensue with the introduction of strictly private or "landed" property. To fulfill this right, he proposed that all members of society should receive a capital grant of fifteen pounds from the government upon reaching adulthood, as well as an old-age income of ten pounds per year after reaching the age of fifty. The source of these grants was to be a "National Fund" financed by inheritance taxes, which he saw as a means of "subtracting from property a portion equal in value to the natural inheritance it has absorbed."[4]

Later in the nineteenth century, another American writer, reform activist Henry George, also urged a strongly articulated version of the major propositions. George, in effect, generalized Ricardian rent theory by putting a spotlight on the effects of urbanization and industrial development on land values. His central judgment began with the well-established fact that land values in urban areas commonly rise dramatically when population growth and economic development occur. Those who simply hold title to land in such circumstances, like rural landowners, do very little to earn increases in value brought about because of broader community and society-wide development. George termed such increased values straightforwardly "the unearned increment." Like Ricardo and Mill, George also saw himself as a strong defender of private property and enterprise. Only by sharply delineating that which an individual personally "earns," he also argued, could one uphold the "real and natural distinction" between "things which are the produce of labor and things which are the gratuitous offerings of nature."[5] George proposed a "single tax" to capture the gain in land values that society in general created—"single" because he believed it could replace all other taxes. He hoped thereby also to increase incentives and productivity because only the unearned income of mere holders of titles to land would be affected by his tax.[6]

Henry George is commonly treated as an outlier by the modern economics profession. However, his influence was extraordinary both in America and Europe. George's 1879 book *Progress and Poverty* sold well over a million copies initially; one estimate puts total worldwide distribution of his works at five million.[7] In the United States a far-flung land-tax movement agitated for state and local policies based upon his ideas.[8] Georgist tax policies were also implemented in England, Australia, New Zealand, Taiwan, and Hong Kong. George himself polled ahead of Theodore Roosevelt in an initial run for mayor in New York City in 1886. After his death four days before the end of his second run for mayor in 1897, tens of thousands of mourners paid tribute to George in what the *New York Times* described as the "largest civic demonstration of the kind . . . since Abraham Lincoln's body was borne in state to the City Hall."[9]

George's views were also shared by leading mainstream economists of the marginalist school. For instance, the English economist Philip Wicksteed, a pioneer of marginal productivity theory, endorsed "public possession" of unearned increments. Wicksteed urged that "the instinct . . . that the increase of wealth due to the communal progress should fall under communal control or should be distributed amongst those who have created it, though quite incapable of being logically confined to the land, can, nevertheless, find in the land an eminently suitable subject on which to fasten."[10] The Swiss architect of market equilibrium theory, Léon Walras, also defended land taxation as a matter of communal inheritance, urging that "in juridical terms humanity is the owner, and the present generation has the land in trust."[11]

In Britain another leading intellectual figure, J.A. Hobson, expanded upon and further developed the distinction between earned and unearned gains. Hobson—one of the main economic theorists of England's Liberal Party when it came to power in 1906—praised George for "the fact that he was able to drive an abstract notion, that of economic rent, into the minds of a large number of 'practical' men."[12] Hobson also endorsed the view that "society is taking an income which belongs to it" in taxing land values. He stressed, however, that "the productive efficacy of social forces" was not confined to "the creation of land values." Indeed, he suggested that the portion of unearned value created by the industrial system was far greater than that which accrued to landowners. Drawing both upon George's ideas and upon traditional rent theory, Hobson held that society had a right to benefit from all socially created value.[13]

In Hobson's work there is also a recognition of the contribution that large-order cultural processes make to economic achievement, and of some of the insights later developed by scholars like Merlin Donald. "Who shall say how far the *Oedipus Tyrannus* was the product of Sophocles," he asked, and "how much of Athens, how much of the Hellenic genius, or how much belongs to humanity?" The influence of the wider culture of Greek tragedy, he suggested, was a microcosm of society's influence on all human output. The contribution of specific individuals can be measured by effort and service, or added worth. The rest can only be understood as coming from what the wider culture contributes. What was true of culture in general was true of economic culture in particular—and that part of economic achievement derived from culture, Hobson held, must also be viewed as unearned surplus and thus by definition a type of "social income."[14]

Hobson held that a new type of industrial rent theory was needed to more fully capture the "productive efficacy of social forces."[15] He suggested that the "unearned increments" in the industrial system included all profits and rents derived from scarcity gains similar to those that the society created in the form of rents on agricultural lands—*plus* payments to factors of production beyond the level necessary to "evoke" the factor, or give it incentive. On the one hand, such surpluses are by definition best able to bear taxation; on the other, as with rising land values, they are generated by social forces—and as the creation of society should be returned to society in some proportionate measure. Mill's dual argument is thus once again echoed in Hobson: the individual deserves what he contributes (but only what he contributes). But society, too, deserves what *it* contributes "by virtue of its own growth and expenditure upon the environment" (but not more, and not what is due the individual or due any other factor by virtue of its genuine productive contribution).[16]

Perhaps the most influential exponent of modern rent-theory ideas related to earned and unearned income was another British writer, Leonard Trelawny Hobhouse. Journalist, political reformer, and social philosopher, Hobhouse was the leading intellectual of the "New Liberalism" that attempted to rethink the liberal tradition in light of modern industrial conditions and to create a new theory of state-centered reform. In his most important work, *Liberalism*, published in 1911, Hobhouse offered a fully developed worldview. "The ground problem in economics," he maintained, "is not to destroy property, but to restore the social conception of property to its right place under conditions suitable to modern needs." The "prosperous business man" should consider "what single step he could have taken" without the "sum of intelligence which civilization has placed at his disposal" and the "inventions which he uses as a matter of course and which have been built up by the collective effort of generations."[17] A key issue was how to distinguish "the social from the individual factors in wealth."[18] Given the ever growing social contribution to economic development, for Hobhouse it was clear that what some called "redistribution" was in the main simply "just compensation," a matter of restoring excess wealth to its underlying nature as social property:

> The true function of taxation is to secure to society the element in wealth that is of social origin, or, more broadly, all that does not owe its origin to the efforts of living individuals. When taxation, based on these principles, is utilized to secure healthy conditions of existence to the mass of the people it is clear that this is no case of robbing Peter to pay Paul. Peter is not robbed. Apart from the tax it is he who would be robbing the State. A tax which enables the State to secure a certain share of social value is not something deducted from that which the taxpayer has an unlimited right to call his own, but rather a repayment of something which was all along due to society.[19]

Like Henry George and other rent-theory individualists, Hobhouse was also careful to distinguish his argument from any form of collective property theory. "[It] is not possible for society to insist on the whole of its claim," he wrote, but "[what] it can do is to shift taxation step by step from the wealth due to individual enterprise to the wealth that depends on its own collective progress, thus by degrees regaining the ownership of the fruits of its own collective work."[20] Indeed, it is only in this way, Hobhouse held, that genuine individualism could be preserved. An "individualism which ignores the social factor in wealth" is no individualism at all, but rather a type of private socialism that "deprive[s] the community of its just share in the fruits of industry and so result[s] in a one-sided and inequitable distribution of wealth."[21]

Sidney Webb, the defining figure of Britain's non-Marxist socialist Fabian Society, contributed a more specific industrial analysis to this basic understanding. Webb pointed out that the demand for a given firm's product was almost always in significant part created by factors outside the firm. The invention of the gas-powered automobile, for instance, created more demand for refined petroleum products than anything John D. Rockefeller (or his vanquished competitors) uniquely achieved within the confines of the oil industry or a particular firm.[22] On close examination, Webb suggested, most business opportunities turn out to be similarly traceable to overarching changes in society, and the profits made in such circumstances were also more like a rent—in the classical sense of a return largely due to a change in external conditions rather than individual effort. Taking advantage of an opportunity created by society, he urged, was not the same thing as creating value.[23]

Although our main concern is with the ideas of important thinkers who expanded upon rent theory to develop a broader understanding of social contributions to wealth, it is worth noting that several of these themes were also taken up by major twentieth-century political figures in both Britain and the United States. The British Liberal Party's "People's Budget" of 1909, for instance, was a powerful example of rent theory in action. Seeking more than £16 million in new revenues—almost entirely from the country's wealthiest families—the People's Budget helped establish the modern principle of "progressive taxation" through a surcharge on higher incomes. It also increased inheritance taxes and imposed licensing fees on automobiles as well as new taxes on gasoline consumption, then both considered to be luxuries. Most controversial of all, it imposed a 20 percent levy on rising land values (whenever land changed hands), and a smaller levy on undeveloped land and mineral deposits.[24] Prime Minister Lloyd George offered a classic statement of the central concepts in what came to be known as his "Limehouse Speech." George's most telling illustration focused on "land which was not very useful . . . a sodden marsh" on London's periphery that once could be rented at £2 or £3 an acre but was now selling at £2,000 to £8,000 an acre. "Who created that increment?" he asked. "Who made that golden swamp? Was it the landlord? Was it his energy? Was it his brains . . . his forethought? It was purely the combined efforts of all the people engaged in the trade and commerce of the Port of London—trader, merchant, shipowner, dock labourer, workman, everybody except the landlord."[25]

Another, perhaps unexpected champion of such arguments was Winston Churchill, at the time a young Liberal cabinet minister. Churchill defended the People's Budget on earned versus unearned rent-theory terms with characteristic bluntness. The "new attitude" of the state toward wealth, Churchill argued, is to ask not only "How much have you got?" but also "How did you get it?"[26] Again, the "unearned increment on the land is on all fours with the profit gathered" by professional monopolists, like grain speculators—reaped "in exact proportion, not to the service but to the disservice done."[27]

In the United States Theodore Roosevelt also sharpened the distinction between earned and unearned in his groundbreaking "New Nationalism" speech of 1910. The "conflict between the men who possess more than they have earned and the men who have earned more than they possess is the central condition of progress." The very survival of civilization, he urged, fundamentally depended on eliminating "special privilege" in the form of unearned wealth. To meet this policy goal Roosevelt called for taxation of high incomes and inherited estates.[28]

Franklin Delano Roosevelt's New Deal also emphasized the difference between individual contribution and social value in connection with progressive taxation measures. "Wealth in the modern world does not come merely from individual effort," Roosevelt urged, "it results from a combination of individual effort and of the manifold uses to which the community puts that effort. The individual does not create the product of his industry with his own hands; he utilizes the many processes and forces of mass production to meet the demands of a national and international market."[29] Various New Deal figures were also mentored or influenced by another leading proponent of societal rent theory, Simon Nelson Patten, president of the American Economic Association for 1908. "After each producer has obtained from the social store a value equal to what he has produced . . . ," Patten wrote, "the store would not be empty. It would still contain the wealth due to superior natural resources and to superior productive instruments" that resulted from social progress. "It is not difficult to see that there is also a surplus or unearned increment" that, he held, should be redistributed through progressive taxation.[30]

Formulations like these offered by various nineteenth- and early twentieth century figures (and many others far too numerous to catalog) expanded upon and deepened the ideas of

Locke, Ricardo, and Mill. Mill's view in particular was suggestive, however, of a related understanding that brought
something else into focus—namely, the long arc of the community's historical development and the cumulative productive inheritance that creates an "increase of wealth which
now flows into the coffers of private persons *from the mere
progress of society.*"[31] With the exception of Hobson—and
here only in a somewhat secondary way—most writers did
not directly confront questions related to the contribution of
long-term historical "progress" or the deeper question of inheritance it suggested. We may or may not agree that a person is due what he himself directly earns, that he does not
deserve what he does not earn, and that what society contributes in turn deserves to be compensated. But what of history? What of the historical contributions—the "technical
progress"—at the core of the modern revolution in economic
growth theory? And what of the judgment that the advances
and investments we inherit from the past contribute far more
to current output than what we uniquely contribute today?

Hobson clearly understood the central question. Modern
industry, he urged, was a form of "social production" involving the cooperation of "a large number of human and nonhuman factors." These factors were not simply contemporary
in nature. All embodied a long accumulation of past advances, including "machinery and other plant which express
a complicated growth of invention running far back into the
past and derived from great numbers of human brains."
There is also an "ancestry" of "labour power" derived from
"past generations of men whose growing knowledge and
practice yielded the training and the habits of industry and of
cooperation essential for the productiveness of labour in the
modern arts of industry."[32] "Society," Hobson urged, was a
"repository of knowledge made available by a nation to its
members throughout its history, and the provider of a common language."[33] By linking past advances to current outputs,

hc suggested, society obtains a right to share in the output at any given time. Despite such arguments, however, Hobson's focus, like that of most of the other thinkers, was largely contemporary, and he did not make the issue of inherited knowledge central to his political argument. It was enough to urge the difference in the here and now between what was earned by one person and what society in the main contributed currently. Immediate forms of unearned income, such as monopoly profits and scarcity rents, were at the top of his list of political targets.[34]

Hobson's reserve, and that of many of his contemporaries, may be compared with the explicit position of the nineteenth-century American writer Edward Bellamy, whose major popular work *Looking Backward* was also a million-copy bestseller:

> All that a man produces today more than his cave-dwelling ancestor, he produces by virtue of the accumulated achievements, inventions, and improvements of the intervening generations, together with the social and industrial machinery which is their legacy. . . . Nine hundred and ninety-nine parts out of the thousand of every man's produce are the result of his social inheritance and environment. The remaining part would probably be a liberal estimate of what by "sacred justice" could be allotted him as his product, his entire product, and nothing but his product.[35]

Three lesser-known nineteenth-century theorists, working largely within a Christian framework, addressed the historical inheritance issues like those underscored by Bellamy frontally and formally—and in a manner that both extended traditional rent theory and was suggestive of modern ideas of the growth residual. Their efforts (and those of their followers) opened up more sophisticated philosophical terrain and clarified additional distinctions of potentially far-reaching significance.

The Scottish philosopher Patrick Edward Dove began, like so many others, with the Lockean principle that "an object is the property of its creator." But again, this also meant that no one could rightfully own what he did *not* create, thus leading Dove (again, like many others) along the familiar path of arguing that the "rent value" of the soil—derived from the "common result of the whole expended labour"—had to be considered "the *common property* of the whole associated community."[36] And "rent" paid to landlords should again therefore be seen as a "tax" on the community, one "that goes on increasing and increasing with the whole labours of the country."[37] Dove held that the "only possible solution of the great question of natural property" was to allocate all rent value to the general benefit of the community.[38]

What is striking about Dove's argument is the next step— the judgment that the "principle of allocating the rent to the community, instead of to individuals" would, among other things, "secure to every labourer his share *of the previous labours of the community.*"[39] Dove emphasized that because the labors of a community create value cumulatively, across generations, it is necessary "at every period" to ensure an equitable distribution of the historically accumulated property of the society. All people of all generations have an equal natural right to a share of the cumulative value, or "whole labours," of the community, he held. By natural right, no one should be born into "a world already portioned out."[40] To redress the ongoing imbalances Dove proposed a policy similar to that which is currently used to allocate the electromagnetic spectrum—an auction of rights to cultivate the land, the proceeds of which would be paid to the community. Rent values that derived from the accumulated efforts of the community would thereby be determined by "perfectly free competition," with the highest bidder paying a cultivation rent "to the nation for the benefit of the whole community."[41]

The French philosopher François Huet also took rent theory into the terrain of historical contribution. His *Le Regne Social du Christianisme*, published a few years after the failed revolution of 1848 and banned by the Catholic Church, sought to reconcile Christianity and socialism through a theory of natural property rights. For Huet the right to property also involved more than raw physical resources. Each person, he held, has an equal right to "enjoy God's gift" of natural resources—which includes all "the fruit amassed by previous generations."[42] A person is entitled to what he creates from external resources in his own lifetime, Huet urged, but the deeper issue of distribution involves each person's "prior right" to an equal share of a society's "patrimonial assets." This, he held, was also "already (by anticipation) owned in common with future generations."[43] Huet repeatedly and forcefully argued that there could be no "exclusive property" in something that no one living created. A person's "acquired assets," those that were the "personal creation of the owner," could be disposed of in any manner the person thought appropriate. However, anything he possessed or had title to that he did not personally create should revert to the general patrimony at his death, for the benefit of all.[44]

Huet did not flinch from the logical implications or from the technical challenges his position inevitably created. One first had to focus upon (and in principle disentangle) that which a person, today, actually could be said to have contributed and "earned" himself—the person's unique contribution. Then it was both necessary and possible to estimate the share that logically came from nature and from past historical contributions. Huet then proposed differentiating the first type of wealth in a twofold system of inheritance: first, any wealth actually acquired by an individual's labor during his lifetime could be freely transferred in bequest or gift to another person, or heir. The recipient could enjoy this gift or bequest as she saw fit. On the other hand, Huet held there could be no moral rationale for *this second* person passing on to the next generation that which she had done nothing to earn during her lifetime. Accordingly, Huet proposed a tax on subsequent gifts and inheritance equal to 100 percent of the amount the person originally inherited, so that all wealth received through such transfers would revert into a common fund upon the death of the recipient:

> Constantly fed by an inexhaustible spring, the general patrimony would be made up, at a given moment, of the old patrimonial assets and of all capital goods, accumulated in each generation which, being capable of gratuitous transfer only once, would join the mass of the first upon the death of the donees.[45]

Huet also proposed a capital endowment system not unlike the "stakeholder grants" suggested in recent years by Yale law professors Bruce Ackerman and Anne Alstott. The strategy emphasized individuals, not the society considered collectively. In Huet's plan the proceeds from gift and inheritance taxes would be reallocated annually in the form of capital grants to individuals reaching their maturity in that year.[46] This would allow each person to enjoy the fruits of his or her labor while also fulfilling everyone's prior right to a share of the profits of the whole society as they expanded over time. This, he urged, was the "natural order of succession"—one in which the individual's right to share in the general patrimony "consecrates the harmony of property with community," while also giving individuals their due by right of productive contribution.[47]

A final important representative of the writers who extended rent theory and began to explore its historical dimensions was a Belgian nobleman who spent most of his years writing in Paris. Hippolyte de Colins's overall position provides one of the most clearly worked out statements of the argument that what we inherit can hardly be said to be earned by the current generation—and that this in turn demands a different moral reckoning. It may accordingly serve as a convenient summary of the trajectory of developing nineteenth- and early-twentieth-century thought on these issues, and on the importance of historical contribution.

Colins accepted Locke's primary argument concerning individual contribution and entitlement, and he also strongly challenged the view that simply expending labor on land or other resources created a right to the total value of the final product. Colins judged that the contribution of current labor was minimal compared with the contribution that came from the past and from natural resources. "These two parts of the general wealth are *infinitely* greater than the part acquired by the existing generation," he urged—and in any just system wealth derived from them belongs to all.[48]

Colins's position was uncompromising: "The only means that society can have of being just in the interpretation of the will of past generations is to ensure that the existing generation—*without distinction among families*—owns the products that the past generations destined for their posterity."[49] But again, this did not mean that individual effort and "desert" were of no consequence. Quite the contrary. Colins stressed that "the labor of each person belongs to himself, and the product of his labor must pass, by inheritance, to his own children." Justice therefore required reconciling the two principles so that "no one could find himself stripped of the portion of wealth that belongs to him from past generations."[50] Colins hoped to develop a school of "rational socialism," seeking a middle ground between capitalist private property and collective ownership. Like Dove and Huet, he urged that the "community" be considered as consisting of individuals, not primarily as a collective body. Hence, individual allocations, rights, and incentives needed to be respected. Colins proposed a three-part policy framework to achieve a just allocation of that which came from the past (and from natural resources) and that which was the product of individual effort in the here and now.

First, all land would be held in trust by the community, with rights to use it allocated each year through competitive bidding. (Individual inheritance of land would be abolished.) Second, private ownership of the stock of capital goods would be permitted as an incentive to further production—with such private wealth considered a privilege, rather than a right, and therefore subject to heavy taxation. Third, as a matter of justice and an equal right of inheritance, those who had less than an equal share of the stock of capital goods, land, and other productive assets derived from nature or from previous generations were to be compensated from taxation of the surpluses of those who had more than an equal share of such historically and socially created wealth.[51]

In subsequent decades, ideas of inheritance were to become part of the mainstream of European political thinking and were also to influence American Progressive thinking and politics in significant ways. The most important development was the philosophy of "solidarism," elaborated by the French statesman Léon Bourgeois. Solidarism—the "official social philosophy of the French Third Republic"—called for social insurance policies financed by progressive taxation on income and property. This was justified, Bourgeois argued, because the common assets generated by social progress created corresponding social debts.[52] In his 1896 book *Solidarité* he wrote:

> Man does not only become the debtor of his contemporaries in the course of his life; from the very day of his birth, he is a debtor. Man is born a debtor of human as-

sociation. On entering such an association, he takes his share of an inheritance built up by his own ancestors and those of all others; at birth, he begins to benefit from an immense capital which previous generations have accumulated.[53]

As historian J.E.S. Hayward observes, this reality cried out for "reparative justice," a program to "redistribute fairly the 'common capital' of society amongst all its members."[54] Although rarely recalled today, Bourgeois's writings and ideas also found their way into American thinking. Most importantly, they contributed to the work of the progressive economist John R. Commons and the Commons-led "Wisconsin School" of economic policy, in turn the major intellectual source for the U.S. Social Security system and other social insurance ideas developed during the New Deal and after.[55]

7

Toward a More Encompassing Theory

Who has made a larger contribution to the operation of General Electric—its chief executives or Albert Einstein or Michael Faraday or Isaac Newton?

—Robert Dahl, *Dilemmas of Pluralist Democracy: Autonomy vs. Control* (1982)[1]

Let us return one final time to the three primary propositions concerning the distinction between earned and unearned income we discussed in chapter 5: From Locke, the argument that an individual has a right to that which he actually creates by his own unique contribution. From Ricardo, the analysis of unearned rent created not by individual contributions but by external forces. From Mill and others, the judgment that gains not due to individual contributions are subject to special consideration from the standpoint of distributive justice— together with the argument that society as a whole creates many values and is or should be the residual claimant of such values. It is clear from elements of the work of Hobson, Hobhouse, Dove, Huet, Colins, Bourgeois, and many others that a fourth proposition can also be seen to be developing among various thinkers—and needs now to be clarified, explicated, and confronted: this is the simple acknowledgment that society's contribution is not only "current" in the sense of active systems and institutions that facilitate everyday life, but, more importantly, it is also inherited, a "gift of the past" in the form of material, intellectual, and cultural assets created and preserved by previous generations. To this we may now add explicit recognition of the research findings reported in Part I—namely, that the most important contribution of society (and of the past) is inherited and ever-expanding knowledge.

Taken together, the four propositions, fully elaborated and linked to modern understanding of the residual, lead to the logically inevitable judgment that since the wealth we today enjoy is largely a gift of the past, and since no one individual contributes more than a minor amount compared to the gift of the past, therefore society as a whole (after due considera-tion of all other issues of policy and incentive)* has a primary moral claim to that (very large) portion of wealth that the in-herited knowledge it has contributed now creates.

A review of the writings of a diverse group of important twentieth-century thinkers, including an unusual array of Nobel laureates, suggests there are reasons to believe we may be moving slowly but steadily toward a full confrontation with the fourth proposition's powerful claim.

One of the most striking early contributions is that of the iconoclastic American economist Thorstein Veblen. With a body of work spanning the late nineteenth and early twenti-eth centuries, Veblen also provides a useful bridge to consid-eration of modern thinkers who have begun to reach toward the fully developed argument. Veblen was one of the first economists to directly confront the central theoretical point concerning knowledge. It was obvious, he held, that society's heritage of learning was the "prime creative factor" in all

* See the conclusion for a discussion of incentives and efficiency.

production—the "accumulated knowledge, skill, and judgment that goes into the work."[2] Labor and capital, he stressed, were always embedded in a long, growing developmental process, a cumulative proficiency endowed mainly by knowledge and habit. As he put it in *Absentee Ownership*, "Tangible assets, considered simply as material objects, are inert, transient and trivial, compared with the abiding efficiency of that living structure of technology that has created them and continues to turn them to account."[3] Passages from other works, especially his 1914 book *The Instinct of Workmanship*, are evocative of cutting-edge research fields today such as social epistemology and cognitive economics. Veblen argued, for instance, that "the higher the degree of intelligence and the larger the available body of knowledge current in any given community, the more extensive and elaborate will be the logic of ways and means interposed between . . . impulses and their realization." This "apparatus of ways and means" for pursuing beneficial economic and other advances is a "legacy of habits of thought accumulated through the experience of past generations."[4] The "joint stock of knowledge," he urged, is "the indispensable foundation of all productive industry."[5]

In Veblen's view capital was not so much a source or creator of value as a kind of conduit or transfer point for society's cumulative learning: "Ownership of the material means [of production] . . . carries with it the usufruct of the community's immaterial equipment of technological proficiency."[6] Again, the "business situation" obscures the "community's immaterial equipment of technological knowledge," and so a "genetic exposition" is necessary to understand how output really grows.[7] The "technological scheme" that "enables" production is itself a "creation of the group life of the community."[8] At the same time, he critically noted, the gains from such socially created capacities are increasingly captured by a tiny elite:

[The] joint stock of technology is the substance of the
community's civilization on the industrial side, and
therefore it constitutes the substantial core of that civilization. Like any other phase or element of the cultural
heritage, it is a joint possession of the community, so far
as concerns its custody, exercise, increase and transmission; but it has turned out, under the peculiar circumstances that condition the use of this technology among
these civilized peoples, that its ownership or usufruct
has come to be effectually vested in a relatively small
number of persons.[9]

Veblen wrote scathingly of the "captains of industry" and
the "great man" theory of accumulation. The same natural
right that once entitled the small farmer to the fruits of his
labor, he held, now unjustly gave the owners of capital, a
small minority, effective title to "the state of the industrial
arts," a creation of the community. This tiny elite constituted
the "vested interests" or the "kept classes." Under modern
conditions, Veblen judged, the right of ownership "promises
to be nothing better than a means of assured defeat and vexa-
tion for the common man." The fundamental reason why this
was occurring, he suggested, was that traditional moral views
of entitlement had not been sufficiently adapted to the modern industrial system.[10]

Veblen did not take the next step. Although he once wrote
that "it may well come to pass, in time, that men will consider
any income unearned which exceeds a fair return for tangible
performance," unlike writers such as Dove, Huet, Colins, and
Bourgeois, he did not attempt to develop either the philosophical or policy implications of his larger view.[11] What is
striking, however, is how prescient Veblen's writings now appear, both because they so clearly anticipate the work of
Solow, Denison, Mokyr, and others on the central economic
importance of inherited knowledge, and because his analytic

understanding resonates so powerfully with contemporary
efforts to clarify a theory of entitlement that explicitly recog-
nizes the full implications of knowledge.

Another early-twentieth-century theorist who contributed
to the developing knowledge thesis—and who did begin to
explore its moral implications—was G.D.H. Cole, a leading
Fabian intellectual and later Oxford professor of social and
political theory. Cole, like Veblen, stressed that "current productive power is, in effect, a joint result of current effort and
of the social heritage of inventiveness and skill incorporated
in the stage of advancement and education reached in the
arts of production." Citizens should share in the yields of
their common heritage, he held, and "only the balance of the
product after this allocation" should be distributed as rewards
or incentives for current individual input.[12] In his *Principles
of Economic Planning* (1935) Cole proposed a social dividend
mechanism to guarantee each individual an equal share
of that part of current productive power that came as an inheritance from the past. Under such an approach, he also
observed, income from individual contribution would inevitably decline relative to social income, since the social and
inherited share of productive power always increased, relative to what any one person could contribute, with the steady
advance of knowledge and industrial productivity.[13]

Edwin Cannan, a major early-twentieth-century figure at
the London School of Economics, also made important contributions that further developed these themes. Although a
critic of Fabian socialism, Cannan nonetheless shared with
Cole an understanding of the centrality of society's "heritage
of improvement"—by which he meant "the net economic
advantage which we and other generations who come late in
the history of mankind, possess in consequence of what has
been done by mankind in the past." One of Cannan's important contributions was a broadening of the central thesis to
include organizational development. The "heritage of im-

provcmcnt," hc wrotc, consists first in "knowledge and skill produced by research and experience, and transmitted from each generation to the next by books and other instruments, by oral instruction and by mere imitation." An ever-increasing supply of goods accumulated over time in the productive domain—buildings, machinery, landscaping, and so on—constituted a second element. Beyond this, however, was a legacy of socially created and inherited "organizations" that enable "large numbers of people . . . to co-operate in production." Cannan held that in ignoring or playing down the various elements in the "heritage," conventional economics had things backward. Most economists had

> worked outwards from the individual to the nation and society, rather losing interest as they went, without testing the results by working backwards from society to the individual, and the consequence has been that capital, unduly glorified, has been allowed to usurp the place which should properly be occupied by the heritage of improvement, to the great detriment both of economic theory and of public policy.[14]

Cannan anticipated Mokyr's "free lunch" judgment in stressing that the knowledge and organizational forms "acquired by the past and transmitted to us" are, in fact, "free goods."[15]

In recent years, Columbia University philosopher Brian Barry has extended and in certain respects amplified the overall argument. "Most of our technology and the capital stock embodying it are not by any stretch of the imagination the sole creation of the present generation," he stresses, and thus "we cannot . . . claim exclusive credit for it." Indeed,

> the whole process of capital formation presupposes an inheritance of capital and technology. To a considerable extent, then, we can say that, from the standpoint of the current generation, natural resources are not as sharply

distinguished from capital and technology as might at first appear. Both are originally inherited, and thus fall outside any special claims based on the present generation's having done something to deserve them.[16]

Barry goes on to emphasize that this insight is especially relevant in advanced countries, where people are literally born into a wealth of "productive capital, good systems of communications, orderly administration, well-developed systems of education and training, and so on." What, specifically, he asks, "have the fortunate inheritors of all these advantages done to give them an exclusive claim to the benefits flowing from them?" Barry's answer is that "any claims that those now alive can make to special advantages derived from the efforts of their ancestors [are] quite limited." *[17]

We noted earlier that the ever-growing contribution of the past inevitably becomes proportionately larger and more valuable, year by year, than the time-bound contribution of any specific "new" generation. Barry likewise suggests that even the limited claims to inheritance of those alive in any particular period "attenuate with time." The present generation might legitimately derive some special advantages from the efforts of the preceding one, and perhaps the one before that. However, the inherited share of what they, in turn, pass on—that part of their wealth that is inherited from their predecessors—"should be regarded as by now forming part of the common heritage of mankind."[18]

Quite apart from the work of these representative political and economic philosophers, perhaps the most striking and unexpected contributions toward an expanded twentieth-

---

* Although beyond the scope of the present work, obviously such issues might also be raised at a global level. An initial statement by Barry can be found in his *Democracy, Power and Justice* (Oxford: Clarendon Press, 1989), chap. 16, in particular pp. 450–55.

century understanding of the fourth distributive proposition are those of certain American conservatives. Frank Knight was one of the leading figures of the free-market Chicago School of economics. In *The Ethics of Competition* (published in 1923 on the basis of a lecture delivered at Harvard), Knight focused his discussion on how individual competence, hence individual contribution, actually develops. Drawing a sharp distinction between a person's *effort* and a person's *"productive capacity,"* Knight argued that

> the ownership of personal or material productive capacity is based upon a complex mixture of inheritance, luck, and effort, probably in that order of relative importance. What is the ideal distribution from the standpoint of absolute ethics may be disputed, but of the three considerations named certainly none but the effort can have ethical validity. From the standpoint of absolute ethics most persons will probably agree that inherited capacity represents an obligation to the world rather than a claim upon it.[19]

Put another way, even what we judge to be contributed and earned by personal effort is itself in significant part the product of inheritance, social influence, and luck *for each person.* Every individual participates personally "in a total accumulated social inheritance [that] is mental or spiritual or 'cultural,' as well as 'material.' " There is "no visible reason," Knight urged, why anyone is "more or less entitled" to benefit from a personal "capacity resulting from impersonal social processes."[20]

Knight's forceful concluding argument takes one further step: it is not simply that current personal effort is less significant compared to inheritance and luck, nor that only effort (among the three factors) merits consideration in an ethical distributive approach. What is striking is Knight's conclusion

that since individual "productive capacity" is itself something one largely inherits, such capacity is not only morally
undeserved by the individual but—as something inherited—
it morally *obligates* the advantaged individual to contribute
some measure of support back to society.

Knight did not work out the kind of redistributive argument that could easily be developed from these judgments.
Others, however, including additional important conservatives, have moved the central issues forward in further unexpected ways. In his wide-ranging book *The Problems of
Jurisprudence*, the well-known contemporary free-market
jurist Richard Posner observes that in "a state of nature people would not have much in the way of life, liberty, or property." He then offers his own version of an inheritance
analysis of the sources of current wealth and well-being:

> The long life, spacious liberties, and extensive property
> of the average American citizen are the creation not
> of that American alone but of society—a vast aggrega-
> tion of individuals, living and dead—and of geographi-
> cal luck (size, topography, location, natural resources,
> climate).

For this reason, Posner argues, conservatives and others
who oppose redistributive strategies are on weak ground
when they stress traditional arguments based on very narrow
Lockean premises. Because they do not take account of the
obvious contributions of the "vast aggregation of individuals,
living and dead" and other factors, such arguments, he says
are "porous." (Posner's own views on redistribution are in the
main pragmatic—i.e., they are based on whether specific
policies reduce incentives or in other ways hinder wealth
maximization.)[21]

Although figures like Knight and Posner have helped open
the discussion of these issues to a broader range of thinkers,

thc most important modcrn contributions to the development of the central ideas have come from a diverse group of
other economists and political writers. We may note, for instance, the straightforward judgment of the American Nobel
laureate economist Kenneth J. Arrow on one critical element
of the argument. Writing in terms that resonate strongly
with the earlier liberal views of Paine, Mill, and Hobhouse,
Arrow observes: "There are large gains to social interaction
above and beyond what . . . individuals and subgroups could
achieve on their own. The owners of scarce personal assets do
not have a private use of these assets which is considerable; it
is only their value in a large system which makes these assets
valuable. Hence, there is a surplus created by the existence of
society as such which is available for redistribution."[22]

The work of another Nobel laureate economist, Douglass
North, advances arguments similar in emphasis to Thorstein
Veblen's central contention. Although North does not deal directly with distributional matters, and although his approach
is more sophisticated in its formal development, for North,
too, "growth in the stock of knowledge" is the fundamental
underlying determinant of modern economic growth.[23] Accordingly, the "focus of our attention . . . must be on human
learning, and in the final analysis, growth must be understood as essentially a cultural process."[24]

North stresses the importance of what he calls the "artifactual structure"—what past generations put in place to preserve and transmit their learning and ideas.[25] How the
artifactual structure relates to economic growth, in turn, reflects the influence of belief systems—about nature, society,
human purpose, and humanity's place in the world and uni-
verse.[26] Knowledge creates growth by reducing uncertainty
and expanding human problem-solving powers. The effects
of capital-labor substitution and other conventional firm behaviors are quite limited by comparison. "Successful economic development will occur," North writes, "when the

belief system that has evolved has created a 'favorable' artifactual structure that can confront the novel experiences that
the individual and society face and resolve positively the
novel dilemmas."[27] Critically,

> the beliefs that individuals, groups, and societies hold
> which determine choices are a consequence of learning
> through time—not just the span of an individual's life
> or of a generation of a society but the learning embod-
> ied in individuals, groups, and societies that is cumula-
> tive through time and passed on intergenerationally by
> the culture of a society.[28]

In chapter 1 we noted the similar views of still another
Nobel laureate, George Akerlof, which are also worth recall-
ing here. "Our current standard of living," Akerlof judged, is
something we "owe" to the past. The fruits of current labor
or current savings "are due almost entirely to the cumulative
process of learning that has taken us from stone age poverty
to twenty-first-century affluence."[29]

Finally, Herbert Simon, arguably the twentieth century's
most important organizational theorist and yet another
American Nobel laureate economist, took the occasion of
his 2000 Gaus Award Lecture before the American Political
Science Association to deal directly with the problem of individual entitlements in a world increasingly dominated by societal contribution. "If we are very generous with ourselves,"
he stated, "I suppose we might claim that we 'earned' as
much as one fifth of [our income]." The rest, he argued,

> is the patrimony associated with being a member of an
> enormously productive social system, which has accu-
> mulated a vast store of physical capital, and an even
> larger store of intellectual capital—including knowl-
> edge, skills, and organizational know-how held by all of
> us—so that interaction with our equally talented fellow

citizens rubs off on us both much of this knowledge and this generous allotment of unearned income.[30]

How we allocate the inherited patrimonial share of output in a given year or period, Simon suggested, was not to be decided through reference to narrow economic formulas. Rather, he urged, it "is a matter of values to be decided by political processes."[31] Elsewhere Simon suggested that, since a very large share of American per capita income was due to "the happy accident that the income recipient was born in the U.S.," the huge gift bestowed as a "patrimony," and received simply by the chance of birth, should be subject to large-order taxation.[32]

That the related views of these diverse economists and philosophers might—taken together—point toward something new and important was fully anticipated by one of America's leading political scientists, Yale professor and former president of the American Political Science Association Robert Dahl. What first caught Dahl's attention was Denison's work pointing to the critical role of advances in knowledge in economic growth. "It is immediately obvious," Dahl observed after reading Denison, "that little growth in the American economy can be attributed to the actions of particular individuals." But then:

> Who ought to receive what shares? And how should the "decision" about shares be made? One answer is that shares in the growth in national income ought to be allocated according to individual or group contributions. If the contributions are traceable to social factors, however, and not to specific individuals or even to definite groups, how are we to make the allocations?[33]

That social factors had to be considered in historical terms was also obvious to Dahl. "A large firm," he pointed out, "is inherently a social and political enterprise. It is inherently *social* in the sense that its very existence and functioning depend on contributions made by joint actions, past and current, that cannot be attributed to specific persons: the arrow of causation is released by 'social forces,' history, culture, or other poorly defined agents." Indeed,

> without the protection of a dense network of laws enforced by public governments, the largest American corporation could not exist for a day. Without a labor force the firm would vanish. It would slowly languish if the labor force were not suitably educated. Who then provides for the education of its skilled workers, its white-collar employees, its executives? One of a firm's most critical resources is language. Language comes free, provided by "society" and millennia of evolution. Concepts, ideas, civic orientations like the famous Protestant ethic, the condition of science and technology: these are social. Who has made a larger contribution to the operation of General Electric—its chief executives or Albert Einstein or Michael Faraday or Isaac Newton?[34]

Dahl's conclusion was perhaps the most radical to be offered in the evolving discussion: "Insofar as a right to property is justified by the principle that one is entitled to use the products of one's own labor as one chooses . . . the principle would lead to the conclusion that the control and ownership of the economy rightfully belongs to 'society.' If so, means must be found for 'society' to exercise the control to which it is entitled by virtue of its collective ownership."[35] In various writings Dahl proposed a range of redistributive measures in general—and also consideration of employee-owned enterprises in particular—as effective ways to achieve such ownership.[36]

●　　●　　●

Dahl also suggested that "changes in the way the economy is likely to be perceived in the future would almost certainly help to make distributive issues more salient."[37] The "ill fit" between conventional "private" views of economic institutions and their "social and public" nature, he observed, "creates a discordance that probably cannot be indefinitely sustained."[38] This judgment helps define one of the most interesting of the emerging issues. We noted above Thorstein Veblen's view that vast inequities had become commonplace in his day because traditional moral views of what was "deserved" had not kept up with, or been adapted to, the early-twentieth-century industrial system. In chapter 1 we noted Daniel Bell's suggestion that a new "knowledge theory of value" was demanded by the new processes at work in the modern economy.[39] Before his death the acclaimed management consultant Peter Drucker urged that the central role of knowledge in the emerging twenty-first-century system defined it as no longer *"a"* resource, but rather *"the"* resource." Drucker also judged that the development of the "knowledge economy" pointed in the direction of a new and different type of economic system.[40] Many other writers have grasped that the very nature of the knowledge economy requires new understandings. Nobel laureate Joseph Stiglitz offers this increasingly accepted conclusion among leading economic thinkers: "Just as the importance of land in production changed dramatically as the economy moved from agriculture to industry, so too does the movement to a knowledge economy necessitate a rethinking of economic fundamentals."[41] To this we must now add the judgment that such a rethinking must include the question of what is contributed and what is inherited, what is earned and what is unearned, and, accordingly, who deserves what, and why.

Conclusion

Earned and Unearned in the Era
of the Knowledge Economy

That which you inherit from your fathers, you must earn in order
to possess.

—Johann Wolfgang von Goethe, *Faust* [1]

In a recent book urging taxation of large estates like that
which his own son will one day leave, Bill Gates Sr. (along
with co-author Chuck Collins) writes: "Success is a product of
having been born in this country, a place where education and
research are subsidized, where there is an orderly market,
where the private sector reaps enormous benefits from public
investment. For someone to assert that he or she has grown
wealthy in America without the benefit of substantial public
investment is pure hubris. . . . What is it worth to operate
within this marvelous system?" [2]

Gates's judgment is a strongly urged statement of one facet
of the larger argument of this study. It is certainly true that
private wealth creation depends fundamentally on publicly
supported education and research, and on public creation and
maintenance of an orderly market. It depends even more
fundamentally, however, on the fact that all current economic
production is overwhelmingly dependent on a long, long
prior history of socially created science, technology, and other
knowledge. There is every reason to reward individuals for
the specific contributions they make. There is no reason to

hand over to them excessively large shares of that which comes to us all as the gift of the past.

The findings of modern economics, economic history, and other fields of scholarly inquiry that have documented the centrality of inherited knowledge in economic progress are not yet widely understood. People speak of the "knowledge economy," but for many the phrase is simply that—a phrase. For others, it is a vague notion that computers, computer-driven production processes, and the Internet are very important, but in ways most would find difficult to explain. In a sense the sun still revolves around the earth; Galileo has done his studies but has not yet been heard. Nor, of course, have many confronted the attendant judgments about what one person can be said to have earned and deserved when inherited knowledge contributes so overwhelmingly to all economic achievement.

The likelihood that this will change—slowly, as always when profound theoretical insights move from academic birthing to real-world impact—is suggested by the steadily developing trajectory of the knowledge economy itself, a trajectory of economic change impacting everyday life and public understanding, day by day, year by year, decade by decade. The scale of the changes we are experiencing is immense. "Industry in the developed countries is moving from metal-bashing to knowledge generation," observes Joseph Stiglitz. "The information . . . revolution is pushing to eliminate the effects of 'weight' and distance. In the days of the pony express, it took many horses, men, and days to send a message from Kansas City to San Francisco whereas today it is done in the blink of an eye by a little quivering in an electromagnetic field."[3]

The United States currently spends ten times more on R&D than it did in 1950 (after adjusting for inflation).[4] U.S. patent applications more than tripled between 1985 and 2005—exploding from 63,874 in 1985 to 207,867 in 2005.

Total patent applications in the United States of both foreign and domestic origins increased at a similar pace, reaching 417,508 per year by 2005.[5] The number of science and engineering positions in the U.S. economy has also increased dramatically—at more than four times the rate of growth for all jobs from 1980 to 2000.[6] A majority of American workers are now employed in office/institutional settings relying heavily on specialized knowledge and information technology: professionals, managers, salespeople, administrative support, and technicians.[7] Less than 11 percent are directly involved in manufacturing.[8]

Keynesian ideas became widely accepted during the 1930s and then dominated American economic judgments for several decades. During the 1940s and 1950s it was considered an act of philosophical extremism to question New Deal social and economic programs; Chicago School economists were ignored. By the 1980s, however, it was routinely argued that government taxes and regulatory interventions were the source of our economic problems. In only a few decades the ideas that largely set the terms of reference for the conservative resurgence in the late twentieth century moved from the extreme margin of public life to its very center, as had Keynesian theories in earlier decades. That other, newer ideas might equally rise to transcendent power in the future is, minimally, the lesson of history—and of how major lines of thought can emerge, develop, and transform public opinion as economic realities change.

In the Note that follows this conclusion we take up a number of detailed philosophical questions that arise when the implications of technological inheritance are fully confronted. One commonly misunderstood issue, however, is worth noting briefly at this point. It is sometimes held that great inventors or great business innovators deserve all the economic gains they can capture because of the contribution they uniquely make to society. If they had not made their contribution, it is implied, society would have suffered greatly. This argument, however, largely ignores what we know about how invention and innovation actually occur. As we have seen, broadly speaking, when science and technology reach a certain point in development, if one person does not achieve the inevitable next-step "breakthrough," almost certainly another person will. From the discovery of DNA to MRI scanners, from the invention of calculating machines to the rise of digital information technologies, the historical record of simultaneous invention reflects a powerful cultural process at the heart of innovation and discovery in which the evolving range and depth of human knowledge virtually guarantees new advances no matter who, individually, gets there "first" or "second" or who wins or loses the patent race. If Alexander Graham Bell had not invented the telephone, someone else would have—and, indeed, Elisha Gray and Antonio Meucci did. If Bill Gates hadn't "invented" the MS-DOS operating system, someone else would have invented a similar system— and, in fact, Gary Kildall did.[9] It may possibly be true (it is impossible to know for sure one way or another) that specific contributions can sometimes advance things a bit faster because of sheer genius in certain cases, or that there may be special, highly unusual exceptions to the general rule. But it is also a fact that both Newton and Leibniz developed versions of the calculus at roughly the same time, and Darwin and Alfred Russel Wallace closed in on similar theories of evolution at very close to the same time. Newton, we may also recall—like Einstein—was one of the strongest proponents of the centrality of knowledge inheritance. As he famously wrote: "If I have seen far, it is because I have stood on the shoulders of giants."[10]

Put another way, every new breakthrough starts from a plateau of knowledge created by others and preserved and passed on by society. Increasingly, at every new stage, *most of the work is already done*, and in most cases the scientist, the inventor, and the business innovator may add something new, but mainly they recombine what others have done in a way that is usually about to become evident to others as well.[11] If Newton, in his lifetime, had to learn everything humanity had learned from the time of the caveman to the late seventeenth century—if he had no knowledge inheritance whatsoever to work with—he could not have contributed much more than an insightful caveman could in his lifetime. That which the entrepreneurs of the knowledge economy have drawn upon is equally massive compared with what they or any one person, today, can possibly contribute.

More may be said: Each year, each decade, each century, what is created and passed on from one generation to the next becomes larger and larger. And accordingly, what any one person at any new point in time actually can be said to personally contribute becomes smaller and smaller *relative to that which comes to her as the free (and constantly growing) gift of the past.* It is not simply that the question of what one individual contributes (and therefore may "deserve") is brought into sharp relief by modern studies of the role of knowledge in economic growth. As each year passes, what Geoffrey Hodgson has called the "mismatch" between "productive realities" and "individualistic formulations" of desert and entitlement inevitably becomes greater and greater.[12]

So, too, the resulting moral contradictions involved in allocating new forms of socially created wealth—above all, the economic value generated by expanding knowledge—through an outmoded system of entitlements can only intensify. Herbert Simon's striking judgment that 80 percent of our wealth is the "patrimony" of a productive society, an inheritance mainly comprised of intellectual and social capital, suggests the scale of the problem with which we are confronted.

•   •   •

The principal "practical" *operational* objection to the argument that society as a whole—not favored individuals and
elites—should benefit most from the knowledge society has
created over many generations is the same objection made to
all proposals for changes in the distribution of income and
wealth—namely, that this might harm the economy, thereby
harming all citizens and society in general. Many studies,
however, now challenge this widely publicized but increasingly questionable understanding. It is argued, for instance,
that high taxation must hinder economic growth—and that
low taxation fosters growth. A recent collection of studies edited by public finance scholar Joel Slemrod, however, points
out that such a view bears very little resemblance to historical
reality. When the annual rate of productivity growth was at
its peak in the United States, for instance—3.1 percent during the period from 1951–1963—so too were the top marginal tax rates at their peak: in 1957 incomes of $400,000 or
more were taxed at a marginal rate of 91 percent. At
$100,000 the marginal rate was 75 percent.[13] The last thirty
years of tax cutting and deregulation, in contrast, have generated mixed productivity growth: rates slowed to less than 1.5
percent per year between 1973 and 1995, and although they
averaged 2–3 percent annually from 1995 to 2004, they did
not match the 3.1 percent rate of the 1950s and early 1960s.[14]
"The fact that the golden years of modern American economic growth occurred during the apex of marginal tax
rates," Slemrod observes, "is, at a minimum, an embarrassing
coincidence for those who believe that avoiding such a policy
is the key to economic success."[15]

Comparative evidence from other advanced nations also
challenges the conventional wisdom. It is true that U.S. productivity growth was higher than that of the European
Union as a whole during the 1995–2004 period.[16] On the other
hand, France, Germany, Norway, Belgium, Great Britain,

Italy, Ireland, and Finland all had higher taxes than the United States between 1970 and 1990—and all had higher productivity growth than the U.S. during this period.[17] Another scholar, Peter Lindert, has studied the longer-term relationship between social spending and economic growth since the eighteenth century in a broad range of countries. "It is well known," he writes, "that higher taxes and transfers reduce productivity. Well known—but unsupported by statistics and history." More taxation to finance social spending also "does not correlate negatively with either the level or the growth of GDP per capita," Lindert points out. Indeed, countries that tax and transfer as much as a third of the national product have not grown any more slowly than countries devoting only a seventh of GDP to social spending. One of the main reasons, he observes, is that social spending on education, on health, on training, and on many other essentials contributes to growth by promoting the development of human capital. "Real-world welfare states benefit from a style of taxing and spending that is in many ways more pro-growth than the policies of most free-market countries."[18]

None of this is to suggest that incentives have no role in behavior or that badly designed government policies are cost-free. The price of gasoline clearly affects the market for large and small automobiles. Some tax incentives may work reasonably well to encourage investment and innovation; others may not. What recent studies suggest is an important but simple point: there is very substantial evidence that carefully designed redistributive policies can be supportive both of greater economic growth and social equality. Furthermore, if the revenues accruing from new tax policies are used to enhance research, education, health, and other factors affecting the quality, skill levels, and technological capacities of the economy in general and the American labor force in particular, such policies may well enhance economic growth.

The most obvious areas for reform include increasing the

income taxation of the top 1–2 percent, raising the current cap on Social Security taxes, increasing corporate taxes (especially on windfall gains in connection with oil industry profits), and increasing inheritance taxes on large estates. Private inheritance of large amounts of capital in particular violates the principle that what one deserves should be related to what one contributes and earns—both because an heir does nothing directly to earn his or her inheritance, and because that inheritance itself, like all wealth, derives overwhelmingly from the contributions of inherited knowledge. Estimates of how much individual wealth depends on personal inheritance range from a low of 20 percent to roughly 80 percent; the latter (by Laurence Kotlikoff) includes all unearned wealth transfers to children after they reach the age of eighteen (including, for example, college tuition paid by parents) as well as the appreciating value of gifts and bequests after transfer.[19]

Proceeds from new taxation might be allocated to a variety of public purposes ranging from universal health care to the maintenance and development of the nation's failing infrastructure. Particularly appropriate uses might be to support educational and research institutions that generate and pass on knowledge at all levels, to offer tuition relief (and possibly something akin to a new "GI Bill" to expand opportunities for college education), and to provide much more generous underpinnings for low and moderate incomes—perhaps modeled on a greatly expanded version of the current Earned Income Tax Credit.[20]

In addition to these and other redistributive policies there are a number of newer strategies that do not in any event significantly impact incentives related to work or investment. Among the most important are so-called asset-based approaches, which emphasize the wealth people accrue, have, and invest—as opposed to the income people receive, and spend or save. Harvard economist Richard Freeman writes:

Our main strategy—be we left or right—for fighting
income inequality under capitalism should be to assure
a fair initial distribution of physical and human capital
themselves. Equality of income obtained in the first instance via greater equality in those assets, rather than as
an after-the-fact (of earning or luck) state redistribution of income from rich to poor, would enable us to better square the circle of market efficiency and egalitarian
aspiration.[21]

A forward-looking proposal that also alters ownership (and
echoes ideas of some of the nineteenth-century theorists reviewed in chapter 6) has recently been put forward by Yale
law professors Bruce Ackerman and Anne Alstott. This would
allocate a "capital stake" of $80,000 to every citizen on reach-
ing adulthood—to be used for any purpose an individual
chose (in most cases, probably for college education). The
program would initially be financed by a 2 percent annual
wealth tax, thus simultaneously challenging the top beneficiaries of the current system with a strategy that could provide
large numbers with the means of acquiring knowledge. The
capital stake would be recouped at death through an inheritance tax.[22]

Another promising, rapidly growing asset-based approach
is the employee-owned firm, currently encouraged by certain
federal tax policies. When properly structured, such enterprises (especially small- and medium-sized firms) are demon-
strably more, rather than less, efficient than comparable
privately owned traditional firms.[23] An obvious reason is that
people tend to work better and harder when they have a stake
in the outcome. Robert Dahl's argument that ownership—
not simply income redistribution—must now become important is given substance by the little-noted fact that there
are approximately ten thousand firms now operating in the
United States that are wholly or substantially owned by em-

ployees. Policies to provide further support for such firms could both help broaden the ownership of wealth and simultaneously achieve greater economic efficiency.[24]

The main goal of this work has been to explore a new way of thinking about the implications of the knowledge economy, rather than to delineate the many possible policies that might flow from the larger judgments. Numerous variations on the themes here outlined have been widely discussed by specialists working in diverse areas of policy concern—and are likely, we believe, to be expanded upon as growing understanding of the need for change develops.

In 1982 the average CEO of an American company received 42 times the compensation received by the average worker. In 2004 CEO compensation was estimated to be 431 times higher than that of the average worker.[25] In 2005 the top 1 percent of Americans received 15.6 percent of the nation's post-tax income, more than the bottom 120 million Americans taken together.[26] The concentrated ownership of productive wealth is even more extreme: in 2004 the top 1 percent of wealth holders owned over 60 percent of all individually owned business equity and financial securities and nearly half of all non–retirement account stocks, mutual funds, and trusts. An only slightly larger elite group—the top 5 percent—owned just under 70 percent of financial wealth and nearly 60 percent of all net worth. In 2004 Bill Gates's net worth alone was more than twice the direct stock holdings of the entire bottom half of the U.S. population.[27]

The full meaning of statistics like these is rarely confronted. "Tectonic shifts" in the economy have produced what Paul Krugman, Kevin Phillips, and others have called a "new plutocracy." Krugman observes that the "rich have always been different from you and me, but they are far more different now than they were not long ago—indeed, they are as different now as they were when F. Scott Fitzgerald made his famous remark." Political scientist Alan Wolfe adds: "There really are only two classes in America now—the top 2 percent and everybody else."[28] Experts have long understood that the United States is the most unequal of all the advanced nations. Changes in recent years, however, have produced outcomes that are both extraordinary and disturbing.

The shift toward extreme concentrations of income and wealth at the top has occurred at a time of growing economic and social pain—especially, recently, among America's middle class as wages stagnate, manufacturing jobs disappear, pensions are cut back, medical costs rise, property taxes skyrocket, and college tuition payments soar. Real hourly wages have hardly increased for three decades; for many, real wages have gone down. A generation ago the typical one-earner family spent 54 percent of its income on the basics of housing, health insurance, transportation, and taxes. Today such expenses—plus child care, needed to allow both parents to work—consume 75 percent of the family's combined income.[29] Tuition at public four-year universities has risen more than 180 percent in inflation-adjusted dollars in the past twenty-five years. Families planning for retirement face steadily increasing insecurity: 40 percent of workers had traditional private "defined benefit" pension plans in the mid-1980s; a mere 20 percent had such plans in 2004.[30]

The growing pain of the middle class is occurring side by side with the ongoing pain of America's poor, and especially America's minority poor. Today nearly 37 million Americans still live below the official poverty line. A U.S. Department of Agriculture study of the period 1999–2004 found the number of Americans who were "food insecure"—meaning they had to cut back on food requirements due to a lack of income—had increased from 31 million to 38.2 million. For children the numbers are more dramatic still: in 2005 more than one third of all African American children were being brought up in poverty conditions.[31]

An obvious question is: How long can the claims of those at the top to very large shares of the gift of the past continue to be sustained as the economic difficulties facing vast numbers of Americans continue to increase? How long can the benefits conferred by many generations of development continue to be siphoned off by elites rather than allowed to flow back to society and to the people at large?

The core lesson of the modern revolution in economic understanding is that perhaps as much as 90 percent of the twentieth-century productivity gains that lie behind our contemporary prosperity may derive from knowledge broadly understood. If we include the much longer buildup of knowledge that comes to us from the contributions of generation upon generation of scholars, researchers, technicians, and craftsmen who created the basic concepts and instruments of modern mathematics, genetics, chemistry, and physics (to name only a few pivotal realms of productive knowledge)— and those who also created the institutions that helped preserve and transmit knowledge, from the first alphabet, printing press, and books and libraries to public schooling, universities, computer databases, and the Internet—we must recognize with Mokyr not only that the relationship between economic performance and expanding knowledge is "obvious if not trite," but that inherited knowledge is the primary source of the wealth and income we enjoy in our own time. All of this comes to us today as a "free lunch," the generous gift of the past.

Seth Shulman, author of *Owning the Future*, has put the central moral point in sharp terms: the elites who hold most of the rights to modern technologies, he writes, "are legally sanctioned, but the legitimacy of their claims often remains dubious because of the debt they owe to innovations that have been made possible only by years or decades of collective advances." [32]

American history includes regular eruptions of transcendent change against large odds. Often such change has been driven by economic pain, on the one hand, and by the simultaneous development of new, morally charged understandings on the other. The Jeffersonian "second revolution" of the 1790s; the Populist revolt of the 1890s; the powerful electoral ratification of the New Deal; the equally powerful social challenges to race and gender discrimination in the 1960s— all suggest possibilities that often lie buried within the deeper reaches of this nation's heritage and quiet potential . . . until they explode into powerful forces of change.

As the ongoing advances of the knowledge economy continue to teach us the extraordinary possibilities—and sources—of this nation's bountiful development, the question of precisely why so few deserve to benefit so greatly while so many are in pain may well become impossible to evade. If so, the ultimate gift of the past may be renewed moral and political understanding of the responsibilities that come with a simple acknowledgment of the enormity of our common inheritance.

A Note on the Philosophical Argument

What may be called the knowledge inheritance theory of distributive justice includes the following basic claims: (1) An individual deserves compensation commensurate with the economic value attributable to his or her distinctive personal contribution. (2) A person does *not* strictly deserve what she or he does *not* create: any wealth and income a person may have that is not a result of those distinctive contributions is "unearned income" and, morally speaking, undeserved. (3) Society broadly understood also has a right to benefit from the wealth it helps to create, much of which is captured illegitimately and without warrant by privileged individuals. (4) By far the most important source of modern prosperity is societal wealth in the form of cumulative knowledge and inherited technology, which under the first three principles means that (5) a substantial portion of current wealth and income should be reallocated to all members of society equally or, at a minimum, to promote greater equality.*

* The terms "desert" and "entitlement" are often used interchangeably. In this note "desert" (or "deservingness") refers to a moral concept that is "pre-institutional," based on essential judgments of right and wrong. Entitlement here refers to a legal or institutional concept deriving its legitimacy from established rules. Thus: Bernice worked at the firm for thirty-five years, so she *deserves* a generous retirement benefit. Steve caused a security breach in the company's computer system, so he *deserves* to be fired. Mary is *entitled* to her father's estate under the legal terms of his will; the federal minimum wage *entitles* all workers to at

It may be useful for the sake of further philosophical clarity to illustrate these principles by way of a simple example: an individual who invests the effort to pick up an apple resting on an unowned piece of ground has a strong moral claim to own the entirety of that apple. While that moral claim is not always in itself decisive (claims based on desert must be balanced against, for instance, claims based on need, in particular the needs of those unable to make productive contributions), in ordinary circumstances we can reasonably say that the person who makes the effort to gather an apple from the ground has a claim to eat it, whereas an equally able-bodied person who did not make that effort does not.*

In contrast, from the perspective of the knowledge inheritance view, a person who helps design the operating system for an Apple computer does not have a similarly strong moral claim to the *entirety* of the revenues generated from the subsequent production of Apple computers. The operating system designer has a moral claim to some reward for her effort and its contribution to the existence of Apple computers; but the existence of Apple computers obviously rests on not just her contributions but that of many other people, living and dead, including (a) the other persons working directly to build an Apple computer; (b) the complex of legal and political structures that provide the background stability in which economic advances can take place; (c) the other public and

---

least $5.85 for every hour worked. A useful definition of "desert" is that of David Miller, who writes, "When primary desert judgments are made, some agent A is said to deserve some benefit B on the basis of an activity or performance P. . . . The important thing is that P should be in the relevant sense A's performance, that is, A should be responsible for P." David Miller, *Principles of Social Justice* (Cambridge, MA: Harvard University Press, 1999), p. 133.

* As we shall see, however, to the extent that the apple picker is already engaged in a system of social cooperation, his claim must be balanced against social claims: if the apple picker is living not in a state of nature but in a society with a police force that protects him from highway robbery, he might, for instance, be legitimately obliged to transfer one of every ten apples picked to help pay for the police service.

private entities that paid for the research and developed computer technology to the point where an Apple computer became an achievable accomplishment; (d) the educational, research, and other institutions that helped train succeeding generations and transmit knowledge over the centuries; and (e) the long train over many generations of contributors to the scientific, mathematic, metallurgical, and engineering knowledge that ultimately led to the idea and reality of the computers we use today.

The idea that other persons working on the creation of an Apple computer, not just the operating system designer, have a claim to the revenues generated by Apple computers—point (a) above—is not in dispute. What is in dispute is whether the firm itself—Apple Incorporated—should have a justifiable moral claim to the profits generated by the sale of Apple computers *as strong as that which the individual person picking up an apple has to that apple.* It is the argument of this book that the case of Apple computers is different from the case of an individual picking up an apple—in a morally relevant way—precisely because the creation of something as complex as a personal computer rests so fundamentally on (b), (c), (d), and (e). While some political philosophers (as noted below) have stressed the role of (b) in enabling economic activity in order to argue for a social claim to wealth, contemporary political philosophers have paid far less attention to factors (c), (d), and (e).

To say that Apple Incorporated, its employees and shareholders, does *not* have an exclusive desert claim to the wealth created by Apple computers leaves many questions unanswered. For instance, it is possible to acknowledge that those who now capture the largest benefits from our shared technological inheritance do not *deserve* to capture such benefits, but nonetheless contend that they should be *entitled* to them anyway. It might be thought, for instance, that strong incentives are needed to encourage innovative productive activity, or that there is simply no practical way to distribute the bene-fits of our knowledge economy other than allowing entrepre-neurs who draw upon our shared technological knowledge to control whatever they can get. Less sophisticated versions of this view might hold that entrepreneurs and corporations are entitled to *all* market returns; more sophisticated versions might acknowledge point (b) but say that once firms have paid sufficient taxes to contribute to the ongoing workings of the political and legal institutions that make wealth creation possible, they should be entitled to keep the remaining wealth.

The knowledge inheritance theory developed in this book takes a different approach. While (as noted in the conclusion) it allows for reasonable incentives to reward effort, it holds not only that the distinctive contributions of individuals to current economic activity and progress are minuscule com-pared to the enormous gift of the past upon which those contributions rest, but that properly recognizing this gift es-tablishes a social claim to the wealth that it generates, a moral claim that is presently largely unrecognized. Put another way, the knowledge inheritance theory agrees with tradi-tional arguments—and widely held, common-sense popular views—that *how* and *by whom* economic value is created should affect how that economic value is distributed. The knowledge inheritance account thus departs from some lib-eral philosophical conceptions of distributive justice that sug-gest that the production process is one thing and the distributive process is another, and that who produces wealth and income simply has no bearing on how it should be dis-tributed. Such conceptualizations have always struck both conservative critics and many ordinary people as implausible, insofar as they suggest that my picking up an apple off the ground does not give me a strong claim to that apple, or that distribution should have no relationship whatsoever to effort and contribution.[1]

The knowledge inheritance view departs from conventional understandings of desert, however, by stressing that in any realistic account of how economic value in the knowledge economy is actually created, the *current* efforts of individuals and firms represent a rather small input relative to the vast input provided by the gift of the past. Recognizing the magnitude of that input provides grounds for society to morally claim a larger share of the benefits generated by current knowledge-based advances, as a matter of desert. If we really take seriously *how* those of us who are alive now arrived at our current wealth, and to what we owe our prosperity, we cannot fail to recognize the enormous role that the past buildup of knowledge plays in making that prosperity possible.

The knowledge inheritance theory makes the further claim that this past buildup of knowledge should be treated as a *common inheritance*. Just as no individual or privileged group has the right to enclose commonly owned land without the consent of the rest of the community, so too no particularly privileged group has the right to claim the lion's share of the benefits produced by the common inheritance of knowledge at the same time that others are largely or completely excluded. The knowledge endowed to us by the past should not be used as a moneymaking vehicle by one small subset of society while others are excluded.

This point becomes particularly clear when we consider that the knowledge produced by the past is owed *not* only to the specific inventors and researchers whose work advanced that knowledge, but to the many other non-scientists whose work (growing food, building houses, providing public safety, printing books, cleaning offices) made the specialized work of those inventors possible. In short, the growing stock of knowledge we inherit from the past is itself the product not of a small class of people, but of society (understood as a complex system of social cooperation) as a whole. Consequently, it makes no sense for a small group of persons to benefit disproportionately from that growing stock of knowledge. Put another way, if the gift of the past is seen as a never-ending series of "free lunches," there is no moral justification for distributing those free lunches to those few who are already exceptionally well-fed while neglecting the many who are not.[2]

This does not mean that current efforts to create economic value and add to the stock of human knowledge should not be suitably rewarded. It does mean that the value (and corresponding claims) of such efforts must be kept in proper perspective: the great bulk of our prosperity is due not to our own efforts or genius, but to the efforts and knowledge accumulation of those who came before us.

The aim of this philosophical note is to sketch some of the key similarities and differences between the knowledge inheritance view and other prominent theories of distributive justice. While a comprehensive effort to compare the knowledge inheritance theory to the many competing academic theories of distributive justice is beyond the scope of the present volume, we believe it may be useful to briefly outline some important distinctions between the knowledge inheritance approach and four of the best-known theories. These are: the labor theory of property; libertarian natural rights theory; marginalist productivity theory; and "liberal" distributive justice theory (particularly as developed by John Rawls). The first three of these theories have diminishing influence in academic life today. Although the latter is closer in certain respects to the theory presented here, it does not address many of the issues involved in knowledge inheritance.

The first of the competing arguments is the labor theory of property—also sometimes called labor-entitlement theory. This view holds that who owns what must depend, in the first

instance, on who made what.* As previously noted, John
Locke's theory of property outlined in chapter 5 of his *Second
Treatise of Government* rested legitimate ownership on labor
input or, more broadly, on productive contribution. In arguing
that property rights derived from productive contributions,
Locke galvanized reformers by establishing a moral distinction between mere ownership, in a legal sense, and morally
legitimate entitlement. One of the most influential advocates
of the labor theory of property, Thomas Hodgskin, exceeded
Marx in certain respects in developing a serious moral critique of capital. Labor's "right to the whole product,"
Hodgskin argued, derives from the wellsprings of natural
law: "The natural idea of property is a mere extension of that
of individuality; and it embraces all the mental as well as
all the physical consequences of muscular exertion."[3] The
classical labor theory of property was mainly applied in the
struggle between workers and employers in industrial manufacturing. Hodgskin, a passionate advocate for trade unions
and workers' rights, skillfully attacked the "artificial rights"
of capital created by human laws:

> Laws being made by others than the labourer, and being
> always intended to preserve the power of those who
> make them, their great and chief aim for many ages,
> was, and still is, to enable those who are not labourers to
> appropriate wealth to themselves. In other words, the
> great object of law and of government has been and is,
> to establish and protect a violation of that natural right
> of property they are described in theory as being in-
> tended to guarantee.[4]

---

* This is not to be confused with the labor theory of value, formulated by Adam
Smith and David Ricardo and given its fullest analytical treatment by Karl Marx.
The labor theory of value is ultimately a theory of price based on the idea that
labor is the sole source of the exchange value of goods.

The Fabian and New Liberal reformers discussed in Part II rejected the full or explicit labor theory of property. They nevertheless implicitly embraced a certain kind of Lockean entitlement theory by focusing on "unearned increments" within the market system. As we have noted, Mill and, later, Hobhouse, on implicit Lockean grounds, argued that society should tax away the socially created share of individual wealth in order to protect private property and preserve its true (individualistic) moral foundations. In some ways this social view of entitlement went further than the popular labor radicalism of the period. Ultimately, in the view of writers like Mill and Hobhouse (and before them, Thomas Paine), anything that a person could not produce alone in nature had to be considered a social surplus—a consequence of society—and therefore be targeted for social benefit. Underlying this view was the moral principle, shared by both the Mill and Hobhouse theories, as well as more radical labor theories, of distinguishing earned from unearned gains (however defined). Whether in terms of labor property theory or related social theories, "the repudiation of unearned income," Anton Menger observed in 1899, was "the fundamental revolutionary conception . . . playing the same dominant part as the idea of political equality in the French Revolution and its offshoots."[5]

The argument of Part II accepts the distinction between earned and unearned income. However, following modern growth accounting in its emphasis on the importance of knowledge, it builds upon—and then departs in significant ways from—labor property theory: labor and capital are both seen as increasingly subordinate to advances in knowledge. Labor, like capital, is viewed as only one element of a much broader evolution of productive power across society. Although the conflict between labor and capital is viewed as important, the much larger problem is defined as our failure to account for the very significant portion of national income that comes not from current labor or capital, but from inherited technological progress and advances in knowledge.

In more recent times theories that stand in clearest opposition to the knowledge inheritance approach have been broadly aligned in two camps: natural-right libertarianism, most notably represented by the philosopher Robert Nozick; and a more mainstream economic libertarianism, which infers the moral legitimacy of inequality from standard marginalist economic theory. The natural-right position has a diminished number of academic adherents today, but it strongly influenced the ideological development of the modern conservative movement in American politics. Nozick's study *Anarchy, State, and Utopia* (1974), which won the National Book Award, argues against "patterned" or "end-result" concepts of justice in favor of a "historical" concept of legitimate entitlement.[6] (In this last sense, Nozick's model bears a resemblance to the labor theory, which also stresses the importance of examining history—who created what—to establish who should own what.) In Nozick's historical model the legitimacy of any distribution of goods is simply a question of how goods were acquired and transferred in a given period of time.

Three basic rules of entitlement apply. The first is "just original acquisition" from nature. Private owners may keep what they appropriate from nature, subject to minimum constraints. Specifically, Nozick significantly alters Locke's "sufficiency proviso" regulating the just initial acquisition of property. For Nozick what is important is not whether "enough and as good" land is left for others, "and more than the yet unprovided could use," as Locke termed it in his *Second Treatise on Government* (chap. 5, sec. 27, 33), but whether an appropriation of an unowned object worsens the situation of others.[7] Nozick recommends taking a very broad view in answering that question, by asking whether "the situation of persons who are unable to appropriate [is] worsened by a system allowing appropriation and permanent property"; in his view, the answer to that question is almost always no.[8] Nozick's version of the proviso rests on the assumption that the baseline against which the merits of private ownership should be judged is leaving things in a state of common use ("lyeing waste in common," as Locke put it), where people just take whatever they need or want from an unimproved common stock.[9]

Nozick's second rule of entitlement holds that goods justly acquired from nature on these terms can accumulate over time in private hands if they are justly transferred between individuals. A transfer is just if it occurs through voluntary exchange (i.e, not through force or fraud) and if the holding is transferred from someone who was entitled to it in the first place. Thus, there is no moral distinction between what a person receives from others (through gifts, bequests, etc.) and what he himself produces. Whether someone's gains are earned or unearned is judged strictly and narrowly by these "historical" criteria of just original acquisition and just transfer.

Nozick also proposes a third rule, that of "rectification." This is not systematically treated, but it applies to cases of what Nozick considers illegitimate acquisition or transfer—things like resource monopoly, forced labor, fraudulent schemes, etc. Nozick argues, in fact, that no redistributive policy can be rejected until it is shown that "rectification" is completely unwarranted in a given distribution of goods. "One *cannot* use the analysis and theory presented here [in *Anarchy, State, and Utopia*] to condemn any particular scheme of transfer payments, unless it is clear that no considerations of rectification of injustice could apply to justify it. . . . Past injustices might be so great as to make necessary in the short run a more extensive state in order to rectify them."[10]

Nozick's theory of entitlement accords with a far-right libertarian political perspective. At the core of this is an ex-

pansive concept of "self-ownership," based on the idea that
"every person is morally entitled to full private property in
his own person and powers."[11] Nozick extends Locke's concept
of self-ownership to the income and assets a person may come
to own.[12] A person's justly acquired property is an extension of
his own bodily self, and so is protected by the same fundamental liberty that protects his "self" from harm or coercion.
Following this principle Nozick goes so far as to describe taxation as "on a par with forced labor."[13]

In contrast to labor theorists like Hodgskin (who arguably
drew on a stricter reading of Locke), Nozick further holds
that self-ownership can also extend to the products of others'
labor—so long as that labor is voluntarily supplied in a
process of exchange (for wages, a share of the crop, etc.). He
explicitly argues, in fact, that a person need not be the *creator*
of his holdings (by whatever criteria) for his ownership of
them to be considered legitimate. The bare fact of possession,
assuming just acquisition from nature and voluntary transfers, suffices as a basis of entitlement in Nozick's view: "Some
of the things he uses he just may *have*, not illegitimately."[14]

The overall result, G.A. Cohen points out, is an almost un-
limited license for private accumulation:

> Nozick believes not only that people own themselves, but
> that they can become, with equally strong moral right,
> sovereign owners of indefinitely unequal amounts of
> such raw external resources as they can gather to them-
> selves as a result of proper exercise of their own and/or
> others' self-owner personal powers. When, moreover,
> private property in external resources is rightly gener-
> ated, its morally privileged origin insulates it against ex-
> propriation or limitation.[15]

A number of critics have emphasized that Nozick relies on
a narrowly grounded view of entitlements—to the exclusion

of desert ("deservingness") or other moral considerations such as need. Moreover, his rules of entitlement set a very low threshold for weighing the benefits of property rights against any burdens they might create. Michael Sandel adds that Nozick's theory of entitlement "never says why people are entitled to their [natural] assets in any sense of entitlement strong enough to get the argument going."[16] (The theory of entitlement is offered "without foundations," Thomas Nagel similarly argues.[17]) Put another way, the position is essentially self-justifying: it asserts a very large and individualist claim as if it is morally self-evident.

In contrast with Nozick, the argument presented in Part II holds the common view that deservingness, according to some measure of productive contribution, should be the basis of entitlement. None of this is to deny the possibility of refining the principle of "self-ownership"—for example, by differentiating between the value someone receives from society and the value that person adds. Thus, by the logic of self-ownership, it is also possible to argue that a person's inalienable "natural right" to property is limited to what he can create *alone in nature*—which today, of course, means very little compared to what can be achieved in society, one of the underlying precepts of the knowledge inheritance understanding. (Benjamin Franklin put a sharp edge on the essential point in a 1783 letter to Robert Morris: "He that does not like civil Society on these Terms, let him retire and live among Savages."[18])

Interestingly, in other passages Nozick pursues lines of thought that seem clearly to echo the substance of the inheritance view. In fact, he raises precisely the question at the core of this position: "Why should one's entitlement extend to the whole object," he asks, regarding just acquisition from nature, "rather than just to the *added value* one's labor has produced?" His answer is simply that (in his view) "no workable or coherent value-added property scheme has yet been devised."[19] Nozick also argues that if a form of goods came like "manna from heaven" (his term—meaning not "made or produced or transformed" by people now living) then the claim of one person over another would have to be demonstrated through some rule of justice other than his theory of individual entitlement.[20] Nozick's concession here—when brought together with modern economic understandings of the historically inherited knowledge-based sources of productivity and growth—again, seems clearly to weaken, even arguably to undermine, his essential position.[21]

As noted, the central judgment of the knowledge inheritance argument is that society must inevitably be deemed the residual claimant of the inherited contributions of past generations. With Dahl it holds that insofar "as a right to property is justified by the principle that one is entitled to use the products of one's own labor as one chooses . . . the principle [given society's contribution] would lead to the conclusion that the control and ownership of the economy rightfully belongs to 'society' "—at least the control and ownership of that (very large) share of the economy's capacity that cannot be attributed to current individual effort. If so, as Dahl stresses, "means must be found for 'society' to exercise the control to which it is entitled by virtue of its collective ownership."[22]

To many people society's moral status may seem obvious, something implicitly assumed in such simple acts as picking up after one's dog or being honest about the taxes one owes. A number of philosophers writing in the libertarian tradition represented by Nozick, however, see it differently. For instance, like his fellow (earlier and recent) Chicago School theorists Frank Knight and Richard Posner, Richard Epstein seems to agree that market incomes cannot really be considered morally deserved in any absolute sense. He also agrees (with Knight) that personal talents, because they come from nature and family circumstances, cannot be a basis for justifying economic inequalities.[23] Epstein further emphasizes the moral problem of productive interdependency. In the case of artistic production, for example, he considers how a Lockean perspective can undermine copyright law by pointing to the web of external sources—the "cultural commons"—from which all writers and artists necessarily draw in finding inspiration and ideas.[24] (This example, while compelling, casts the problem too narrowly: all production draws from stocks of knowledge, techniques, and ideas that form a common inheritance.)

In the end, however, Epstein rejects such challenges to individual entitlement by implicitly denying that "society" (or any other broader claimant) can have any standing at all in connection with these matters. "If I do not deserve the fruits of my labor, genetic endowments and parental endowments," Epstein asks, "then who does?"[25] This question, he claims, offers the *"strongest opposition* to the idea that individuals do not deserve to own their own labor."[26] The strongest argument against social claims (and, implicitly, redistributive policies), in other words, is that undeserved economic differences remain in force, by default, as it were, *simply because* there is no other way (in his view) of justifying allocation to "society" or reallocation on the basis of desert, the only legitimate rivals to simple legal possession. Compare Posner's previously cited judgment that such arguments are "porous" since "the long life, spacious liberties, and extensive property of the average American citizen are the creation not of that American alone, but of society—a vast aggregation of individuals, living and dead—and of geographical luck (size, topography, location, natural resources, climate)."[27] Compare also Knight's view: agreeing that a person's productive capacity is based upon both effort and inheritance (and luck), Knight emphasized that "certainly none but the effort can have ethical validity." Knight, in fact, went beyond the conclusion that society—what he calls "the world"—must inevitably be the residual claimant to that which comes from inheritance; he suggests that most people would even agree that "inherited capacity represents an obligation to the world rather than a claim upon it."[28]

We take up this issue in greater detail later in this note, but broadly speaking, there is a rough analogy between how the knowledge inheritance theory treats what is sometimes called the "knowledge commons" and "society" in this regard, and the way we commonly treat the electromagnetic spectrum.[29] Few would argue that the first person who happened to find a way to exploit the commercial value of the electromagnetic spectrum should be entitled to all of the spectrum and all of the gains it makes possible. That society must inevitably be the residual claimant of such values (and of the spectrum) is not seriously disputed—although how to determine fees to be paid for the right to exploit the spectrum (or minerals on public lands, etc.) is by no means a simple matter.

Another argument sometimes offered by theorists working in the tradition represented by Nozick and Epstein—and also countered implicitly by Posner, Knight, Dahl, the many authors canvassed in Part II, and the overall thrust of the knowledge inheritance view—is that since all individuals have a theoretically equal opportunity to apply their labor to the received (but "inert") social, technological, and cultural inheritance, if one individual can find a way to capture all the gains the inheritance permits by applying his efforts, he should be allowed to keep them. Here the overweighting of individual contribution and effort should be obvious. Ask this question: which is more important, the technological inheritance available to such a person, or the person's effort, intelligence, etc., in producing from the inheritance some practical or marketable end? Clearly inheritance *in a strong sense* is the indispensable precondition of the individual contribution: if Bill Gates were to be kidnapped from his Seattle-area mansion and put on a deserted island where the only factors of production were raw nature and his own physical efforts and intelligence, we would quickly learn how much of his wealth is due to living in an advanced society with access to technological capabilities and vast stores of knowledge. If he managed to survive, he might even see that, indeed, virtually all of this wealth (beyond barest subsistence) is due to such access.

A further subordinate argument in this basic tradition holds that if one person is more talented than another in wresting gains from the technological inheritance, he should again have legitimate claim to all that he can capture so long as all persons have an equal opportunity to do the same. In addition to the challenges to this view presented by the societal and related arguments we have just reviewed, the "equal opportunity" objection, many have demonstrated, is also challenged by (among other things) the simple fact that children of non-elites who are brought up in culturally deprived circumstances and who do not have access to high-quality education, coaching, and financial support obviously do *not* enjoy equal opportunities.[30]

What may be termed a "mainstream *economic* libertarian" approach has been embraced by a number of modern economists. This attempts to justify unequal holdings by linking entitlement to ascribed productivity. The approach draws on what is known as "marginal productivity" theory. First developed in the late nineteenth century, marginal productivity theory sought to explain the different rewards received by each "factor" of production—labor, capital, land, etc.—working together in a cooperative process. In equilibrium the wage or profit to be received by a contributing factor is equal, the theory holds, to the increase in the value of the product if a unit of that factor is added while other factors remain constant. Marginal productivity theory has been challenged in certain respects on technical grounds, but as a general model for understanding how resources are allocated in the production process (aiming for the greatest value at the lowest cost), it is widely accepted in mainstream economics. Beyond this, many if not most economists also believe that each factor "owner" in the production process—the worker who supplies labor, the employer who supplies capital, etc.—is (or should be) compensated roughly in proportion to the value of their contribution to the final product.[31]

Marginal productivity theory has been extended beyond the realm of technical economics in ways that intersect with and impact political and philosophical debates. John Bates Clark, who offered one of the first fully worked-out versions of the theory in his 1899 book *The Distribution of Wealth*, did not hide his normative motivations. As he states explicitly at the outset of the book, "the purpose of this work [is] to show that the distribution of the income of society is controlled by a natural law, and this law, if it worked without friction, would give to every agent of production the amount of wealth which that agent creates."[32] In this view marginal productivity guaranteed not only the *efficient* coordination but the *morality* of the economic system, because it gives "to each what he creates."[33] Again we see the Lockean paradigm at work—indeed, Clark argued that capitalism fulfilled Lockean principles through its own inner workings rather than through any deeper considerations of justice. Understanding marginal productivity or the "fundamental law" of distribution, he later claimed in *Social Justice Without Socialism* (1914), is to get a glimpse of the "glory that may come from a moral redemption of the economic system."[34]

The extension of marginal productivity theory into the realm of moral philosophy was criticized early on by left-leaning contemporaries and, subsequently, by a number of conservatives as well—including Knight and, later, Nobel laureate George Stigler, who called it a "naïve productivity ethics."[35] Many have pointed to the problem of "disentanglement": even if a marginal product (and the efficient contribution of specific factors) can be revealed by varying one factor while the others remain constant, as the theory holds, this measurement does not account for the causal role of the constant factors in *enabling* the marginal product.[36] Writing in the *Quarterly Journal of Economics*, W.M. Adriance called the attempt to ascribe specific shares of a joint product to separate factors a "verbal absurdity." The error lies, he continued, in "not attributing to the cooperation of the rest of the group any part of the so-called 'marginal product.' "[37]

An influential contemporary version of "naïve productivity ethics" was put forward by the British economist P.T. Bauer in the early 1980s. High incomes are "earned," Bauer insisted, because "normally they are produced by their recipients and the resources they own."[38] Ultimately, "some people are gifted, hard-working, ambitious and enterprising, or had far-sighted parents, and they are therefore more likely to become well-off."[39] Nobel laureate Amartya Sen has characterized Bauer's "personal production" theory of wealth as an approach that draws false inferences from marginal productivity theory.[40] Sen points out that there is nothing in "marginalist logic" that establishes an "identification" between a factor's *earnings* and its *contribution* to the total output. Marginal accounting is useful for certain allocation decisions in production, "but it does not 'show' which resource has 'produced' how much of the total output." Nor does it account for the often huge added benefits of increasing the scale of production, which creates value not by anything intrinsic to a particular factor of production, but by raising efficiency (and lowering costs) across the board. Sen also stresses the market's role in determining value: factor earnings depend on the relative prices of the products being produced, thus introducing additional arbitrary elements into personal production theories of entitlement. Furthermore, for the personal production view to be consistent there is a need to distinguish between "what a person produces" and "what is produced by resources that he happens to own."[41]

From the standpoint of the technological inheritance view, what is additionally problematic about the marginalist approach, beyond the severe difficulty of figuring out who contributed exactly what in any complex cooperative enterprise, is that no account is taken of the role of factors external to the firm in making the firm's production process possible to begin with. These include, again, such things as social order, legal systems, and property rights—and more directly, education, public investments, and especially the long historical accumulation of knowledge. Consequently, it is fundamentally misleading in this broader sense as well to speak as if the various factors within the firm (labor, capital) in themselves create economic value; they create economic value given the background conditions and accumulation of knowledge provided by factors external to the firm—i.e., by society.

The most well-known "liberal" or progressive approach to these issues was developed by John Rawls in *A Theory of Justice*, published in 1971. Rawls famously argued against a system of "natural liberty" in which distributive inequalities are considered just simply because they reflect individual differences of talent, effort, and other productive capacities. Because no one deserves the natural assets and family background they are born with, these assets are "arbitrary from a moral point of view," Rawls argued; so, too, are the "distributive shares" they generate in the marketplace. "Intuitively, the most obvious injustice of the system of natural liberty is that it permits distributive shares to be improperly influenced by these factors so arbitrary from a moral point of view."[42]

Rawls does not propose to eliminate people's different natural endowments, but rather to moderate the economic effects of such differences. This is the motivation behind his "difference principle," which holds that the inequality of a society is only legitimate to the extent that it benefits the least well-off. "Rawls' way," Michael Sandel observes, "is not to eradicate unequal endowments but to arrange the scheme of benefits and burdens so that the least advantaged may share in the resources of the fortunate."[43] Rawls strikingly terms this a way "to redress the bias of contingencies in the direction of equality." His difference principle "represents, in effect, an agreement to regard the distribution of natural talents as a common asset and to share in the benefits of this distribution whatever it turns out to be."[44] Rawls called his argument "justice as fairness."

Fairness in Rawls's view has two key components: assuring that morally arbitrary factors such as gender, race, and initial class position have minimal effect on individuals' life chances, and assuring that the overall distribution treats those left least well-off better off than they would be under any other arrangement.[45]

To his critics on the right, Rawls's philosophy is most controversial in its rejection of individualistic entitlement as a basis for market inequalities. But moral skepticism toward highly individualistic views of distribution has deep roots in the "social contract" tradition in Western philosophy. The essential point of this tradition is that it is rational for people to enter into social agreements for reasons of self-preservation. Quite simply, they are better off living under a shared set of limits than they would be in a state of nature where everyone is free to do what they want—what Thomas Hobbes famously described as the "war of all against all." The benefits of social order carry their own sort of price, however. By freeing individuals from the war of all against all, the social contract implicitly entails obligations from individuals for the benefits they receive and, indeed, for maintaining the system they share. Obedience to law is the most basic of these obligations. Taxation is another, because the goods provided by society depend on institutions, procedures, and enforcements that have costs.

As noted in the introduction to Part II, Stephen Holmes

and Cass Sunstein's *The Cost of Rights: Why Liberty Depends on Taxes* is a revealing study of the necessary role of government in protecting and financing not only civil liberties, but also property rights and market processes.[46] It challenges "the widespread but obviously mistaken premise that our most fundamental rights are essentially costless," stressing that in fact the market is interwoven with and cannot function without public systems.[47] A related contribution, *The Myth of Ownership: Taxes and Justice*, by philosophers Liam Murphy and Thomas Nagel, explores the moral principles at work in tax policy.[48] Murphy and Nagel argue that property (be it wealth, income, or any other taxable form) does not have any a priori status in relation to government. Indeed, it logically cannot have an a priori status, they urge, since property is a creation of law without any independent origin apart from how the law structures ownership and property rights. Furthermore, since the division of property (and of income and wealth) exists (*and only exists*) within a system already previously created and structured by past and existing tax policy, there can be no moral claim against taxation on grounds that it has been imposed from "outside" of the private sphere and "outside" of the system that it has helped (and continues to help) establish.[49]

In general, along with Rawls, the knowledge inheritance theory accepts the general conclusions of social contract theory and its judgments concerning the essential benefits of living in society and the importance of government to economic development. However, it goes beyond social contract theory in stressing the centrality (and moral implications) of generation upon generation of socially created and inherited knowledge. Aspects of Rawls's position, in fact, intersect with the knowledge inheritance theory, pointing to the deeper obligation we suggest. For instance, note his striking description of people's "native endowments"—their genetic and family advantages—as a "common asset," a formulation more commonly used in describing natural resources and knowledge.[50] The common social and cultural dimensions of economic life are also obvious and important to Rawls. He writes: "The collective activity of society, the many associations and the public life of the largest community that regulates them, sustains our efforts and elicits our contribution. Yet the good attained from the common culture far exceeds our work in the sense that we cease to be mere fragments: that part of ourselves that we directly realize is joined to a wider and just arrangement the aims of which we affirm."[51]

Despite such observations—and unlike the knowledge inheritance theory and the related theories of Dahl and other authorities previously noted—Rawls's view of *fairness* does not consider social contributions as a potential basis of entitlement. Sandel has offered an explicit challenge on this point, observing that for Rawls it is simply "the *absence* of individual desert [that] creates a presumption in favor of regarding the distribution of talents as a common asset."[52]

Put another way, Rawls's individualistic viewpoint precludes him from grounding his basic argument—that economic inequalities must benefit the least well-off—in any positive claims of social desert. Sandel suggests that such a line of argument could be open to Rawls if he were willing to adopt a stronger conception of community. As it stands, Sandel argues, Rawls has not shown why the community has a positive right to the benefits that flow from the exercise of individuals' talents.*

For the community as a whole to deserve the natural assets in its province and the benefits which flow from them, it is necessary to assume that society has some

---

* To be clear, Sandel here is focusing on how Rawls defends the case for treating personal assets as shared, but what is at stake is the larger question of whether the community has a claim to distribute society's resources and benefits according to principles of justice.

pre-institutional status that individuals lack, for only in this way could the community be said to possess its assets in the strong, constitutive sense of possession necessary to a desert base. But such a view would run counter to Rawls' individualistic assumptions, and in particular to his view that society is not "an organic whole with a life of its own distinct from and superior to that of all its members in their relations with one another."[53]

Instead, Rawls tries to show that rational individuals selecting principles of justice in an "original position" in which they were ignorant of their personal circumstances would agree to treat natural assets as shared. Sandel contends that, nonetheless, Rawls's egalitarian principles must rest, at bottom, on "*some* social claim on the distribution of assets" and the benefits they produce; "otherwise, the parties would be deliberating about how to allocate shares that were not (yet) rightfully *theirs* to allocate."[54]

That social claim might rest, Sandel's work suggests, on a philosophical conception of the self and its attributes as inherently constituted by communities. But, we suggest, it also might rest on empirical observation of the fact that the exercise of individual talents plays only a relatively small role in generating prosperity: what is most important is not individual talents (whether we regard them as individual possessions or in some sense common property), but our common inheritance of knowledge, infrastructure, and technological capability. It is that inheritance that undergirds a social claim to the goods produced by modern economies.

As we have seen, the judgment that society as a whole must be considered the residual claimant of historically contributed benefits has been urged by a very broad range of liberal, conservative, and radical writers whose work does not reach to the issues stressed by Sandel. Numerous political leaders from Winston Churchill to Franklin Delano Roo-

sevelt have also affirmed the fundamental judgment. However, Sandel's argument helps point the way to a fully articulated, positive, desert-based societal claim to the gift of the
past.

All of this returns us once again to Locke. By his labor a person joins a portion of nature to himself and so makes it part of
his person, Locke argued. "It being by him removed from *the
common state Nature placed it in*, it hath by this labour something annexed to it, that excludes the common right of other
men."[55] That private property could lay claim to so much and
exclude "the common right of other men" was due to the
fact—in his judgment at the time—that "nine tenths," or
even "ninety-nine hundredths," of the "products of the
earth" were the "effects of labour," or "wholly to be put on
the account of labour."[56] Stated another way: by virtue of
labor's disproportionate role in creating value, the individual's right to remove property from "the common state nature placed it in" exceeded any rightful competing or original
claim the community might have.

In the seventeenth-century world of labor-intensive, small-
scale agriculture, Locke may not have been far from the mark
in putting so much emphasis on individual labor. In
the twenty-first century, however, the judgment that "nine
tenths" or "ninety-nine hundredths" of the products of the
earth are the "effects of labour" or "wholly to be put on the account of labour" is challenged both by the productive power of
the knowledge economy and by modern understandings of
the underlying sources of economic achievement.[57]

The various arguments we have reviewed—labor entitlement, libertarian "self-ownership," marginalist ethics, and
liberal distributive justice—share the same fundamental difficulty: all fail to recognize the significance of the "gift of the
past," the disproportionate share of current value that we receive simply because we have been born later rather than ear-

lier in human history. Most of our wealth derives from an increase in output that is not commensurate with any increase in effort or cost incurred by those now alive. In failing to recognize the overwhelming contribution of historically inherited knowledge, all the positions also fail to uphold the basic moral judgment of most ordinary people—namely, that each of us has a claim to what he creates or helps create but not to what he has done nothing whatsoever to earn.

Once these points are clear it should not be difficult to understand the central judgments of the knowledge inheritance argument: that society—all of its members equally—must be the residual claimant to the inherited contributions of past generations; that these contributions are of sufficient magnitude to warrant significant social claims on private wealth; and that the moral basis of such claims will only grow stronger as we move further along the trajectory of knowledge-based growth. The critical question is how long a society of extreme and growing inequality, of growing social and economic pain—and, simultaneously, of ever-advancing technological capability and productive knowledge—can ignore the distributive implications of a simple acknowledgment of the enormity of that which comes to us all from those who preceded us in history.

NOTES

Introduction

1. Joel Mokyr, *The Lever of Riches: Technological Creativity and Economic Progress* (New York: Oxford University Press, 1990), p. 3.

2. In 2008 Warren Buffett had a net worth of $62 billion, according to *Forbes*, "The World's Billionaires: #1 Warren Buffett," March 5, 2008, www.forbes.com/lists/2008/10/billionaires08_Warren-Buffett_C0R3.html (accessed April 25, 2008). Warren Buffett quoted in Chuck Collins, Mike Lapham, and Scott Klinger, "I Didn't Do It Alone: Society's Contribution to Individual Wealth and Success," United for a Fair Economy, June 24, 2004, p. 17.

3. Louis Uchitelle, "The Richest of the Rich, Proud of a New Gilded Age," *New York Times*, July 15, 2007. Weill also defends his billion-dollar fortune by pointing to his charitable donations, including $30 million for renovations to Carnegie Hall.

4. Historical GDP data from Richard Sutch, ed., "Gross Domestic Product: 1790–2002," in *Historical Statistics of the United States: Earliest Times to the Present, Millennial Edition* (New York: Cambridge University Press, 2006), vol. 3, table Ca9-19, series Ca11. Also note that Yale economist William Nordhaus estimates a thirteen- to eighteenfold increase in output per person in the shorter time period since 1850; see William D. Nordhaus, "Do Real Output and Real Wage Measures Capture Reality? The History of Lighting Suggests Not," in *The Economics of New Goods*, ed. Timothy Bresnahan and Daniel Raff (Chicago: University of Chicago Press, 1997), p. 29.

5. Angus Maddison, *The World Economy: A Millennial Perspective* (Paris: Development Centre of the Organisation for Economic Co-operation and Development, 2001), p. 351, table E-7. Maddison estimates labor productivity to be $2.25 per hour in 1870, and $34.55 per hour in 1998 (in comparable 1990 international dollars). For the shorter time period from 1870 to 1979, William Baumol calculates from similar data an "1100 percent increase of labor productivity in the United States" (GDP per work-hour); see William J. Baumol, "Productivity Growth, Convergence, and Welfare: What the Long-Run Data Show," *American Economic Review* 76, no. 5 (December 1986), p. 1074.

6. Joel Mokyr, *The Gifts of Athena: Historical Origins of the Knowledge Economy* (Princeton, NJ: Princeton University Press, 2002), p. 2.

7. Robert M. Solow, "Technical Change and the Aggregate Production Function," *Review of Economics and Statistics* 39, no. 3 (August 1957), pp. 312–20. Quote taken from Robert Solow's Nobel Prize lecture to the memory of Alfred Nobel, December 8, 1987, nobelprize.org/nobel_prizes/economics/laureates/1987/solow-lecture.html (accessed August 31, 2006).

8. William J. Baumol, "Rapid Economic Growth, Equitable Income Distribution, and the Optimal Range of Innovation Spillovers," in *Economic Events, Ideas, and Policies: The 1960s and After*, ed. George L. Perry and James Tobin (Washington DC: Brookings Institution, 2000), p. 27.

9. Paul M. Romer, "Endogenous Technological Change," *Journal of Political Economy* 98, no. 5, pt. 2 (October 1990), pp. 83–84.

10. Mokyr, *Lever of Riches*, p. 3.

11. Nathan Rosenberg, *Exploring the Black Box: Technology, Economics, and History* (Cambridge, UK: Cambridge University Press, 1994), p. 16.

12. Congressional Budget Office data show that, in 2005, the top 1 percent received 18.1 percent of pretax household income while the bottom 40 percent got only 12.5 percent. Posttax income was only slightly less unequal: the bottom 40 percent received 14.4 percent while the top 1 percent received 15.6 percent. Remarkably, by 2005, the top 20 percent held a larger share of both pre- and posttax income than everyone else combined. (For this data, see Jared Bernstein, "Updated CBO Data Reveal Unprecedented Increase in Inequality," Economic Policy Institute, Issue Brief #239, December 13, 2007, www.epi.org/content.cfm/ib239.)

13. For wealth numbers, see Edward N. Wolff, "Recent Trends in Household Wealth in the United States: Rising Debt and the Middle-Class Squeeze," Levy Economics Institute of Bard College, Working Paper No. 502, June 2007, pp. 11, 26, tables 2, 8. These figures are for assets directly under individual control. If pensions are included, there is some diminution of concentration. For instance, although individually owned business assets are not altered, when pension assets are included, the top one percent share declines from 44.8 percent to 36.7 percent of such assets.

14. Stanford growth economist Moses Abramovitz has called the "80 percent level" the "familiar" level of the residual from "standard growth accounts" for the period 1929–1966. See Moses Abramovitz, "The Search for the Sources of Growth: Areas of Ignorance, Old and New," *Journal of Economic History* 53, no. 2 (June 1993), p. 229.

15. Derek J. de Solla Price, *Science Since Babylon* (New Haven: Yale University Press, 1975 [1961]), p. 162.

16. For the 1650 figure, see Joel Mokyr, "The Intellectual Origins of Modern Economic Growth," *Journal of Economic History* 65, no. 2 (June 2005), p. 331. For the mid-twentieth-century figure, see Derek J. de Solla Price, *Little Science, Big Science ... and Beyond* (New York: Columbia University Press, 1986 [1963]), p. 8, fig. 1.1, p. 7. For 2000 figure, see Nancy Carey and Natalie M. Justh, "Academic Libraries: 2000," *Education Statistics Quarterly*

5, no. 4 (2000), nces.ed.gov/programs/quarterly/vol_5/5_4/5_1.asp (accessed May 1, 2007).

17. Thomas Paine, *Agrarian Justice* (1796), par. 13.

18. L.T. Hobhouse, *Liberalism and Other Writings* (Cambridge, UK: Cambridge University Press, 1994), p. 91.

19. Richard Posner, *The Problems of Jurisprudence* (Cambridge, MA: Harvard University Press, 1990), p. 345.

20. Herbert A. Simon, "Public Administration in Today's World of Organizations and Markets," *PS: Political Science and Politics* 33, no. 4 (December 2000), p. 756.

21. Brian Barry, *Democracy, Power and Justice* (Oxford: Clarendon Press, 1989), p. 518.

22. Robert A. Dahl, *Dilemmas of Pluralist Democracy: Autonomy vs. Control* (New Haven: Yale University Press, 1982), pp. 182–83, 201, and 181.

23. For important contributions to theories of the Commons, see David Bollier, *Silent Theft: The Private Plunder of Our Common Wealth* (New York: Routledge, 2003); and Peter Barnes, *Capitalism 3.0: A Guide to Reclaiming the Commons* (San Francisco: Berrett-Koehler, 2007).

Part I. The Fruits of Knowledge

1. List quoted from *National System of Political Economy* (1841), in Chris Freeman and Luc Soete, *The Economics of Industrial Innovation* (Cambridge, MA: MIT Press, 1997), pp. 296–97.

1. Knowledge and Economic Growth

1. Simon Kuznets, "Two Centuries of Economic Growth: Reflections on U.S. Experience," *American Economic Review* 67, no. 1, Papers and Proceedings of the Eighty-ninth Annual Meeting of the American Economic Association (February 1977), p. 7.

2. William J. Baumol, Sue Anne Batey Blackman, and Edward N. Wolff, *Productivity and American Leadership: The Long View* (Cambridge, MA: MIT Press, 1989), p. 9.

3. The following discussion, focused as it is on the contributions of knowledge to economic growth, necessarily abstracts from debates over precisely how GDP is measured, and, for instance, questions of the degree to which including the costs associated with environmental damage and the exploitation of nonrenewable resources might alter various estimates. For a discussion, see Herman E. Daly and John B. Cobb Jr., *For the Common Good: Redirecting the Economy Toward Community, the Environment, and a Sustainable Future* (Boston: Beacon Press, 1989).

4. Historical GDP data from Richard Sutch, ed., "Gross Domestic Product: 1790–2002," in *Historical Statistics of the United States: Earliest Times to the Present, Millennial Edition* (New York: Cambridge University Press, 2006), vol. 3, pp. 3-23–3-26, table Ca9-19, series Ca9. U.S. GDP was $12.434 trillion

in 2005 and $13.195 trillion in 2006, finally reaching $13.843 trillion in 2007, according to figures from the Bureau of Economic Analysis, "Table 1.1.5: Gross Domestic Product," National Income and Product Accounts Table, January 30, 2008, www.bea.gov (accessed February 26, 2008). Cargill Inc.'s revenue for 2005 was $71.1 billion. See John Vomholf Jr., "Cargill Earnings Up 18% in Q4," *Minneapolis/St. Paul Business Journal*, August 23, 2005. Real GDP in 1850 was roughly $52 billion (using the CPI index to update from 1996 dollars to 2005 dollars). See Sutch, "Gross Domestic Product."

5. See Robert E. Gallman, "Economic Growth and Structural Change in the Long Nineteenth Century," in *The Cambridge Economic History of the United States*, ed. Stanley L. Engerman and Robert E. Gallman (New York: Cambridge University Press, 2000), vol. 2, pp. 2–6. According to estimates reported by Angus Maddison, U.S. GDP was $12.5 billion in 1820, compared to $38.4 billion for France, $26.3 billion for Germany, and $36.2 billion for the United Kingdom (all in 1990 international dollars). By 1870, the United States ($98.4 billion) had eclipsed France ($72.1 billion) and Germany ($71.4 billion) and was closing in on the United Kingdom ($100.1 billion). See Angus Maddison, *The World Economy: A Millennial Perspective* (Paris: Development Centre of the Organisation for Economic Co-operation and Development, 2001), p. 184, table A1-b. Gallman claims, "Aggregate annual output was greater in the United States than in the three main World War I belligerents—the United Kingdom, Germany, and France—combined" (p. 6). OECD historical statistics from Maddison suggest that the United States was still approaching their combined GDP in 1913. According to OECD estimates, U.S. GDP was $9.765 trillion in 2000, while OECD European countries totaled $8.976 trillion (at 2000 prices and 2000 exchange rates). See Organisation for Economic Co-operation and Development, "Gross Domestic Product," OECD data table, www.oecd.org/dataoecd/48/4/37867909.pdf (accessed February 26, 2008).

6. For older numbers, see Maddison, *World Economy*, p. 352, table E-8. Current numbers are Nonfarm Business Output per hour data available at the U.S. Bureau of Labor Statistics. See data.bls.gov/cgi-bin/surveymost and www.bls.gov/news.release/pdf/prod2.pdf (accessed September 6, 2006).

7. Maddison, *World Economy*, p. 351, table E-7.

8. Historical GDP per capita data came from Sutch, ed., "Gross Domestic Product: 1790–2002," pp. 3-23–3-26, table Ca9-19, series Ca11. Current GDP per capita is estimated to be $43,000 using GDP data from the Bureau of Economic Analysis ($13 trillion in 2006) and from the U.S. Census (the U.S. population just surpassed 300 million people).

9. Historical life expectancy numbers taken from Michael R. Haines, ed., "Expectation of Life at Birth, by Sex and Race: 1850–1998," *Historical Statistics of the United States, Millennial Edition*, table Ab644-911, series Ab644. That series puts life expectancy at 38.3 years in 1850 and 76.7 years in 1998. The 2004 figure (77.8 years) is reported by the U.S. Census Bureau, "Table 98. Expectation of Life at Birth, 1970 to 2004, and Projections, 2010 and 2015," *Statistical Abstract of the United States: 2008*, 127th ed. (Washington, DC: U.S.

Census Bureau, 2007), www.census.gov/compendia/statab/tables/08s0098 .pdf (accessed February 27, 2008).

10. Robert William Fogel, *The Fourth Great Awakening and the Future of Egalitarianism* (Chicago: University of Chicago Press, 2000), p. 44.

11. John Stuart Mill, *Principles of Political Economy* (1848), bk. I, chap. X, par. 4.

12. Moses Abramovitz and Paul A. David, "American Macroeconomic Growth in the Era of Knowledge-Based Progress: The Long-Run Perspective," in *Cambridge Economic History of the United States* (see note 5), vol. 3, chap. 1, p. 1.

13. As Maurice Dobb notes, the leading Ricardo scholar Mark Blaug in fact argues that the "alleged 'pessimism' of Ricardo was entirely contingent upon the maintenance of the tariff on raw produce." See Maurice Dobb, *Theories of Value and Distribution Since Adam Smith* (Cambridge, UK: Cambridge University Press, 1973), p. 90.

14. Thorstein Veblen, *The Engineers and the Price System* (Kitchener, ON: Batoche Books, 2001 [1921]), p. 19.

15. Ibid.

16. Schumpeter quoted in W.W. Rostow, "Technology and the Economic Theorists," in *Favorites of Fortune: Technology, Growth, and Economic Development Since the Industrial Revolution*, ed. Patrice Higonnet, David S. Landes, and Henry Rosovsky (Cambridge, MA: Harvard University Press, 1991), pp. 406–8.

17. Richard R. Nelson, *The Sources of Economic Growth* (Cambridge, MA: Harvard University Press, 1996), p. 90.

18. See Robert M. Solow, "Technical Change and the Aggregate Production Function," *Review of Economics and Statistics* 39, no. 3 (August 1957), pp. 312–20. Solow's growth model was presented in "A Contribution to the Theory of Economic Growth," *Quarterly Journal of Economics* 70, no. 1 (February 1956), pp. 65–94.

19. Here we rely on the explanation given in Rod Coombs, Paolo Saviotti, and Vivien Walsh, *Economics and Technological Change* (Totowa, NJ: Rowman & Littlefield, 1987), pp. 24–29.

20. David S. Landes, "Introduction: On Technology and Growth," in *Favorites of Fortune* (see note 16), p. 8.

21. For a good overview of the debate and terminology, see Moses Abramovitz, "The Search for the Sources of Growth: Areas of Ignorance, Old and New," *Journal of Economic History* 53, no. 2 (June 1993), pp. 217–43.

22. Robert M. Solow, "Technical Change and the Aggregate Production Function," *Review of Economics and Statistics* 39, no. 3 (August 1957), p. 316.

23. Abramovitz, "The Search for the Sources of Growth," p. 218.

24. This is the term Solow uses in his 1987 Nobel Prize lecture, which provides a lucid summary of the rise of neoclassical growth theory and the discovery of the residual, available online at nobelprize.org/nobel_prizes/ economics/laureates/1987/solow-lecture.html (accessed August 30, 2006).

What is sometimes called "growth accounting," Harvard economist Zvi Griliches argues, developed from "two traditions" that were brought together in Robert Solow's critical papers of the late 1950s: theoretical work involving production functions (especially by Paul Douglas), on the one hand, and the work of the National Bureau of Economic Research (NBER) and others in "national income measurement" on the other. In the 1940s and early 1950s several economists (including Raymond Goldsmith and Solomon Fabricant) worked under the direction of Simon Kuznets at the NBER to construct real output and capital series for major sectors of the national economy (on this, see Zvi Griliches, "The Discovery of the Residual: A Historical Note," *Journal of Economic Literature* 34, no. 3 [September 1996], pp. 1324–26). Solow's 1957 study relies on Raymond Goldsmith's capital time series data and John Kendrick's output per labor-hour series (in 1953 Kendrick had been asked by NBER to "systematize and develop" the measurement of productivity and economic growth); see Griliches, "The Discovery of the Residual," pp. 1326–27. Other economists working with similar data in the 1950s produced residual estimates comparable to Solow's. In 1954, for instance, Fabricant found a residual of 92 percent in measuring per capita output growth between 1870 and 1950. Moses Abramovitz presented a paper at the American Economic Association in 1955 in which he estimated that the combined per capita input of labor and capital explained only 10 percent of the growth in per capita output over the previous eight decades. For these contributions, see Solomon Fabricant, "Economic Progress and Economic Change," National Bureau of Economic Research, New York, 1954, cited in Zvi Griliches, *R&D, Education, and Productivity: A Retrospective* (Cambridge, MA: Harvard University Press, 2000), p. 13, table 1.1; and Abramovitz, "The Search for the Sources of Growth," pp. 217–18.

25. David Warsh, *Knowledge and the Wealth of Nations: A Story of Economic Discovery* (New York: W.W. Norton, 2006), p. 147. For another useful discussion of these issues, see Barry Bluestone and Bennett Harrison, *Growing Prosperity* (New York: Houghton Mifflin, 1999).

26. Moses Abramovitz and Paul David, "Technological Change and the Rise of Intangible Investments: The US Economy's Growth-Path in the Twentieth Century," in *Employment and Growth in the Knowledge-based Economy* (Paris: Organisation for Economic Co-operation and Development, 1996), pp. 37–38.

27. John W. Kendrick, "Productivity," in Glenn Porter, ed., *Encyclopedia of American Economic History: Studies of the Principal Movements and Ideas* (New York: Scribner, 1980), vol. 1, pp. 163–64, table 4.

28. Edward F. Denison, *Trends in Economic Growth, 1929–1982* (Washington, DC: Brookings Institution, 1985), p. 28.

29. Ibid., p. 30, unnumbered table. Other significant factors, such as "improved resource allocation" (11 percent) and "economies of scale" (11 percent) draw on new organizational knowledge, but these components, in Denison's model, are distinct from the more general advance of knowledge in the production process.

30. Ibid. In his effort to break down the residual into discrete measurable components, Denison uses a highly technical model. One feature of this that may be confusing to non-specialists is the fact that, in some cases, the percentages attached to the various determinants of growth add up to more than 100 percent of growth. In the case of growth per person employed between 1929 and 1982, for example, in addition to the 94 percent Denison attributes to knowledge and education, he attributes 10 percent to capital, 20 percent to economies of scale, and 19 percent to improved resource allocation—for a total of 143 percent of total growth! The reason for this surprising result is actually quite simple: other determinants had a *declining* impact over this period. In particular, the impact of labor input per person employed was -23 percent, reflecting declining average work hours across this period.

31. There was a substantial drop in the measured residual between the early 1970s and roughly 1995, amid a substantial downturn in productivity growth. These trends remain a puzzle for economists, but there is a fair (but not universal) degree of agreement that many of the well-documented productivity gains since the mid-1990s can be attributed to technological innovations in information technology; see J. Bradford DeLong, "Productivity Growth in the 2000s," National Bureau of Economic Research, March 2002, pp. 1–5. Edward Denison calculated that the growth rate of the residual dropped by 72 percent between 1973 and 1978 compared to the previous twenty-five years, and was negative between 1978 and 1982. He concluded that "it is not possible that an index measuring the contributions of advances in knowledge would have behaved this way" and thus that other "miscellaneous determinants" were responsible for the "erratic movement" of the residual (Denison, *Trends in American Economic Growth*, p. 29). University of Pennsylvania economist Edwin Mansfield also found that there is "no strong evidence" that a reduction in technological advance made a "very large" contribution to the productivity slowdown (cited in ibid., pp. 40–41). Zvi Griliches suggested that growth in the service sector acted as a "brake" to the acceleration in productivity because "productivity in services industries grew much more slowly than productivity in goods-producing industries after the late 1960s." On this, see Zvi Griliches, ed., *Output Measurement in the Service Sectors*, National Bureau of Economic Research, Studies in Income and Wealth, vol. 56 (Chicago: University of Chicago Press, 1992). A recent Brookings Institution study supported Griliches's explanation, finding that advances in information technologies boosted service-sector productivity and played a "crucial part" in post-1995 productivity growth. See Barry P. Bosworth and Jack E. Triplett, "Services Productivity in the United States: Griliches' Services Volume Revisited," Brookings Institution, September 19, 2003.

32. Simon Kuznets, *Modern Economic Growth: Rate, Structure and Spread* (New Haven: Yale University Press, 1966), p. 286.

33. Among the main sources of such growth, Field argues, were public investment in transportation infrastructure and utilities, coupled with a wave of "disembodied technical change"—mainly in the form of basic scientific

advances in production processes and energy use, as well as more efficient factory designs. Field suggests that it is no coincidence that the New York World's Fair of 1939–1940, arguably the greatest such event of the twentieth century, took place at the end of this period of technologically driven growth. Alexander J. Field, "Technological Change and U.S. Productivity Growth in the Interwar Years," *Journal of Economic History* 66, no. 1 (March 2006), pp. 203–36.

34. John W. Kendrick, "Total Capital and Economic Growth," *Atlantic Economic Journal* 22, no. 1 (1994), pp. 1–18, esp. p. 6, table 2B; see also Carol Corrado, Charles Hulten, and Daniel Sichel, "Intangible Capital and Economic Growth," NBER Working Paper Series No. 11948, National Bureau of Economic Research, January 2006, p. 19, table 3. Kendrick also measures shares of growth broken down along tangible/intangible lines. Between 1929 and 1990, intangible capital (mostly in the "human" forms of education and training) contributed 69 percent to the growth of the private business economy. "Nonhuman Tangible Capital"—primarily structures and equipment—contributed only 24 percent. This figure is larger than other estimates of the share of growth due to conventional capital accumulation, but it should be noted that by 1990, according to Kendrick, nearly half of tangible capital investment came from nonbusiness sectors such as government, nonprofit institutions, and households (cf. tables 1B and 8).

35. Lev's figures (which in part, of course, also reflect quite independent stock market shifts) are reviewed in Peter J. Wallison, "Enhanced Business Reporting Gets a Start," American Enterprise Institute, republished as a special report in the *New Republic*, December 20, 2004. Wallison's main point is to push for new accounting standards for intangible assets—a problem ignored by the recent Sarbanes-Oxley accounting reform legislation passed in the wake of the corporate scandals of 2000–2002.

36. Martin Wolf observes that U.S. output, measured in tons, is roughly the same as it was a century ago, yet the value of this output is twenty times greater. Martin Wolf, "The Bearable Lightness," *Financial Times*, August 12, 1998.

37. Margaret M. Blair, ed., *Unseen Wealth: Report of the Brookings Task Force on Intangibles* (Washington, DC: Brookings Institution, 2001).

38. Landes, "Introduction," p. 8.

39. For a discussion of the disputes concerning the size and measurement of the residual, see Warsh, *Knowledge and the Wealth of Nations*, chap. 11.

40. See the work of Dale Jorgensen and Zvi Griliches, in particular "The Explanation of Productivity Change," *Review of Economic Studies* 34, no. 3 (July 1967), pp. 249–83.

41. For endogenous growth theory, see Paul Romer's seminal papers: "Increasing Returns and Long-Run Growth," *Journal of Political Economy* 94, no. 5 (1986), pp. 1002–37; and "Endogenous Technological Change," *Journal of Political Economy* 98, no. 5 (October 1990), pp. S71–S102. See also the

general discussion of Romer's work in Warsh, *Knowledge and the Wealth of Nations.*

42. One important school of endogenous growth theory, associated with Robert Lucas, focuses on the role of "human capital" and the "investments" individuals make in getting an education. Such investments (endogenous because economically motivated) improve productivity (and therefore growth) by increasing the skill and knowledge of workers in the economy. Viewing human capital simply as a function of private investment in education, however, ignores the no less important question of where the knowledge and learning that create "human capital" come from: the educational institutions, the libraries and databases, and the broader history and culture of learning that underwrite the "return" on educational investments in the form of individual skills and reasoning, as well as sheer exposure to new information and ideas. Lucas himself, drawing on Jane Jacobs's urban studies, emphasizes the "external" effects of human capital—essentially, the benefits people derive from others' human capital in cooperative environments like the classroom, the shop floor, and the commercial district. Such (major) effects are not reliably measured by integrating educational investments into narrowly focused input-output models of growth. Robert E. Lucas Jr., "On the Mechanics of Economic Development," *Journal of Monetary Economics* 22, no. 1 (1988), pp. 36–37.

43. Robert M. Solow, "Perspectives on Growth Theory," *Journal of Economic Perspectives* 8, no. 1 (Winter 1994), pp. 48–53. A paper written for a 2007 symposium celebrating the fiftieth anniversary of the 1956 growth model picks up on this judgment by Solow. It points out that although there has been a massive effort to endogenize technological change, there is still no clear model or theory of how or why it occurs—and concludes that "it is hard, even today, to question the wisdom of Solow's modeling assumptions." In general, the narrow "innovation-centric" focus of much of the earlier literature, they note, is losing ground to a more historical focus on less mechanical factors such as institutions. Kieran McQuinn and Karl Whelan, "Solow (1956) as a Model of Cross-Country Growth Dynamics," *Oxford Review of Economic Policy* 23, no. 1 (2007), p. 59.

44. Joel Mokyr, *The Gifts of Athena: Historical Origins of the Knowledge Economy* (Princeton, NJ: Princeton University Press, 2002), p. 2.

45. Mokyr traces the Industrial Enlightenment back to Francis Bacon in the early seventeenth century. See Joel Mokyr, "The Intellectual Origins of Modern Economic Growth," *Journal of Economic History* 65, no. 2 (June 2005), passim.

46. Joel Mokyr, *The Lever of Riches: Technological Creativity and Economic Progress* (New York: Oxford University Press, 1990), pp. 90, 131–41.

47. Carl Boyer, *A History of Mathematics*, 2d ed. (New York: Wiley, 1991), pp. 228–29, 28–34.

48. Ibid., chap. 4–7.

49. Abbot Payson Usher, *A History of Mechanical Inventions* (Cambridge,

MA: Harvard University Press, 1962), p. 114; Jon Lackman, "Is It Time to Revamp the Periodic Table?" *Slate*, July 19, 2005, www.slate.com/id/2122919; Mokyr, *Lever of Riches*, p. 218.

50. Stephen Broadberry and Bishnupriya Gupta, "Cotton Textiles and the Great Divergence: Lancashire, India and Shifting Comparative Advantage, 1600–1850," Discussion Paper No. 5183, Centre for Economic Policy Research (London), August 2005, table 10.

51. Eric Mayer, "Lecture 8: Industrialism in England 1700–1850," lecture for "World History from 1500," Victor Valley College (California), summer 2006, www.emayzine.com/lectures/indust~2.htm (accessed January 19, 2007).

52. Mervyn King, "The Governor's Speech at Salts Mill, Bradford," speech delivered June 13, 2005, *Quarterly Bulletin* (Bank of England), Autumn 2005, pp. 382–84; Mayer, "Lecture 8."

53. Mokyr, *Lever of Riches*, pp. 92–94; Doug Peacock, "Engineers: Abraham Darby and a Dynasty of Iron-Founders," Cotton Times Web site, www.cottontimes.co.uk/darbyo.htm (accessed February 15, 2007); Frederick Engels, "The Eighteenth Century," *Vorwärts!* no. 72 (September 7, 1844), www.marxists.org/archive/marx/works/1844/condition-england/ch01 .htm (accessed February 15, 2007); Thomas J. Misa, *A Nation of Steel: The Making of Modern America, 1865–1925* (Baltimore: Johns Hopkins University Press, 1999), p. 32, fig. 1.12.

54. Jeremy Atack, Fred Bateman, and William N. Parker, "The Farm, the Farmer, and the Market," in *Cambridge Economic History of the United States* (see note 5), vol. 2, p. 269, table 6.3.

55. Ibid., pp. 268–70.

56. Akerloff response in William J. Baumol, "Rapid Economic Growth, Equitable Income Distribution, and the Optimal Range of Innovation Spillovers," in *Economic Events, Ideas, and Policies: The 1960s and After*, ed. George L. Perry and James Tobin (Washington, DC: Brookings Institution, 2000), p. 35.

57. Ibid., p. 27.

58. Abramovitz and David, "Technological Change and the Rise of Intangible Investments," p. 35.

59. Simon Kuznets, "Two Centuries of Economic Growth: Reflections on U.S. Experience," *American Economic Review* 67, no. 1 (February 1977), p. 7.

60. Bell asserts this in a new foreword to his recently reissued classic *The Coming of Post-Industrial Society* (New York: Basic Books, 1999 [1973]), pp. xv–xvii.

61. Maddison, *World Economy*, p. 351, table E-7.

62. Projection is based on the GDP growth of the twentieth century; GDP per capita increased by a factor of 7.7 over the twentieth century. See Sutch, "Gross Domestic Product."

2. Deep Knowledge and External Memory

1. Jack Cohen and Ian Stewart, *The Collapse of Chaos: Discovering Simplicity in a Complex World* (New York: Viking, 1994), p. 352.

2. Joel Mokyr, "The Intellectual Origins of Modern Economic Growth," *Journal of Economic History* 65, no. 2 (June 2005), p. 287.

3. Douglass C. North, *Understanding the Process of Economic Change* (Princeton, NJ: Princeton University Press, 2005), p. viii.

4. Without the developments that occurred between 1960 and 1990 alone, Nobel laureate agronomist Norman Borlaug estimates, global production "would have moved into marginal grazing areas and plowed up things that wouldn't be productive in the long run. We would have had to move into rolling mountainous country and chop down our forests." See "Billions Served: Norman Borlaug Interviewed by Ronald Bailey," *Reason*, April 2000, www.reason.com/news/show/27665.html.

5. See Michael Balter, "Was Lamarck Just a Little Bit Right?" *Science*, April 7, 2000, p. 38.

6. Joel Mokyr, *The Gifts of Athena: Historical Origins of the Knowledge Economy* (Princeton, NJ: Princeton University Press, 2002), pp. 227–28. For a communications perspective on Mendel's use of math and statistics, see James Wynn, "Alone in the Garden: How Gregor Mendel's Inattention to Audience May Have Affected the Reception of His Theory of Inheritance in 'Experiments in Plant Hybridization,' " *Written Communication* 24, no. 1 (2007), pp. 3–27.

7. Max Tegmark and John Archibald Wheeler, "100 Years of Quantum Mysteries," *Scientific American*, February 2001, p. 69.

8. Francis Bacon, *The New Organon*, ed. Lisa Jardine and Michael Silverthorne (Cambridge, UK: Cambridge University Press, 2000), p. 53.

9. Ibid., pp. 36–37.

10. First published in 1991, Donald's *Origins of the Modern Mind: Three Stages in the Evolution of Culture and Cognition* (Harvard University Press) was among the most influential works of cognitive theory published in the 1990s and more recently has begun to influence related fields such as knowledge management and institutional economics. The influential journal *Behavioral and Brain Sciences* published a précis of the book, followed by a set of open peer commentaries and a follow-up response from Donald in 1993 (vol. 16, no. 4, pp. 737–91). A further set of commentaries was published in *Behavioral and Brain Sciences* 19, no. 1 (1996), pp. 155-64. More recent interdisciplinary influence is evident in Syed Z. Shariq, "How Does Knowledge Transform as It Is Transferred? Speculations on the Possibility of a Cognitive Theory of Knowledgescapes," *Journal of Knowledge Management* 3, no. 4 (1999), pp. 243–52; see also North, *Understanding the Process of Economic Change*, pp. 31, 35.

11. See Merlin Donald, *Origins of the Modern Mind: Three Stages in the Evolution of Culture and Cognition* (Cambridge, MA: Harvard University Press, 1991), chap. 8.

12. See Merlin Donald, "Précis of Origins of the Modern Mind: Three Stages in the Evolution of Culture and Cognition," *Behavioral and Brain Sciences* 16, no. 4 (1993), p. 739; his *Origins of the Human Mind*, pp. 160–61; and North, commenting on Donald, in *Understanding the Process of Economic Change*, pp. 34–35.

13. There is some evidence that chimps and apes are capable of more innovative thought without direct outside stimulus. For example, a recent archaeological study demonstrated that chimps used tools more than four thousand years ago to crack nuts, and researchers in West Africa recently reported the widespread use of fashioned weapons by female chimps for hunting. See John Noble Wilford, "Archaeologists Find Signs of Early Chimps' Tool Use," *New York Times,* February 13, 2007; and Rick Weiss, "For First Time, Chimps Seen Making Weapons for Hunting," *Washington Post*, February 23, 2007.

14. Donald, "Précis," p. 741.

15. Ibid., p. 745.

16. A major breakthrough in deciphering ancient Egyptian, the Rosetta Stone translates the same passage into three scripts: Egyptian hieroglyphics, Egyptian demotic script (a shorthand used for administrative purposes), and Greek script (the direct ancestor of modern alphabetical systems).

17. Donald, *Origins of the Modern Mind*, chap. 8, pp. 308–9.

18. Frank E. Manuel and Fritzie P. Manuel, *Utopian Thought in the Western World* (Cambridge, MA: Belknap Press, 1979), p. 466.

19. Donald, *Origins of the Modern Mind*, p. 312.

20. Merlin Donald, *A Mind So Rare: The Evolution of Human Consciousness* (New York: W.W. Norton, 2001), p. 313.

21. Andy Clark, "Economic Reason: The Interplay of Individual Learning and External Structure," reprinted in *The Frontiers of the New Institutional Economics*, ed. John N. Drobak and John V.C. Nye (San Diego: Academic Press, 1997), p. 283.

22. Donald, *Mind So Rare*, p. 309.

23. Derek J. de Solla Price, *Little Science, Big Science . . . and Beyond* (New York: Columbia University Press, 1986), p. 13.

24. Donald, *Mind So Rare*, pp. 298, 326.

25. North, *Understanding the Process of Economic Change*, p. 36.

26. Mokyr, "The Intellectual Origins," p. 331.

27. See www.mathpages.com/home/kmath414.htm for an explanation of the anagram.

28. Mokyr, "The Intellectual Origins," pp. 332–35.

29. Price, *Little Science, Big Science*, pp. 5–6.

30. Michael Heylin, "Science Is Becoming Truly Worldwide," *Chemical and Engineering News* 82, no. 24 (July 14, 2004), pubs.acs.org/cen/science/8224/8224sci2.html.

31. The seminal work was Price's book *Little Science, Big Science*, published by Columbia University Press in 1963. For Price's views on the growth of science, see Jonathan Furner's appreciation of the book at polaris.gseis.ucla.edu/jfurner/03jolis-pt1-compact.pdf, pp. 8-9.

32. Nancy Carey and Natalie M. Justh, "Academic Libraries: 2000," *Education Statistics Quarterly* 5, no. 4 (2000), nces.ed.gov/programs/quarterly/vol_5/5_4/5_1.asp (accessed April 17, 2007).

33. In 2005–2006 there were an estimated 6,441 "Title IV" postsecondary institutions in the United States ("Title IV" denotes eligibility for federal student aid programs). This figure includes four-year and two-year degree-granting institutions as well as non-degree-granting professional and vocational schools. See government data at National Center for Education Statistics, "Table 2. Title IV Institutions, by Level and Control of Institution and State or Other Jurisdiction: Academic Year 2005–06," March 7, 2007, nces.ed.gov/ipeds/factsheets/pdf/fct_title_IV_03072007_4.pdf. In fall 2004, there were approximately 17.7 million students enrolled in Title IV institutions (Laura G. Knapp, Janice E. Kelly-Reid, and Roy W. Whitmore, *Enrollment in Postsecondary Institutions, Fall 2004; Graduation Rates, 1998 & 2001 Cohorts; and Financial Statistics, Fiscal Year 2004*, NCES 2006-155, U.S. Department of Education [Washington, DC: National Center for Education Statistics, 2006], p. 4, table 1, nces.ed.gov/pubsearch/pubsinfo.asp?pubid=2006155).

34. Brandon Shackelford, *National Patterns of Research and Development Resources: 2003*, NSF 05-308 (Arlington, VA: National Science Foundation, 2005), p. 24, fig. 11. For detailed numbers, see app. B, tables B-3 and B-4, www.nsf.gov/statistics/nsf05308/pdf/appb.pdf (accessed September 12, 2006). Industry funds 16.7 percent of basic science research and carries out only 14.3 percent.

35. Fritz Machlup, *The Production and Distribution of Knowledge in the United States* (Princeton, NJ: Princeton University Press, 1962), p. 79, table IV-6. For recent numbers, see U.S. Department of Education, "Biennial Survey of Education in the United States," *Digest of Education Statistics: 2005*, NCES 2006-030, National Center for Education Statistics, table 25, nces.ed.gov/programs/digest/d05/tables/dt05_005.asp?referrer=list (accessed March 20, 2008).

36. Machlup, *Production and Distribution of Knowledge in the United States*, pp. 81.

For more recent data on the number of scientists, see National Science Foundation, "Scientists, Engineers, and Technicians in the United States: 2001," Detailed Historical Tables, Division of Science Resource Statistics, Directorate for Social, Behavioral, and Economic Sciences, May 2005. For postsecondary teachers, see Bureau of Labor Statistics, U.S. Department of Labor, *Occupational Outlook Handbook, 2006–07 Edition*, www.bls.gov/oco/print/ocos066.htm (accessed August 30, 2006).

37. Anna Bernasek, "What's the Return on Education?" *New York Times*, December 11, 2005.

38. Mokyr stipulates this at the outset of *Gifts of Athena*, p. 2.

39. Friedrich A. Hayek, *The Constitution of Liberty* (Chicago: University of Chicago Press, 1978 [1960]), pp. 43, 27, and 22. Hayek is often carelessly grouped with Milton Friedman as a right-wing libertarian. In fact, his often

profound considerations of collective knowledge and norms in human development place him closer (in some respects) to the "communitarian" philosophies of Burke, Ruskin, Veblen, and even Hobson. Hayek's critique of the welfare state evolved beyond the libertarianism of Friedman and other free-market economists favored by the Republican right of recent decades. The welfare state's main threat, Hayek believed, was its distortion effects in trying to alter economic relations without the benefit of the diffuse social knowledge embodied in exchange processes. Whatever its threat to abstract individual liberty, the state simply does not (and cannot) *know enough* to succeed economically, Hayek ultimately believed.

40. Mokyr, "The Intellectual Origins," p. 287.

41. Richard Nelson is a leading political economist at Columbia University. Katherine Nelson is a professor of developmental psychology at the City University of New York. See Katherine Nelson and Richard R. Nelson, "On the Nature and Evolution of Human Know-how," *Research Policy* 31, no. 5 (July 2002), p. 719.

3. How Does Technological Progress Occur?

1. "Timeline of Communication Techonology," Wikipedia, en.wikipedia .org/wiki/Timeline_of_communication_technology (accessed September 15, 2006).

2. The interjection "Eureka!" derives from the Greek word *heuriskein*, meaning "to find." It is famously attributed to Archimedes, who allegedly ran naked through the streets of Athens shouting "Eureka!" after discovering the hydrostatic principle of buoyancy while taking a bath.

3. Review of *They Made America* by Harold Evans, *Publishers Weekly*, September 13, 2004.

4. Abbott Payson Usher, *A History of Mechanical Inventions* (Cambridge, MA: Harvard University Press, 1962 [1929]), p. 61. For a detailed explanation of Usher's theory of cumulative invention (interestingly contrasted with Schumpeter's views), see Vernon W. Ruttan, "Usher and Schumpeter on Invention, Innovation, and Technological Change," *Quarterly Journal of Economics* 73, no. 4 (November 1959), pp. 596–606. Notably, Usher was Solow's economic history teacher in graduate school. Of Usher's influence, Solow writes: "Long runs of history offer the economist or historian or economic historian the chance to figure out how changes in the 'noneconomic' background factors have an influence on behavior in the narrowly economic realm. It is a little like being able to extend the range of temperatures or pressures available in a laboratory." See Robert M. Solow, "How Did Economics Get That Way and What Way Did It Get," *Daedalus*, Fall 2005, pp. 87–100.

5. Robert K. Merton, *The Sociology of Science* (Chicago: University of Chicago Press, 1973), p. 213.

6. Wilkins and Franklin in fact published their photographic findings in the same issue of *Nature* (no. 171, 1953) in which Watson and Crick first published the structure of DNA. Franklin's seminal role in the discovery of DNA

structure was increasingly recognized after her death. It was only after he saw her photographic evidence (shown to him by Wilkins without Franklin's knowledge) that Watson became convinced of the helical structure of DNA and was able to model it. See Denise Grady, "50 Years Later, Rosalind Franklin's X-Ray Fuels Debate," *New York Times*, February 25, 2003.

7. Allyn A. Young, "Do the Statistics of the Concentration of Wealth in the United States Mean What They Are Commonly Assumed to Mean?" *American Economic Review* 7, no. 1 (March 1917), Supplement, Papers and Proceedings of the Twenty-Ninth Annual Meeting of the American Economic Association, p. 146.

8. The title of Bell's first telephone patent was in fact "Improvement in Telegraphy" and described "an approach to harmonic telegraphy" rather than "a complete or fully functional system." See Edward Evenson, *The Telephone Patent Conspiracy of 1876* (Jefferson, NC: McFarland & Company, 2000), p. 72.

9. It is popularly believed that the fact that Bell was "no. 5" and Gray "no. 39" in the day's log entries proves that Bell was the first to arrive at the patent office. In fact there is no way to know for sure who "got there first" because the logs were generally completed at the end of the day due to the high number of patents sent by mail to the office. See ibid., pp. 75–76. Whether or not Bell stole Gray's design is explored in a recent book: Seth Shulman, *The Telephone Gambit: Chasing Alexander Graham Bell's Secret* (New York: W.W. Norton, 2008).

10. Professor Basilio Catania, the former head of Italy's Central Research Laboratories in Telecommunications, presented detailed legal and scientific evidence of Meucci's priority in the invention of the telephone at New York University in 2000. These findings were published in Basilio Catania, "Antonio Meucci, Inventor of the Telephone: Unearthing the Legal and Scientific Proofs," *Bulletin of Science, Technology & Society* 24, no. 2 (April 2004), pp. 115–37. For a review of the U.S. government's anti-monopoly challenge to the original Bell patents (beginning in 1885), see also another Catania article (translated from the Italian), "The United States Government vs. Alexander Graham Bell," trans. Filomena Ricciardi, October 1999, www.esanet.it/chez _basilio/us_bell.htm (accessed March 20, 2008).

11. The text of the resolution is available online at www.esanet.it/chez_ basilio/us_congr_min.htm (accessed February 28, 2007).

12. Thomas would later become the first woman elected president of the American Sociological Association. William F. Ogburn and Dorothy Thomas, "Are Inventions Inevitable? A Note on Social Evolution," *Political Science Quarterly* 37, no. 1 (March 1922), pp. 83–98.

13. Robert K. Merton, "Singletons and Multiples in Scientific Discovery," *Proceedings of the American Philosophical Society* 105, no. 5 (1961), pp. 475–76. The Macaulay case is especially interesting for us. In his 1828 essay on Dryden, Macaulay cites the theory of economic rent as a simultaneous discovery. It was variously proposed by Malthus and Ricardo, among others, in the early nineteenth century. In chapter 5, we examine Ricardian rent

theory as an important foundation for modern redistributive policy. For Macaulay, the example of multiple rent theories illustrated a kind of determinism or necessity in all such major developments.

14. A typical popular statement of this view is that of the British physicist Lancelot Law Whyte in "Simultaneous Discovery," *Harper's Magazine*, February 1950.

15. Ogburn and Thomas, "Are Inventions Inevitable?" pp. 93–98.

16. Ibid.

17. Alfred Kahn, "Fundamental Deficiencies of the American Patent Law," *American Economic Review* 35, no. 4 (September 1940), p. 479.

18. For news coverage of the Nobel Prize dispute, see Nicholas Wade, "Doctor Disputes Winners of Nobel in Medicine," *New York Times*, October 11, 2003; Horace Freeland Judson, "No Nobel Prize for Whining," *New York Times*, October 20, 2003; and David Montgomery, "In a Funk Over the No-Nobel Prize," *Washington Post*, October 10, 2003, p. C01.

19. Damadian's Web page, www.fonar.com/nobel.htm, contains text files of the newspaper ads as well as other documents relating to the controversy.

20. "Raymond Damadian," *Who Made America?* PBS, www.pbs.org/wgbh/theymadeamerica/whomade/damadian_hi.html (accessed April 19, 2008).

21. S.C. Gilfillan, *Inventing the Ship: A Study of the Inventions Made in Her History Between Floating Log and Rotorship* (Chicago: Cuneo Press, 1935). Among them, Nathan Rosenberg and Joel Mokyr: Rosenberg contrasts the cumulative theory with Schumpeter's emphasis on discontinuity or "creative destruction"—whose chief agent is the heroic entrepreneur. A large body of case studies, from the American railroad system, to synthetic fabrics, to petroleum refining, illustrate the cumulative theory, Rosenberg argues. See Nathan Rosenberg, *Inside the Black Box: Technology and Economics* (Cambridge, UK: Cambridge University Press, 1982), pp. 6–8. Mokyr has noted that although shipbuilding has inherent environmental and functional constraints that bias it toward the kind of gradual, cumulative change proposed by Gilfillan, it is nevertheless clear that a significant share of technological progress occurs in this way. Joel Mokyr, *The Lever of Riches: Technological Creativity and Economic Progress* (New York: Oxford University Press, 1992), p. 12 and chap. 11, passim.

22. Gilfillan, *Inventing the Ship*, pp. 22–24.

23. Ibid., pp. 93–94.

24. Ibid., p. 194.

25. Ibid., p. 196.

26. Pliny the Elder's account can be found in *The Natural History*, bk. 36, chap. 66. Although unproven to be about aluminum, Pliny's account is referenced in many places, including "The Element Aluminum," World of Molecules Web site, www.worldofmolecules.com/elements/aluminum.htm (accessed March 6, 2007).

27. On Hall's efforts, see Norman C. Craig, "Charles Martin Hall—The

Young Man, His Mentor, and His Metal," *Journal of Chemical Education* 63, no. 7 (1986), pp. 557–59.

28. Ibid., p. 558.

29. Ibid., p. 557. Craig notably concludes his article on Hall by drawing attention to the "simultaneous invention" of electrolytic aluminum processing by Hall and Héroult. What this illustrates, he argues, is that major discoveries often occur when "the time is right," due to a convergence of many independent factors (ibid., p. 559).

30. Margaret B.W. Graham traces the importation of Duralumin technology from Germany to the U.S. and Britain in her article "R&D and Competition in England and the United States: The Case of the Aluminum Dirigible," *Business History Review* 62, no. 2 (Summer 1988), pp. 261–85.

31. "Superalloys: A Primer and History," TMS Online, www.tms.org/Meetings/Specialty/Superalloys2000/SuperalloysHistory.html (accessed March 7, 2007).

32. "The History of Hydropower Development in the United States," Bureau of Reclamation Hydropower Web site, U.S. Department of the Interior, revised October 5, 2004, www.usbr.gov/power/edu/history.html (accessed May 17, 2007).

33. Usher quoted in Martin L. Weitzman, "Recombinant Growth," *Quarterly Journal of Economics* 113, no. 2 (May 1998), p. 335.

34. The *Playboy* interview with Bill Gates is available online at ei.cs.vt.edu/~history/Bill.Gates.html (accessed April 20, 2007).

35. For a detailed account of Douglas Engelbart's contributions to the development of personal computers see Thierry Bardini, *Bootstrapping: Douglas Engelbart, Coevolution, and the Origins of Personal Computing* (Palo Alto: Stanford University Press, 2000), in particular chap. 4 on the development of the graphical user interface. Charles Babbage was the first to adapt the punch-card concept for data processing in the mid-nineteenth century. For this story, see Michael E. Hobart and Zachary S. Schiffman, *Information Ages: Literacy, Numeracy, and the Computer Revolution* (Baltimore: Johns Hopkins University Press, 1998), chap. 7. By the late nineteenth century, William Morris was using Jacquard looms to weave some of his most brilliant designs, while Herman Hollerith, a U.S. Census Bureau employee, adapted punch-card techniques for the first effective tabulating machines. Hollerith took his tabulating machine into the private sector in 1896, which led to the founding of International Business Machines (IBM) in 1911. According to James Essinger, both Babbage and Hollerith were influenced by the Jacquard loom. James Essinger, *Jacquard's Web: How a Hand Loom Led to the Birth of the Information Age* (New York: Oxford University Press, 2004).

36. This according to economist Diane Coyle, *The Weightless World: Strategies for Managing the Digital Economy* (Cambridge, MA: MIT Press, 1998), p. ix.

37. Paul Romer, "In the Beginning was the Transistor," *Forbes ASAP*, December 2, 1996, pp. 43–44; reprinted in the *Hoover Digest*, no. 2 (1997),

www.hoover.org/publications/digest/3541736.html (accessed April 20, 2007).

38. On the inheritance behind transistors, see Brian Winston, *Media Technology and Society: A History from the Telegraph to the Internet* (London: Routledge, 1998), chap. 11.

39. Winston, *Media Technology and Society*, pp. 207–9.

40. Richard C. Levin, "The Semiconductor Industry," in *Government and Technical Progress: A Cross-Industry Analysis*, ed. Richard R. Nelson (New York: Pergamon Press, 1982), p. 13.

41. Barbara Goody Katz and Almarin Phillips, "The Computer Industry," in *Government and Technical Progress* (see note 40), pp. 198–200.

42. From the *Playboy* interview with Bill Gates.

43. "Timeline of Electricity—Electronic Inventions," About.com, inventors. about.com/library/inventors/blelectric2.htm; "Otto von Guericke 1602–1686," About.com, inventors.about.com/library/inventors/bl_otto_von_guericke.htm; "Michael Faraday," About.com, inventors.about.com/library/inventors/blfaraday.htm. See also Bernard S. Finn, "Origin of Electrical Power," *Powering the Past: A Look Back*, Smithsonian Institution, amer icanhistory.si.edu/powering/past/prehist.htm (accessed April 20, 2007).

44. Finn, "Origin of Electrical Power"; Bruce R. Schulman, *Interactive Guide to the World's Columbian Exposition: Chicago, Illinois, May–October 1893* (published by author, 2002), users.vnet.net/schulman/Columbian/columbian.html (accessed April 20, 2007).

45. S.C. Gilfillian, *The Sociology of Invention* (Cambridge, MA: MIT Press, 1970 [1935]).

46. Ibid., pp. 5–6.

47. Katherine Nelson and Richard R. Nelson, "The Cumulative Advance of Human Know-how," *Philosophical Transactions: Mathematical, Physical and Engineering Sciences* 361, no. 1089 (August 15, 2003), pp. 1647, 1651.

48. Rosenberg, *Exploring the Black Box*, p. 16.

49. Albert Einstein, *Living Philosophies* (New York: Simon & Schuster, 1931), p. 3.

4. Public Foundations of Private Wealth

1. Harvey Brooks, "National Science Policy and Technological Innovation," in *The Positive Sum Strategy: Harnessing Technology for Economic Growth*, ed. Ralph Landau and Nathan Rosenberg (Washington, DC: National Academy Press, 1986), p. 119.

2. Ibid., p. 121.

3. For federal share of investment in basic research, see Brandon Shackelford, "U.S. R&D Continues to Rebound in 2004," National Science Foundation Infobrief, NSF 06-306, January 2006, p.3, table 1. For recent federal spending on R&D and basic research, see Ronald Meeks, "Federal Support for R&D and R&D Plant Projected at $110 Billion for FY 2005," National Science

Foundation Infobrief, NSF 06-300, November 2005, p. 2, table 1. (The estimates for the last fifteen years are total federal expenditure from 1990 to 2005 in constant 2000 dollars.)

4. National Academy of Sciences, *Funding a Revolution: Government Support for Computing Research* (Washington, DC: National Academy Press, 1999), chap. 3, par. 3, (p. 2 of 16 printed pages), available online at books.nap.edu/readingroom/books/far/ch3.html (accessed April 3, 2007).

5. Ibid., fig. 3.15, books.nap.edu/readingroom/books/far/ch3_f15.html (accessed April 3, 2007).

6. For 2003 numbers on federal funding of computer science, see National Science Foundation, Division of Science Resources Statistics, *Federal Funds for Research and Development: Fiscal Years 2003–05*, NSF 06-313 (Arlington, VA: National Science Foundation, 2006), table 19, http://www.nsf.gov/statis tics/nsf06313/pdf/tab19.pdf (accessed September 8, 2006).

7. Kenneth Flamm, *Creating the Computer: Government, Industry, and High Technology* (Washington, DC: Brookings Institution, 1988), pp. 260–61, table A-1.

8. G. Steven McMillan, Francis Narin, and David L. Deeds, "An Analysis of the Critical Role of Public Science in Innovation: The Case of Biotechnology," *Research Policy* 29 (2000), p. 5, table 1. The number cited here refers to citations of "papers originating solely at public science institutions (universities, medical schools, research institutes)" (p. 5). The authors define "public science" as "scientific research performed in and supported by governmental, academic, and charitable research institutions" (p. 1).

9. Ibid., p. 1.

10. National Science and Technology Council, "The National Nanotechnology Initiative: Research and Development Leading to a Revolution in Technology and Industry, Supplement to the President's 2007 Budget," July 2006, p. 35, table 2, www.nano.gov/NNI_07Budget.pdf (accessed April 23, 2007).

11. For projections, see Mihail C. Roco and William Sims Bainbridge, eds., "Societal Implications of Nanoscience and Nanotechnology," National Science Foundation, March 2001, p. 3, www.wtec.org/loyola/nano/NSET.Societal .Implications/nanosi.pdf (accessed September 7, 2006).

12. Richard C. Levin, "The Semiconductor Industry," in *Government and Technical Progress: A Cross-Industry Analysis*, ed. Richard R. Nelson (New York: Pergamon Press, 1982), p. 61.

13. John Orton, *The Story of Semiconductors* (New York: Oxford University Press, 2004), p. 99.

14. Levin, "The Semiconductor Industry," pp. 62–63.

15. Edwin Mansfield, "Academic Research Underlying Industrial Innovations: Sources, Characteristics, and Financing," *Review of Economics and Statistics* 77, no. 1 (February 1995), pp. 63–64.

16. Janet Abbate, *Inventing the Internet* (Cambridge, MA: MIT Press, 1999), p. 186.

17. Ibid., p. 191.

18. Ibid., p. 195.

19. Ibid., pp. 195–96.

20. Harold Evans profiles Whitney in *They Made America* (New York: Little, Brown, 2004), pp. 50–55. In 1799, Whitney wrote to Secretary of the Treasury Oliver Wolcott concerning his musket contract, describing his emerging theory of machine production. "One of my primary objects, is to form tools so the tools themselves shall fashion the work and give to every part its just proportion—which when once accomplished will give expedition, uniformity and exactness to the whole," he explained. He used the metaphor of an engraving, "from which may be taken a great number of impressions imperceptibly alike." Ibid., p. 54.

Whitney's originality has become a matter of controversy among scholars in recent decades, as evidence of earlier precision manufacturing workshops in France and elsewhere has come to light. See Robert S. Woodbury, "The Legend of Eli Whitney and Interchangeable Parts," *Technology and Culture* 1, no. 3. (Summer 1960), pp. 235–53.

This appears to be yet another example of simultaneous invention. As Evans explains, fifteen years before Whitney first demonstrated to officials the fruits of his method in 1801 (the highlight of which was assembling a musket's precision firelock mechanism from a random selection of parts), Thomas Jefferson visited the workshop of French gun-maker Honore LeBlanc in Paris. There he was presented, he later reported, "with the parts of fifty locks taken to pieces, and arranged in compartments," and he put several together himself, "fitted in a most perfect manner" (Evans, *They Made America*, p. 54).

21. Library of Congress, "Homestead Act," Web exhibit, www.loc.gov/rr/program/bib/ourdocs/Homestead.html (accessed December 10, 2007).

22. For detailed information on the Morrill Act and the development of land-grant colleges, see National Association of State Universities and Land-Grant Colleges, *The Land Grant Tradition*, March 1995, www.eric.ed.gov/ERICDocs/data/ericdocs2sql/content_storage_01/0000019b/80/14/70/2e.pdf (accessed March 20, 2008). See also the Department of State, "Backgrounder on the Morrill Act," exchanges.state.gov/EDUCATION/ENGTEACHING/pubs/AmLnC/br27.htm (accessed March 3, 2008). Far beyond their agricultural roots, public universities today have a large and diverse economic impact in many states. In Michigan, for example, the net economic impact of its fifteen public universities was estimated to be $39 billion in 1999. This represents a huge (nearly thirtyfold) return on the state's $1.5 billion appropriation for public universities that year, far exceeding any other type of public investment. See SRI International, *The Economic Impact of Michigan's Public Universities*, SRI Project #PDH 02-019, May 2002, p. 19, www.pcsum.org/pdfs/impact_study_2002.pdf (accessed February 2, 2007).

23. On the development of these and other U.S. agricultural investments, see R.E. Evenson, "Agriculture," in *Government and Technical Progress* (see note 12), chap. 5, pp. 233–82.

24. John C. Culver and John Hyde, *American Dreamer: The Life and Times of Henry A. Wallace* (New York: W.W. Norton, 2000), p. 149.

25. Ken Russell and Leah Sandall, "Corn Breeding: Lessons from the Past," Plant and Soil Sciences eLibrary, University of Nebraska–Lincoln, Plantandsoil.unl.edu/croptechnology2005/pagesincludes/printModule.jsp? informationModuleId=1075412493 (accessed December 5, 2007).

26. Agricultural Research Service, "Improving Corn," U.S. Department of Agriculture, www.ars.usda.gov/is/timeline/corn.htm; Agricultural Research Service, "More and Better Citrus," U.S. Department of Agriculture, www.ars.usda.gov/is/timeline/citrus.htm (accessed December 10, 2007).

27. Vernon W. Ruttan, "Technical Change and Innovation in Agriculture," in *Positive Sum Strategy* (see note 1), pp. 335–36.

28. Evenson, "Agriculture," p. 267.

29. David C. Mowery and Nathan Rosenberg, "The Commercial Aircraft Industry," in *Government and Technical Progress* (see note 12), p. 128. NACA was reconstituted as today's more familiar "NASA" (National Aeronautical and Space Administration) in 1958.

30. Ibid., p. 129.

31. Ibid. This text cites J.C. Hunsaker, "Research in Aeronautics," in *Research—A National Resource*, National Resources Planning Board (Washington, DC: U.S. GPO, 1941), p. 139.

32. Mowery and Rosenberg, "The Commercial Aircraft Industry," p. 132.

33. Ibid., p. 110.

34. Ibid., p. 131, p. 134, table 3.7.

35. Ibid., p. 114.

36. Townes recalled the early days of maser/laser research in a speech celebrating the fortieth anniversary of the Office of Naval Research. See Office of Naval Research, *Naval Research Reviews* 47, no. 1 (1996), pp. 26–28, www.onr.navy.mil/about/history/docs/50years_pi.pdf (accessed April 25, 2007).

37. David Bollier, *Public Assets, Private Profits: Reclaiming the American Commons in an Age of Market Enclosure* (Washington, DC: New America Foundation, 2001), p. 62.

38. U.S. General Accounting Office, "'Technology Transfer: NIH-Private Sector Partnership in the Development of Taxol," Highlights of GAO-03-829, a report to the Honorable Ron Wyden, U.S. Senate, June 2003, www.gao .gov/highlights/d03829high.pdf (accessed March 3, 2008).

39. Bollier, *Public Assets, Private Profits*, p. 63.

40. National Center for Health Statistics, *Health, United States, 2006: With Chartbook on Trends in the Health of Americans* (Hyattsville, MD: U.S. Department of Health and Human Services, 2006), p. 176, table 27, www.cdc .gov/nchs/data/hus/hus06.pdf (accessed April 25, 2007).

41. Richard A. Easterlin, "Twentieth-Century American Population Growth," in *The Cambridge Economic History of the United States*, ed. Stanley L. Engerman and Robert E. Gallman (Cambridge, UK: Cambridge Uni-

versity Press, 2000), vol. 3, pp. 518–21. See also Richard A. Easterlin, "How Beneficent Is the Market? A Look at the Modern History of Mortality," in *The Reluctant Economist* (Cambridge, UK: Cambridge University Press, 2004), chap. 7. Easterlin draws on Edwin Chadwick's landmark public health study, *The Sanitary Condition of the Labouring Population of Great Britain* (1842), which cites reports of British towns where entrepreneurs "retailed" dung "by cartfuls" from large accumulations stored "amidst the habitations of the poorer classes," complete with "extensive privy attached to the concern" (Easterlin, "How Beneficient Is the Market?" p. 120).

42. Relative GDP share calculated using the Measuring Worth relative-value calculator, an online service at www.measuringworth.com/uscompare.

43. These states are Arkansas, Colorado, Iowa, Kansas, Louisiana, Minnesota, Missouri, Montana, Nebraska, North Dakota, Oklahoma, South Dakota, and Wyoming. See U.S. Census Bureau, "Louisiana Purchase Bicentennial," *Facts for Features*, May 12, 2003. State economic output calculated by the Bureau of Economic Analysis, "Gross Domestic Product by State (2005)," www.bea.gov/newsreleases/regional/gdp_state/gsp_newsrelease.htm (accessed February 1, 2007).

44. Martin Reuss and Paul K. Walker, *Financing Water Resources Development: A Brief History* (Washington, DC: U.S. Army Corps of Engineers, 1983), p. 12. See also "Improving the Nation's Transportation System," from U.S. Army Corps of Engineers, "Brief History," www.hq.usace.army.mil/history/brief.htm (accessed April 25, 2007); and U.S. Army Corps of Engineers, "Taming the Des Moines River Rapids," www.mvr.usace.army.mil/Brochures/TamingTheDesMoinesRiverRapids.asp (accessed April 26, 2007).

45. U.S. Army Corps of Engineers, "Engineering the Falls: The Corps Role at St. Anthony Falls," www.mvp.usace.army.mil/history/engineering (accessed April 26, 2007).

46. Reuss and Walker, *Financing Water Resources Development*, p. 2.

47. Department of the Army, *United States Army Annual Financial Statement: Fiscal Year 2004*, pp. 220–22, www.defenselink.mil/comptroller/cfs/fy2004/FY_2004_Army_Financial_Report.pdf (accessed January 10, 2007).

48. U.S. Department of Defense, *U.S. Army Corps of Engineers, Civil Works*, 1998, p. 7, www.dod.gov/comptroller/cfs/fy1998/60_ACECFO98.PDF (accessed April 26, 2007).

49. Department of the Army, *United States Army Annual Financial Statement: Fiscal Year 2004*, p. 221.

50. "East Meets West: Chinese-Americans and the Transcontinental Railroad," About.com, americanhistory.about.com/library/weekly/aa120101a.htm (accessed December 10, 2007).

51. Bruce Levine et al., *Who Built America? Working People and the Nation's Economy, Politics, Culture, and Society* (New York: Pantheon Books, 1989), vol. 1, p. 517.

52. Albert Fishlow, "Internal Transportation in the Nineteenth and Early Twentieth Centuries," in *Cambridge Economic History of the United States* (see note 41), vol. 2, pp. 548–94; Paul Wallace Gates, *History of Public Land*

Law Development (Washington, DC: U.S. GPO, 1968), chap. 14—17, cited in Allan Kulikoff, *The Agrarian Origins of American Capitalism* (Charlottesville: University Press of Virginia, 1992), p. 53.

53. Thomas Ott, "Streamliners Timeline," *American Experience: Streamliners: America's Lost Trains*, PBS, www.pbs.org/wgbh/amex/streamliners/timeline (accessed July 26, 2007); Paul W. Gates, "An Overview of American Land Policy," in *American Law and the Constitutional Order*, ed. Lawrence M. Friedman and Harry N. Scheiber (Cambridge, MA: Harvard University Press, 1988), p. 126.

54. Fishlow, "Internal Transportation in the Nineteenth and Early Twentieth Centuries," p. 601.

55. Jeremy Atack and Peter Passell, *A New Economic View of American History: From Colonial Times to 1940* (New York: W.W. Norton, 1994), p. 166, table 6.6.

56. Jeff Madrick, *Why Economies Grow: The Forces That Shape Prosperity and How We Can Get Them Working Again* (New York: Basic Books, 2002), p. 72.

57. Ibid. Labor shortages also played a role, many historians argue.

58. See Richard R. Nelson and Gavin Wright, "The Rise and Fall of American Technological Leadership: The Postwar Era in Historical Perspective," *Journal of Economic Literature* 30, no. 4 (December 1992), p. 1940.

59. The Sears, Roebuck catalog, launched in the 1890s, pioneered this form, billing itself as the "Book of Bargains" and the "Cheapest Supply House on Earth." See "History of the Sears Catalog," www.searsarchives.com/catalogs/history.htm.

60. Madrick, *Why Economies Grow*, p. 71.

61. Ibid., p. 70.

62. Gavin Wright, "The Origins of American Industrial Success, 1879—1940," *American Economic Review* 80, no. 4 (September 1990), p. 665.

63. Ibid., pp. 664—65.

64. See the detailed official history: Mary C. Rabbitt, "The United States Geological Survey: 1879—1989," U.S. Geological Survey Circular 1050, U.S. Department of the Interior, pubs.usgs.gov/circ/c1050/index.htm.

65. David F. Noble, *America by Design: Science, Technology, and the Rise of Corporate Capitalism* (New York: Alfred A. Knopf, 1977), p. 70.

66. Manufacturing Extension Partnership, *Making a Difference for America's Manufacturers*, National Institute of Standards and Technology, U.S. Department of Commerce, www.mep.nist.gov/impacts/making-a-difference.pdf (accessed March 21, 2008).

67. Bro Uttal, "Inside the Deal That Made Bill Gates $350,000,000," *Fortune*, July 21, 1986, p. 23.

68. The renowned Peruvian development economist Hernando de Soto similarly argues that "when things enter the world, their description within a property system brings out surplus value." Global Envision interview with de Soto, www.globalenvision.org, March 1, 2004 (interview no longer online).

And further: "In the West, we never realized that capital is a dormant value hidden in the assets and talents we own and which legal property brings to life." Hernando de Soto, *The Mystery of Capital: Why Capitalism Triumphs in the West and Fails Everywhere Else* (New York: Basic Books, 2003), back cover.

69. Lucian Hughes, "Nothing New Under the Sun? Perhaps Not, But All That Sunlight Has Created a Flourishing System," *STS Nexus* 2, no. 2 (Spring 2002), www.scu.edu/sts/nexus/2.2spring2002/LHughesArticle.cfm (accessed April 30, 2007). Emphasis added.

70. Randall Stross, "Google, Shmoogle," *New York Times*, August 29, 2004, p. 5.

71. Stephen Holmes and Cass R. Sunstein, *The Cost of Rights: Why Liberty Depends on Taxes* (New York: W.W. Norton, 1999). We discuss their work further in "A Note on the Philosophical Argument" in this book.

72. North, *Understanding the Process of Economic Change*, chap. 5.

Introduction to Part II

1. Interview with Warren Buffett, Finance @ Knowledge Zone, Cool Avenues, www.coolavenues.com/know/fin/inter_warren.php3 (accessed January 1, 2008).

2. Kenneth J. Arrow, "Classificatory Notes on the Production and Transmission of Technological Knowledge," *American Economic Review* 59, no. 2 (May 1969), p. 35.

5. Unearned Income

1. Adam Smith, *An Inquiry into the Nature and Causes of the Wealth of Nations*, ed. Edwin Cannan (Chicago: University of Chicago Press, 1976 [1904]), bk. 1, chap. 6, p. 56.

2. William Godwin, *An Enquiry Concerning Political Justice* (1798), bk. 8, chap. 1, available online at www.english.upenn.edu/Projects/knarf/God win/pjtp.html (accessed April 25, 2007).

3. *The Institutes of Justinian*, trans. J. B. Moyle (London: Oxford Clarendon Press, 1906), bk. 1, title 1, p. 3. Alternate translation from the Medieval Sourcebook available at www.fordham.edu/halsall/basis/535institutes.html: "JUSTICE is the constant and perpetual wish to render every one his due."

4. Smith, *Wealth of Nations*, bk. 1, chap. 6, p. 56.

5. John Locke, *Two Treatises of Government* (Cambridge, UK: Cambridge University Press, 1994), *Second Treatise*, chap. 5, sec. 40, p. 296. Emphasis in original.

6. A good general discussion of Locke's theory of property is found in Thomas A. Horne, *Property Rights and Poverty: Political Argument in Britain, 1605–1834* (Chapel Hill: University of North Carolina Press, 1990), pp. 48–65.

7. John Stuart Mill, *Principles of Political Economy*, ed. J.M. Robson (Toronto: University of Toronto Press, 1965), p. 29.

8. See Mark Blaug, *Ricardian Economics: A Historical Study* (New Haven: Yale University Press, 1958), chap. 2.

9. According to George Stigler, in 1793 the price of wheat in England was 51 shillings per quarter. By 1812 it had risen to 152 shillings. See his *Essays in the History of Economics* (Chicago: University of Chicago Press, 1965), p. 173.

10. Blaug, *Ricardian Economics*, p. 8.

11. Ibid., p. 10.

12. Barbara Fried, *The Progressive Assault on Laissez Faire: Robert Hale and the First Law and Economics Movement* (Cambridge, MA: Harvard University Press, 1998), p. 121.

13. David Ricardo, *The Principles of Political Economy and Taxation* (London: J.M. Dent & Sons, 1962 [1821]), pp. 46–47.

14. Ibid., p. 33, par. 2. Emphasis added.

15. Ibid., p. 40, par. 2. But see, again, the clear distinction between natural and contributed value in Smith's view of landlords: "Landlords, like all other men, love to reap where they never sowed, and demand a rent *even for its natural produce*." Smith, *Wealth of Nations*, bk. 1, chap. 6, par. 8.

16. Ricardo, *Principles of Political Economy and Taxation*, p. 34, par. 2.

17. Ibid.

18. Ricardo cited in Blaug, *Ricardian Economics*, p. 13.

19. David Ricardo, *The Works and Correspondence of David Ricardo: Vol. 8, Letters 1819–1821*, ed. Pierro Sraffa with the collaboration of M.H. Dobb (Indianapolis: Liberty Fund, 2005), p. 194, oll.libertyfund.org/title/211 (accessed February 24, 2008).

20. Ricardo quoted in Stigler, *Essays in the History of Economics*, p. 182.

21. Jones quoted in Blaug, *Ricardian Economics*, p. 151.

22. Ibid. Emphasis on "*may*" in Blaug.

23. Scrope commenting on rent theory and other Ricardian themes taken up in the 1820s, from the *Quarterly Review* of 1831, as quoted in Blaug, *Ricardian Economics*, p. 149.

24. The changing resource base is the focus of E.A. Wrigley, "The Divergence of England: The Growth of the English Economy in the Seventeenth and Eighteenth Centuries," *Transactions of the Royal Historical Society*, sixth series, no. 10 (2000), pp. 117–41.

25. The classic historical study of this period is E.P. Thompson, *The Making of the English Working Class* (New York: Vintage, 1966).

26. Thomas Hodgskin, *Labour Defended Against the Claims of Capital* (New York: Augustus M. Kelly, 1963 [1825]), pp. 80–81. We discuss the radical labor entitlement theories further in "A Note on the Philosophical Argument" in this book.

27. John Stuart Mill, "Land Tenure Reform" (1871), *Collected Works* (Toronto: University of Toronto Press, 1967), vol. 5, p. 691.

28. Ibid.

29. Ibid.

30. John Stuart Mill, *Principles of Political Economy*, in *Collected Works*, ed. John M. Robson (Toronto: University of Toronto Press, 1965), vol. 3, bk. 5, chap. 2, sec. 6, p. 821.

31. Pierre-Joseph Proudhon, *What Is Property?* ed. and trans. Donald R. Kelley and Bonnie G. Smith (Cambridge, UK: Cambridge University Press, 1994), p. 136.

32. Mill, *Principles of Political Economy*, vol. 3, bk. 5, chap. 2, sec. 5, p. 819.

33. Ibid.

34. Mill, *Principles of Political Economy*, vol. 2, bk. 2, chap. 1, sec. 3, p. 207.

35. Ibid., p. 208.

36. Ibid.

37. John Gray discusses Mill's theory of inheritance taxation in "John Stuart Mill: Traditional and Revisionist Interpretations,"*Literature of Liberty* 2, no. 2 (April–June 1979), pp. 23–24.

38. Karl Marx and the entire Marxist tradition, of course, might well be considered an application of certain aspects of rent theory in its view of "surplus value." Since labor is the source of the whole yield for Marx, the surplus above what is paid in wages involves exploitation, or what might be judged a "rent" extracted by the capitalist.

6. Unearned Income Extended

1. L.T. Hobhouse, *Liberalism and Other Writings*, ed. James Meadowcroft (Cambridge, UK: Cambridge University Press, 1994), p. 91.

2. For an exploration of academic discussion of the issue, see "A Note on the Philosophical Argument" in this book.

3. *The Writings of Thomas Paine*, ed. Moncure Daniel Conway (New York: G.P. Putnam's Sons, 1895), vol. 3, p. 340.

4. Ibid., pp. 340, 331–32.

5. Henry George, *Progress and Poverty* (New York: Robert Schalkenbach Foundation, 1955), p. 337.

6. Ibid., pp. 433–39.

7. Michael Kazin, *The Populist Persuasion* (New York: Basic Books, 1995), p. 32; Henry George Jr., "Introduction to the Twenty-Fifth Anniversary Edition," in *Progress and Poverty* (1905 ed.), available online at www.schalken bach.org/library/george.henry/pp-intro-Anniversary-Edition-1905.html.

8. Portland, Oregon, for example, had a spirited land-tax movement in the early 1900s. See Robert D. Johnston, *The Radical Middle Class: Populist Democracy and the Question of Capitalism in Progressive Era Portland, Oregon* (Princeton, NJ: Princeton University Press, 2003), chap. 11.

9. "Pageant for Mr. George," *New York Times*, October 31, 1897.

10. Philip H. Wicksteed, *The Common Sense of Political Economy* (London: George Routledge & Sons, 1944 [1910]), vol. 2, bk. 3, chap. 2, p. 688.

11. Renato Cirillo, "The 'Socialism' of Léon Walras and his Economic

Thinking," *American Journal of Economics and Sociology* 39, no. 3 (July 1980), p. 299.

12. Barbara Fried, *The Progressive Assault on Laissez Faire: Robert Hale and the First Law and Economics Movement* (Cambridge, MA: Harvard University Press, 1998), p. 125.

13. As H.V. Emy writes, "Capital value, especially with regard to property and land, could be regarded as due in part to the action of the community itself," and for Hobson this was a "major justification for policies of progressive taxation." See H.V. Emy, *Liberals, Radicals, and Social Politics, 1892–1914* (Cambridge, UK: Cambridge University Press, 1973), p. 108. The concept of recapturing social value, Michael Freeden summarizes, was "the key to the financial policy of the social reformers" of the early twentieth century. See Michael Freeden, "J.A. Hobson as a New Liberal Theorist: Some Aspects of His Social Thought Until 1914," *Journal of the History of Ideas* 34, no. 3 (July–September 1973), p. 433.

14. For his most detailed discussion of "social income," see J.A. Hobson, *The Industrial System: An Inquiry into Earned and Unearned Income* (New York: Charles Scribner's Sons, 1910), chap. 14. See also Michael Freeden, "J.A. Hobson and Welfare Liberalism," *Political Quarterly* 69, no. 4 (1998), pp. 446–47.

15. Hobson, *Industrial System*, p. 225. Although broadly in agreement with Henry George's analysis of unearned increments, here Hobson addresses the limitations of George's single-tax approach.

16. Emy, *Liberals, Radicals, and Social Politics*, p. 195.

17. Hobhouse, *Liberalism and Other Writings*, pp. 91–92.

18. Ibid., p. 91.

19. Ibid., p. 97.

20. Ibid., p. 93.

21. Ibid., p. 92.

22. Leaving aside the vast spillover effects of the internal combustion engine, Rockefeller's Standard Oil was also plainly a creation of ruthless monopolistic tactics. Ida Tarbell's *The History of the Standard Oil Company*, published in 1904, brought the facts to light and helped make Standard Oil the poster child of the trust-busting movement before World War I.

23. See David M. Ricci, "Fabian Socialism: A Theory of Rent as Exploitation," *Journal of British Studies* 9, no. 1 (November 1969), pp. 107–10.

24. Brian Short, *Land and Society in Edwardian Britain* (Cambridge, UK: Cambridge University Press, 1997), p. 19. As Short notes, the land duties "were aimed above all at those who made profits through development on land which had increased in value owing to some intrinsic locational factor in the site."

25. A transcript of the speech, given on July 30, 1909, is available online at the Liberal Democrat History Group, www.liberalhistory.org.uk/item_single.php?item_id=47&item=history (accessed March 21, 2008).

26. Winston Spencer Churchill, *Liberalism and the Social Problem* (New York: Haskell House Publishers, 1973), p. 377.

27. Winston Spencer Churchill, *The People's Rights* (London: Cape, 1970), p. 120.

28. The speech is available online at www.theodore-roosevelt.com/trnationalismspeech.html (accessed May 7, 2007). As he declared in the "New Nationalism" speech, "I believe in a graduated income tax on big fortunes, and in another tax which is far more easily collected and far more effective— a graduated inheritance tax on big fortunes, properly safeguarded against evasion and increasing rapidly in amount with the size of the estate."

29. Quote is taken from a 1935 message Roosevelt delivered to Congress. The message was reprinted in the House Ways and Means Committee report on the Revenue Act of 1935 and is currently posted on the Department of the Treasury Web site at www.treas.gov/education/faq/taxes/historyrooseveltmessage.shtml (accessed May 7, 2007).

30. Simon N. Patten, "Another View of the Ethics of Land-Tenure," *International Journal of Ethics* 1, no. 3 (April 1891), pp. 366–69. Patten was a mentor to Rexford Tugwell and others who would later become part of FDR's New Deal "brain trust" in the 1930s.

31. Mill, "Land Tenure Reform," p. 691. Emphasis added.

32. J.A. Hobson, *Work and Wealth: A Human Valuation* (1914), unpaginated, available online at socserv2.socsci.mcmaster.ca/~econ/ugcm/3113/hobson/workwealth.html (accessed May 7, 2007).

33. Hobson quoted in Freeden, "J.A. Hobson and Welfare Liberalism," p. 447.

34. As Hobson explained in *Industrial System*, pp. 230–31: "Our analysis of the actual working of the industrial system has shown the emergence of large quantities of waste surplus. It is to the social utilisation of this waste surplus that the taxing power of the state is rightly directed. For the economic rents, the extra profits, interest, salaries, &c., which are got by the use of economic force in creating monopolies or artificial scarcities, are not merely failing to perform the true functions of a surplus, as the fund of progress . . . they are damaging efficiency, by enabling whole classes of persons to be consumers without producing."

35. Edward Bellamy, "What Nationalism Means," *Contemporary Review* 58 (July 1890), p. 18. Note Bellamy's striking inversion of Locke's view (discussed in "A Note on the Philosophical Argument" in this book) that individual labor is 99 percent responsible for economic output. Under modern conditions, as Bellamy understood them, Locke's theory of entitlement would apply to only a small portion of overall wealth. It is clear from Bellamy's terms that "sacred justice" refers to the right-wing Lockean tradition of individual property rights.

36. From Dove's *The Elements of Political Science* (1854), pt. 2, chap. 5, "On Property," excerpted in *The Origins of Left Libertarianism*, ed. Peter Vallentyne and Hillel Steiner (New York: Palgrave, 2000), pp. 140–41.

37. Ibid., p. 142.

38. Ibid., p. 140.

39. Ibid., p. 152. Emphasis added.

40. On this point and for a good general discussion of Dove's approach see John Cunliffe, "The Neglected Background of Radical Liberalism," *History of Political Thought* 11, no. 3 (Autumn 1990), pp. 471–72 and passim.

41. Cunliffe, "The Neglected Background," p. 471.

42. See John Cunliffe, "The Liberal Case for a Socialist Property Regime: The Contribution of Francois Huet," *History of Political Thought* 18, no. 4 (Winter 1997), p. 708.

43. Huet cited in *Origins of Left Libertarianism* (see note 36), pp. 106–8.

44. Ibid., p. 107. "The common sense of nations has always distinguished between *patrimonial assets*, which are gratuitously transferred, and *acquired assets*, which come either from personal work or at least from savings of the fruits of the patrimony. For these savings require care, and are also the personal creation of the owner."

45. Ibid., p. 112. Interestingly, the right-wing libertarian philosopher Robert Nozick (whose views we examine more closely in "A Note on the Philosophical Argument" in this book) proposes a similar policy in his collection of essays *The Examined Life: Philosophical Meditations* (New York: Simon & Schuster, 1989), pp. 28–33, noting that inheritance should not be allowed to "cascade down the generations." The Italian socialist philosopher Eugenio Rignano proposed a similar inheritance-tax concept and plan, which were widely debated in Italy as well as England in the 1920s. See Guido Erreygers and Giovanni Di Bartolomeo, "The Debates on Rignano's Inheritance Tax Proposal," Working Paper No. 85, Dipartmento Di Economia Pubblica (Rome, 1985), dep.eco.uniroma1.it/docs/working_papers/Wp85.pdf.

46. Alstott and Ackerman propose a 2 percent annual wealth tax. Today federal estate and gift taxes do not generate enough revenue for a substantial basic capital program.

47. *Origins of Left Libertarianism* (see note 36), p. 113.

48. Ibid., p. 132. On this point see also John Cunliffe, "The Liberal Rationale of 'Rational Socialism,'" *Political Studies* 36, no. 4 (December 1988), p. 658.

49. *Origins of Left Libertarianism* (see note 36), p. 131. Emphasis added.

50. Ibid., p. 131.

51. Cunliffe, "The Liberal Rationale of 'Rational Socialism,'" pp. 656–57.

52. J.E.S. Hayward, "The Official Social Philosophy of the French Third Republic: Léon Bourgeois and Solidarism," *International Review of Social History* 6 (1961), pp. 19–48.

53. Bourgeois quoted in Hayward, "The Official Social Philosophy," p. 29.

54. Ibid.

55. See Arthur J. Altmeyer, "The Development and Status of Social Security in America," in *Labor, Management, and Social Policy: Essays in the John R. Commons Tradition*, ed. Gerald G. Somers (Madison: University of Wisconsin Press, 1993), available online at www.ssa.gov/history/aja1963.html. Altmeyer was appointed chairman of the Social Security Board in 1937 and later served as commissioner of the Social Security Administration.

7. Toward a More Encompassing Theory

1. Robert A. Dahl, *Dilemmas of Pluralist Democracy: Autonomy vs. Control* (New Haven: Yale University Press, 1982), p. 184.

2. Thorstein Veblen, *Absentee Ownership: Business Enterprise in Recent Times; The Case of America* (Boston: Beacon Press, 1967 [1923]), p. 62.

3. Ibid., p. 65.

4. Veblen quoted in Geoffrey Hodgson, *Economics and Utopia: Why the Learning Economy Is Not the End of History* (New York: Routledge, 1999), p. 228.

5. Thorstein Veblen, *The Engineers and the Price System* (New Brunswick, NJ: Transaction Books, 1983 [1921]), p. 56.

6. Thorstein Veblen, *The Instinct of Workmanship* (New York: B.W. Huebsch, 1918 [1914]), p. 151.

7. Ibid., pp. 227–28.

8. Ibid., p. 144.

9. Thorstein Veblen, *The Vested Interests and the Common Man* (New York: Viking, 1946 [1919]), p. 57.

10. Ibid., pp. 61–62.

11. Ibid., p. 170.

12. G.D.H. Cole, *Money: Its Present and Future* (London: Cassel, 1945), p. 144.

13. Walter Van Trier, "Who Framed 'Social Dividend?' " U.S. Basic Income Guarantee Network, March 2002, available online at http://www.usbig.net/papers.html (accessed May 8, 2007).

14. Edwin Cannan, "Capital and the Heritage of Improvement," *Economica* 1, no. 4 (November 1934), pp. 381–82.

15. Ibid., p. 385.

16. Brian Barry, *Democracy, Power and Justice* (Oxford: Clarendon Press, 1989), p. 518.

17. Ibid., pp. 451–52.

18. Ibid., p. 452.

19. Frank H. Knight, "The Ethics of Competition," *Quarterly Journal of Economics* 37, no. 4 (August 1923), pp. 598–99. Emphasis added.

20. Frank H. Knight, *Freedom and Reform* (New York: Harper & Bros., 1947) pp. 382, 151.

21. Richard Posner, *The Problems of Jurisprudence* (Cambridge, MA: Harvard University Press, 1990), pp. 344–45.

22. Kenneth J. Arrow, "Nozick's Entitlement Theory of Justice," *Philosophia* 7, no. 2 (June 1978), pp. 278–79.

23. Douglass C. North, *Understanding the Process of Economic Change* (Princeton, NJ: Princeton University Press, 2005), p. 101.

24. Ibid., p. viii.

25. Ibid., pp. 50–51.

26. Theological developments of the late Middle Ages and early Renaissance, reflecting changing attitudes toward knowledge and the natural world,

have gained the attention of economists in recent years. See Erik S. Reinert and Arno Mong Daastøl, "Exploring the Genesis of Economic Innovations: The Religious Gestalt-Switch and the Duty to Invent as Preconditions for Economic Growth," *European Journal of Law and Economics* 4, no. 2–3 (May 1997), pp. 233–83.

27. North, *Understanding the Process of Economic Change*, p. 69.

28. Douglass C. North, "Economic Performance Through Time," Nobel Prize lecture, December 9, 1993, available online at nobelprize.org/nobel_prizes/economics/laureates/1993/north-lecture.html (accessed May 7, 2007).

29. Comment by George Akerlof on William J. Baumol, "Rapid Economic Growth, Equitable Income Distribution, and the Optimal Range of Innovation Spillovers," in *Economic Events, Ideas, and Policies: The 1960s and After*, ed. George Perry and James Tobin (Washington, DC: Brookings Institution, 2000), p. 35.

30. Herbert A. Simon, "Public Administration in Today's World of Organizations and Markets," *PS: Political Science and Politics* 33, no. 4 (December 2000), p. 756.

31. Ibid., p. 756.

32. Letter from Herbert A. Simon, reproduced as "Herbert Simon, the Flat Tax and Our Common Patrimony," *Basic Income: Newsletter of the Basic Income European Network*, no. 29 (Spring 1998). Simon estimates here that the "patrimony" is at least two-thirds of per-capita income.

33. Dahl, *Dilemmas of Pluralist Democracy*, pp. 182–83.

34. Ibid., pp. 183–84. Italics in original.

35. Ibid., p. 201.

36. See ibid., pp. 202–5; Robert A. Dahl, *Democracy and Its Critics* (New Haven: Yale University Press, 1989); and Robert A. Dahl, *A Preface to Economic Democracy* (Berkeley: University of California Press, 1985).

37. Dahl, *Dilemmas of Pluralist Democracy*, p. 181.

38. Ibid., p. 185.

39. Bell asserts this in a new foreword to his recently reissued classic *The Coming of Post-Industrial Society* (New York: Basic Books, 1999 [1973]), pp. xv–xvii.

40. Peter F. Drucker, *Post-Capitalist Society* (New York: HarperCollins, 1993), pp. 45, 20.

41. Joseph E. Stiglitz, "Public Policy for a Knowledge Economy," Department for Trade and Industry and Center for Economic Policy Research, London, January 27, 1999, www.worldbank.org/html/extdr/extme/knowledge-economy.pdf (accessed December 10, 2007).

Conclusion: Earned and Unearned in the Era of the Knowledge Economy

1. *Faust* quote cited in David Bollier, "Why We Must Talk About the Information Commons," 2004, community-wealth.org/_pdfs/articles-publications/commons/article-bollier.pdf.

2. William H. Gates Sr. and Chuck Collins, *Wealth and Our Common-wealth* (Boston: Beacon Press, 2002), pp. 122–23. Compare Warren Buffett's comment on loopholes and deductions in the tax code that often allow the very rich to pay taxes at a lower rate than many working people: speaking at a 2007 event in New York to an audience filled with bankers and real estate developers, Buffett first observed that "the 400 of us [here] pay a lower part of our income in taxes than our receptionists do, or our cleaning ladies, for that matter"—and then offered a million dollars to any fellow magnate who could prove he had higher tax rates than his secretary. Evan Thomas and Daniel Gross, "Taxing the Super Rich," *Newsweek*, Web exclusive, 2007, www.newsweek.com/id/32992.

3. Joseph Stiglitz, "Public Policy for a Knowledge Economy," Department of Trade and Industry and Center for Economic Policy Research, London, January 27, 1999, p. 25, www.worldbank.org/html/extdr/extme/knowledge-economy.pdf (accessed December 10, 2007).

4. Research and development expenditures totaled $28.3 billion in 1953 and $293.3 billion in 2006 (in 2000 dollars). See National Science Board, "U.S. Inflation-Adjusted R&D Expenditures, by Performing and Funding Sectors: 1953–2006," in *Science and Engineering Indicators 2004* (Arlington, VA: National Science Foundation, 2004), vol. 2, app. table 4-4, www.nsf.gov/statistics/seind08/append/c4/at04-04.pdf (accessed February 27, 2008).

5. The first set of numbers cited refers to "utility" patent applications of U.S. origin, by far the largest category of patent applications. The 2005 total figure refers to all utility, design, and plant patent applications of both U.S. and foreign origin, which increased from 126,788 in 1985 to 417,508 in 2005. U.S. Patent and Trademark Office, Electronic Information Products Division, Patent Technology Monitoring Team (PTMB), *U.S. Patent Statistics Chart: Calendar Years 1963–2006* (Alexandria, VA: U.S. Patent and Trademark Office, 2007), www.uspto.gov/go/taf/us_stat.htm (accessed May 15, 2007). For data comparing 1992 and 2002 patent figures in the United States and Europe, see *Science, Technology and Industry (STI) Scoreboard 2005* (Paris: Organisation for Economic Co-operation and Development, 2005), executive summary, p. 9. According to this report, "More than 442,000 patent applications were filed in Europe and the United States in 2002, compared to around 224,000 a decade earlier."

6. National Science Board, "Overview: S&E Workforce Trends," in *Science and Engineering Indicators 2004* (see note 4), vol. 1, p. O-9, www.nsf.gov/statistics/seind04/pdf/overview.pdf.

7. Daniel Bell, *The Coming of Post-Industrial Society* (New York: Basic Books, 1999 [1973]), pp. xv–xvi.

8. According to the most recent estimates of the Bureau of Labor Statistics, manufacturing jobs represent 10.8 percent of all employment; see www.bls.gov/iag/manufacturing.htm (accessed May 15, 2007).

9. In 1980 Bill Gates's then-fledgling Microsoft Corporation signed a deal with IBM to create an operating system for its new line of personal computers. This deal, the launching point for today's Microsoft empire, was made

after an initial attempt by IBM to recruit Gary Kildall, who had already written the most widely used operating system of the time, called Control Program/Microcomputer, or CP/M. When IBM turned to Gates in 1980, he bought the rights to another system, QDOS, written by Tim Paterson of Seattle Computer Products. QDOS, which became Microsoft's PC-DOS (later renamed MS-DOS), was what many judge to be a thinly disguised clone of CP/M. The story of how Gates outmaneuvered Kildall for the IBM deal is not fully known. Harold Evans suggests that Kildall wrongly assumed that Gates would not "cut [his] throat." Evans calls Kildall the "true founder of the personal computer revolution and the father of PC software," arguing that Gates effectively stole Kildall's system and could have been stopped in his tracks for copyright infringement if current legal standards existed then. Evans also argues that Kildall's operating system (which he continued to develop) was superior to Microsoft's, particularly for its (then highly innovative) multitasking capabilities: "Multitasking was thus delayed in America for a decade by the IBM-Microsoft hegemony." See Harold Evans, *They Made America* (New York: Little, Brown, 2004), pp. 402–19. Whether it was Gates or Kildall or Tim Paterson (among other competitors) who "won the race" for marketable PC operating software in the 1980s, it is clear that *this technology would have emerged anyway, in roughly the same time frame, because the available knowledge and the existing computer culture made it feasible and the growing market demand made it profitable.* Neither the knowledge nor the demand that drove the process would have been meaningfully altered or even slowed had Bill Gates never been born. A further note, this one involving public support: Kildall developed a good deal of his work while teaching at the Naval Postgraduate School in Monterey, California, in the early 1970s.

10. He was referring to Galileo's influence (and that of Kepler and Copernicus) on his theories of gravity and motion, but calculus likewise rests on earlier foundations in algebra. We may note, additionally, that sometimes those who get there "first" can retard further advances, as noted above, a charge sometimes levied at the particular operating system that Microsoft's early dominance made so ubiquitous.

11. Harvard economist Martin L. Weitzman has outlined a model for what he calls "recombinant" economic growth. Inspired also by Henri Poincaré's reflections on "mathematical creation," Weitzman attempts to model the way that old ideas are "reconfigured" in alternative ways to make new ideas. What this means for growth theory is the possibility of measuring "fixed-factor augmentation" by "recombinant knowledge," thus providing the basis for an "idea-based growth model." Compared to other factors, such as natural resources, the production of knowledge must be modeled differently, Weitzman argues. "New ideas arise out of existing ideas in some kind of cumulative interactive process that intuitively seems somewhat different from prospecting for petroleum," resting rather on a "pattern-fitting or combinatoric feel." Our ability to "generate new ideas" is not the key to long-term growth. Rather, "our abilities to process to fruition an ever-increasing abundance of potentially fruitful ideas" is the key, Weitzman concludes. See Martin L. Weitzman,

"Recombinant Growth," *Quarterly Journal of Economics* 113, no. 2 (May 1998), pp. 331–60.

12. Geoffrey Hodgson, "Knowledge at Work: Some Neoliberal Anachronisms," *Review of Social Economy* 63, no. 4 (December 2005).

13. Joel B. Slemrod, ed., *Does Atlas Shrug: The Economic Consequences of Taxing the Rich* (Cambridge, MA: Harvard University Press, 2000), p. 3.

14. For estimates of the last three decades see Andrew Balls, "Productivity Growth and Employment," *NBER Digest*, November 2005. For estimate of the 1950s, see Slemrod, *Does Atlas Shrug*, p. 3.

15. Slemrod, *Does Atlas Shrug*, p. 3.

16. OECD Productivity database, September 2006, available online at www.oecd.org/topicstatsportal/0,2647,en_2825_30453906_1_1_1_1_1,00 .html (accessed March 12, 2007). Between 1995 and 2004, U.S. GDP per hour increased on average 2.4 percent per year; the European average was 1.5 percent per year.

17. "Labour Productivity Growth—Data: GDP, Annual Hours Worked, Total Employment, Total Hours Worked, GDP per Hour Worked," OECD Productivity Database. For a recent review of comparative trends, see Bart van Ark, Mary O'Mahoney, and Marcel P. Timer, "The Productivity Gap Between Europe and the United States: Trends and Causes," *Journal of Economic Perspectives* 22, no. 1 (Winter 2008), pp. 25–44.

18. Peter H. Lindert, *Growing Public: Social Spending and Economic Growth Since the Eighteenth Century* (Cambridge, UK: Cambridge University Press, 2004), p. 227.

19. In a well-known 1988 debate in the *Journal of Economic Perspectives*, Laurence Kotlikoff calculated that 80 percent of private wealth in the United States is due to personal inheritance. Franco Modigliani found a much lower share of 20 percent. As Jens Beckert summarizes, "this broad divergence is explained by different definitions of what an inheritance is, and what present-day effects on wealth come from an inheritance in the past." Modigliani narrowed the definition of inheritance to actual bequests and large gifts and only their real value in transfer. As noted, Kotlikoff used a more expansive definition that includes all wealth transfers to children after they reach the age of eighteen (including, for example, college tuition paid by parents) as well as the appreciating value of gifts and bequests after transfer. Another study by Denis Kessler and André Masson, using the approach of estimating reductions in private wealth that would result if inheritances were confiscated, concludes that inheritances account for 35–40 percent of private wealth in the United States and France. Summarizing these studies, Beckert (a director at the Max Planck Institute in Germany) concludes that "in spite of this broad range of calculations, it is clear that inheritances account for a substantial share of private wealth." See Jens Beckert, *Inherited Wealth* (Princeton, NJ: Princeton University Press, 2008), pp. 14–15.

20. Jerome M. Segal, *Graceful Simplicity: Toward a Philosophy and Politics of Simple Living* (New York: H. Holt, 1999).

21. Richard B. Freeman, "Solving the New Inequality," *Boston Review*, December 1996/January 1997, p. 14.

22. Bruce Ackerman and Anne Alstott, *The Stakeholder Society* (New Haven: Yale University Press, 1999). Ultimately, Ackerman and Alstott hope the stakeholder grant will become largely self-financing. At the end of life, the $80,000 would be returned to the state.

23. Steve Dubb et al., *Building Wealth: The Asset-Based Approach to Solving Social and Economic Problems* (College Park, MD, and Washington, DC: The Democracy Collaborative and the Aspen Institute, 2005), pp. 55–68. See also John Logue and Jacquelyn Yates, *The Real World of Employee Ownership* (Ithaca, NY: Cornell University Press, 2001), pp. 32–34, 72–109, and 132–57; see especially p. 32 for a discussion of a 1985 General Accounting Office study that is still seen as a benchmark study of the employee stock ownership plan (ESOP) field. Further data on employee ownership productivity can also be found in Joseph Blasi, Douglas Kruse, and Aaron Berstein, *In the Company of Owners* (New York, NY: Basic Books, 2003); see especially pp. 153–57.

24. The National Center for Employee Ownership (NCEO) provides the most up-to-date figures on the extent of ESOPs. See NCEO, *A Statistical Profile of Employee Ownership* (Oakland, CA: NCEO, 2007), www.nceo.org/library/eo_stat.html (accessed January 10, 2008). As of May 2007, the NCEO estimates the number of ESOP companies to be 9,650, with 10.5 million employee owners. For a review of further policies and longer-term strategies, see Gar Alperovitz, *America Beyond Capitalism: Reclaiming Our Wealth, Our Liberty, and Our Democracy* (Hoboken, NJ: John Wiley & Sons, 2005).

25. United for a Fair Economy, "Executive Excess 2005, Defense Contractors Get More Bucks for the Bang, 12th Annual CEO Compensation Survey," August 30, 2005, p. 13, www.faireconomy.org/press/2005/EE2005.pdf. See also United for a Fair Economy, "CEO Pay Charts 1990–2005," www.faireconomy.org/news/ceo_pay_charts.

26. Congressional Budget Office data show that, in 2005, the top 1 percent received 18.1 percent of pretax household income while the bottom 40 percent got only 12.5 percent. Post-tax income was only slightly less unequal: the bottom 40 percent received 14.4 percent while the top 1 percent received 15.6 percent. By 2005 the top 20 percent held a larger share of both pre- and post-tax income than everyone else combined. (For this data, see Jared Bernstein, "Updated CBO Data Reveal Unprecedented Increase in Inequality," Economic Policy Institute, Issue Brief #239, December 13, 2007, www.epi.org/content.cfm/ib239.) Other recent estimates of pretax income for the top 1 percent suggest a range of between 17 percent and 21.5 percent. See Thomas Piketty and Emmanuel Saez, "The Evolution of Top Incomes: A Historical and International Perspective," *American Economic Review* 96, no. 2 (May 2006), p. 201. See tables, particularly table 3, available online at emlab.berkeley.edu/users/saez/TabFigOUPvolume2.xls.

27. Including pension-related assets, the top 1 percent still owns over a third (36.7 percent) of all stocks, mutual funds, and trusts. For wealth num-

bers, see Edward R. Wolff, "Recent Trends in Household Wealth in the United States: Rising Debt and the Middle-Class Squeeze," Levy Economics Institute of Bard College, Working Paper No. 502, June 2007, pp. 11, 26, tables 2, 8. According to Federal Reserve economist Arthur B. Kennickell ("Currents and Undercurrents: Changes in the Distribution of Wealth, 1989–2004," January 30, 2006), in 2004 the bottom half of the U.S. population's direct holdings of publicly traded stocks totaled $21.3 billion. In that year Bill Gates's net worth was $48 billion, most of which comes from Microsoft stock and other investments. See *Forbes*, "The 400 Richest Americans," September 24, 2004, www.forbes.com/2004/09/22/rl04land.html (accessed April 29, 2008).

28. Paul Krugman, "For Richer," *New York Times Magazine*, October 20, 2002, p. 62. Alan Wolfe quoted in Rick Lyman, "Every Four Years, Blue Bloods Put on a Blue Collar," *New York Times*, October 5, 2003, p. D14.

29. Elizabeth Warren and Amelia Warren Tyagi, "What's Hurting the Middle Class," *Boston Review*, September/October 2005, bostonreview.net/BR30.5/warrentyagi.html (accessed March 4, 2008).

30. College Board, *Trends in College Pricing 2007* (Washington, DC: College Board, 2007), p. 10, table 3a; Hal R. Varian, "Burden Growing on Pension Group," *New York Times*, December 16, 2004; Carmen DeNavas-Walt, Bernadette D. Proctor, and Cheryl Hill Lee, *Income, Poverty, and Health Insurance Coverage in the United States: 2006*, U.S. Census Bureau, Current Population Reports, P60-233 (Washington, DC: U.S. GPO, 2007), p. 11.

31. Carmen DeNavas-Walt, Bernadette D. Proctor, and Cheryl Hill Lee, *Income, Poverty and Health Insurance Coverage in the United States: 2004*, U.S. Census Bureau, Current Population Reports, P60-229 (Washington, DC: U.S. GPO, 2005), p. 46, table B-1; Mark Nord, Margaret Andrews, and Steven Carlson, *Household Food Security in the United States 2004*, Economic Research Report 11 (Washington, DC: U.S. Department of Agriculture, 2005); Bryan Hall, "Hunger and Food Insecurity Increase for 5th Straight Year," *Center on Hunger and Poverty Bulletin*, October 2005; Sarah Fass and Nancy K. Cauthen, "Who Are America's Poor Children? The Official Story," National Center for Children in Poverty, Columbia University Mailman School of Public Health, December 2006, p. 206, www.nccp.org/pub_cpt06a.html (accessed April 6, 2007); Arloc Sherman, "African American and Latino Families Face High Rates of Hardship," Center on Budget and Policy Priorities, November 21, 2006; Carmen DeNavas-Walt, Bernadette D. Proctor, and Cheryl Hill Lee, *Income, Poverty, and Health Insurance Coverage in the United States: 2005*, U.S. Census Bureau, Current Population Reports, P60-231 (Washington, DC: U.S. GPO, 2006), p. 25.

32. Seth Shulman, *Owning the Future* (Boston: Houghton Mifflin, 1999), p. 155.

A Note on the Philosophical Argument

1. See David Miller, *Principles of Social Justice* (Cambridge, MA: Harvard University Press, 1999), pp. 61–92, for a useful discussion of popular views of

distributive justice. Miller cites evidence showing that very large majorities in the United States and the United Kingdom favor linking earnings with effort and performance, but that there is also very substantial support (on desert grounds) for narrowing inequalities and in particular increasing the earnings of the lowest-paid workers.

2. See Introduction, pp. 1, 5, for Mokyr's use of the term "free lunch."

3. See Thomas Hodgskin, *The Natural and Artificial Right of Property Contrasted* (Clifton, NJ: Augustus M. Kelley, 1973 [1832]), pp. 29–30.

4. Ibid., pp. 48–49.

5. Anton Menger, *The Right to the Whole Produce of Labour* (New York: Augustus M. Kelley, 1970 [1899]), p. 160.

6. Robert Nozick, *Anarchy, State, and Utopia* (New York: Basic Books, 1974), pp. 149–60.

7. Ibid., pp. 175, 178. In contrast to Nozick's more utilitarian interpretation, Locke's description of "enough and as good" states that private appropriation of resources cannot have the effect of limiting others' access to and enjoyment of the same resources: "Nor was this appropriation of any parcel of Land, by improving it, any prejudice to any other Man, since there was still enough, and as good left; and more than the yet unprovided could use. So that, in effect, there was never the less left for others because of his inclosure for himself." See John Locke, *Two Treatises of Government* (Cambridge, UK: Cambridge University Press, 1988), Second Treatise, chap. 5, sec. 33.

8. Nozick, *Anarchy, State, and Utopia*, p. 177.

9. The alternative of cooperative production—or an efficient cultivation under some system of joint ownership—is not considered by Nozick. As G.A. Cohen has stressed, this assumption—that the only alternative to private property is unproductive common use—sets a very low threshold for meeting the sufficiency proviso of not worsening others' position. See G.A. Cohen, *Self-Ownership, Freedom, and Equality* (Cambridge, UK: Cambridge University Press, 1995), pp. 74–91. Nozick himself argues that, given the (assumed) vast benefits of private property, the sufficiency proviso would likely only apply in extreme situations of resource monopoly such as appropriating the only water hole in a desert full of people (Nozick, *Anarchy, State, and Utopia*, pp. 179–80).

10. Nozick, *Anarchy, State, and Utopia*, p. 231. This statement may possibly reference the colonialism, territorial conquest, and slavery that fueled the rise of Europe and the United States. It might in theory even plausibly justify reparations. Any major transfer program of the kind Nozick appears to allow would have a dramatic nullifying effect, clearly, on the laissez-faire agenda of his philosophy.

11. Cohen, *Self Ownership, Freedom, and Equality*, pp. 116–17.

12. To be clear: Locke views God as the ultimate owner of the self; hence the individual's self-ownership is not without restrictions (e.g., suicide is prohibited).

13. Nozick, *Anarchy, State, and Utopia*, p. 169.

14. Ibid., p. 225.

15. Cohen, *Self-Ownership, Freedom, and Equality*, p. 69. Emphasis added.

16. Michael J. Sandel, *Liberalism and the Limits of Justice* (Cambridge, UK: Cambridge University Press, 1982), pp. 99–100. Sandel's critique, drawing on Rawls, is worth quoting at length here:

> Nozick is prepared to accept that people may not deserve their natural assets, but claims they are entitled to them nonetheless. "If people have X, and their having X (whether or not they deserve to have it) does not violate anyone else's (Lockean) right or entitlement to X, and Y flows from (arises out of, and so on) X by a process that does not itself violate anyone's (Lockean) rights or entitlements, then the person is entitled to Y." But he does not show why this is so, nor is he clear on what precisely the difference between desert and entitlement consists in. Rawls and Feinberg agree that "desert is a *moral* concept in the sense that it is logically prior to and independent of public institutions and their rules." Entitlements, by contrast, are claims that can only arise under the rules or qualifying conditions of institutions already established, what Rawls describes as legitimate expectations founded on social institutions. It is a consequence of this view that, for the purpose of designing or assessing social institutions, people's entitlements, being *derivative* from institutions, are without moral or critical force. Assessing the justice of an institution in the light of what people were entitled to would be like judging the validity of a rule in the light of claims arising under the rule; to recall our earlier discussion, it would be appealing to a standard of appraisal thoroughly implicated in the object of appraisal. It is for this reason that the concept of entitlement cannot provide a first principle of justice. As Rawls explains, it "presupposes the existence of the co-operative scheme, and so is irrelevant to the question whether in the first place the scheme is to be designed in accordance with the difference principle or some other criterion."
>
> Nozick never comes to terms with this difficulty. In making his argument, he explicitly adopts the language of entitlement rather than desert, but does not acknowledge its lesser moral force. In Nozick's usage, the concept of entitlement does the same work as desert, but without its pre-institutional credentials ever being established. He begins with the premise that "people are entitled to their natural assets," and proceeds to argue that they are entitled to the benefits that flow from them. But he never says why people are entitled to their assets in any sense of entitlement strong enough to get the argument going.

17. Thomas Nagel, "Libertarianism Without Foundations," *Yale Law Journal* 85, no. 1 (November 1975), pp. 136–49.

18. In a letter to the financier Robert Morris (December 25, 1783), Franklin wrote: "All the Property that is necessary to a Man, for the Conservation of the Individual and the Propagation of the Species, is his natural Right, which none can justly deprive him of: But all Property superfluous to such purposes

is the Property of the Publick, who, by their Laws, have created it, and who may therefore by other Laws dispose of it, whenever the Welfare of the Publick shall demand such Disposition. He that does not like civil Society on these Terms, let him retire and live among Savages." In *The Founders' Constitution*, ed. Philip B. Kurland and Ralph Lerner, online edition (Chicago: University of Chicago Press, 2000), vol. 1, chap. 16, doc. 12, press-pubs.uchicago.edu/founders/documents/v1ch16s12.html.

19. Nozick, *Anarchy, State, and Utopia*, p. 175. Emphasis in original.

20. Ibid., pp. 198, 219.

21. Nozick might contest the characterization of our knowledge inheritance as "manna from heaven," as opposed to a collection of particular goods that come into the world attached to particular people with particular claims. That view is implausible, however, precisely because so much of the knowledge drawn on in modern production processes is in fact general, unowned, and not attached to any particular person. Consider Nozick's central example of just appropriation—a "medical researcher" who synthesizes a new drug from otherwise widely available chemicals in nature. If the researcher obtains a monopoly on the supply of this new drug, this is legitimate, in Nozick's view, because the sufficiency proviso of not leaving others worse off is not violated (both because the natural materials remain available and because others would not have had the drug at all without the researcher's work); see ibid., p. 181. Nozick simply does not consider the fact that, in creating the drug, the researcher not only appropriated materials from nature but likely depended on knowledge created by others and preserved by society to do so. Moreover, if the knowledge contained in the drug was financed with tax revenues provided by other members of society (as with government funding of pharmaceutical research), these claims will be that much stronger. Finally, as we have seen, the idea that society would not have had the drug had this particular individual not come along is challenged by modern studies of how discoveries, invention, and innovation actually occur. In case after case, the evidence is that when socially developed knowledge reaches a certain point, if one individual does not make the inevitable breakthrough almost certainly another will.

22. Robert A. Dahl, *Dilemmas of Pluralist Democracy: Autonomy vs. Control* (New Haven: Yale University Press, 1982), p. 201.

23. Richard A. Epstein, "Liberty Versus Property? Cracks in the Foundations of Copyright Law," John M. Olin Law and Economics Working Paper No. 204, University of Chicago, April 2004, pp. 7–8.

24. "In light of this commons," Epstein argues, "it is possible to mount a desert-like attack on copyrights, as with other mental activity, by noting that all individuals are constantly subject to a wide range of external influences, which enrich their works." Ibid., p. 28.

25. Ibid., pp. 8–9.

26. Ibid., pp. 8–9. Emphasis added.

27. Richard Posner, *The Problems of Jurisprudence* (Cambridge, MA: Harvard University Press, 1990), p. 345.

28. Frank H. Knight, "The Ethics of Competition," *Quarterly Journal of Economics* 37, no. 4 (August 1923), pp. 598–99. Emphasis added.

29. On the many forms of "commons," see David Bollier, *Public Assets, Private Profits: Reclaiming the American Commons in an Age of Market Enclosure* (Washington, DC: New America Foundation, 2001); and David Bollier, *Silent Theft: The Private Plunder of Our Common Wealth* (New York: Routledge, 2003).

30. For research on the impact of social and cultural advantages in maximizing economic opportunities, see Kenneth Arrow, Samuel Bowles, and Steven Durlauf, eds., *Meritocracy and Economic Inequality* (Princeton, NJ: Princeton University Press, 2000), esp. chaps. 2, 3, 7, and 8. For a particular focus on the positive impact of early childhood investments in disadvantaged communities, see the special report "Life Chances: The Case for Early Investment in Our Kids," *American Prospect*, December 2007. For a revealing ethnographic perspective on how socioeconomic differences affecting parenting and childhood experiences help determine long-term life-chances, see Annette Lareau, *Unequal Childhoods: Class, Race, and Family Life* (Berkeley: University of California Press, 2003). See also, generally, James Lardner and David A. Smith, eds., *Inequality Matters: The Growing Economic Divide in America and Its Poisonous Consequences* (New York: The New Press, 2005).

31. For an introduction to the marginal productivity theory, see Robert F. Dorfman, "Marginal Productivity Theory," in *The New Palgrave: A Dictionary of Economics*, ed. John Eatwell, Murray Milgate, and Peter Newman (London: Macmillan, 1987), vol. 3, pp. 323–25.

32. John Bates Clark, *The Distribution of Wealth: A Theory of Wages, Interest, and Profits* (New York: Macmillan, 1931 [1899]), p. v.

33. Ibid., p. 9.

34. John Bates Clark, *Social Justice Without Socialism* (Boston: Riverside Press, 1914), pp. 35–36.

35. Stigler argued that Clark's indefensible normative judgments led to the widespread belief that neoclassical economics (the analytical system built on marginalist theory) was simply apologetics posing as science. Note Stigler's view that Clark's theory was a "made-to-order foil for the diatribes of Veblen." See George Stigler, *Production and Distribution Theories, 1870–1895* (New York: Macmillan, 1941), p. 297.

36. "The fixed factors exert a causative influence, even when unchanged," John Pullen writes. This and other criticisms are discussed in his working paper "A Linguistic Analysis of the Marginal Productivity Theory of Distribution; or, the Use and Abuse of the Proprietorial 'Of,' " University of New England School of Economics, Working Paper No. 2001–4, February 2001, p. 19, www.une.edu.au/economics/publications/ECONwp01-4.PDF.

37. Walter M. Adriance, "Specific Productivity," *Quarterly Journal of Economics* 29, no. 1 (November 1914), pp. 157, 160.

38. P.T. Bauer, *Equality, the Third World, and Economic Delusion* (Cambridge, MA: Harvard University Press, 1981), p. 12.

39. Ibid., p. 8.

40. Amartya Sen, "Just Deserts," *New York Review of Books*, March 1, 1982.

41. Ibid.

42. John Rawls, *A Theory of Justice* (Oxford: Oxford University Press, 1971), p. 72.

43. Michael J. Sandel, *Liberalism and the Limits of Justice* (Cambridge, UK: Cambridge University Press, 1982), p. 70.

44. Rawls, *Theory of Justice*, pp. 100–101.

45. See John Rawls, *Justice as Fairness: A Restatement*, ed. Erin Kelly (Cambridge, MA: Belknap Press, 2001). We can also distinguish the technological inheritance account from another strand of philosophical liberalism commonly termed "luck egalitarianism." Luck egalitarianism, associated with the writings of Ronald Dworkin, G.A. Cohen, and Richard Arneson, holds that egalitarians should strive to minimize the impact of factors over which individuals have no control on their economic holdings, while at the same time assuring that individuals' economic holdings are "effort sensitive." The thought is that inequalities resulting from initial class position, racial and gender prejudice, or simple bad luck are not morally acceptable, but that inequalities resulting from differences in effort and choices are. The technological inheritance account provided here shares both those moral intuitions, but strongly denies any supposition that actually existing inequalities result primarily from differences in the efforts of persons now alive. On the account offered here, what any one person has is not primarily a result of her own effort (whether it be relatively great or relatively small) but a consequence of living in a wealthy society that has received extraordinarily rich endowments from the past. Consequently, while the technological inheritance view certainly allows for incentives and other mechanisms intended to induce and reward effort, it does not explain differences in economic position by moralistic reference to differences in current effort, nor would it justify excluding persons from sharing in the benefits of that inheritance on the basis of differences in effort. Put another way, while it makes sense to distribute labor market income (earnings) with reference to effort and ability (i.e., via a principle of desert), it also makes sense to distribute the unearned gift of the past according to other principles related to equality. (For a useful discussion of why desert is the most relevant distributive criterion in some cases, equality in others, and need in still others, see Miller, *Principles of Social Justice*.)

46. Stephen Holmes and Cass R. Sunstein, *The Cost of Rights: Why Liberty Depends on Taxes* (New York: W.W. Norton, 1999).

47. Ibid., p. 25.

48. Liam Murphy and Thomas Nagel, *The Myth of Ownership: Taxes and Justice* (New York: Oxford University Press, 2002).

49. Ibid., pp. 8–9.

50. Rawls, *Theory of Justice*, p. 101.

51. Ibid., p. 529.

52. Sandel, *Liberalism and the Limits of Justice*, p. 98. Emphasis added.

53. Ibid., p. 101.

54. Ibid., p. 102.

55. Locke, *Second Treatise of Civil Government*, chap. 5, sec. 26, p. 288.

56. Ibid., chap. 5, sec. 40, p. 296.

57. Some "left-libertarians" have urged a similar critique of labor entitlement and "self-ownership" views, but they have given less systematic attention to issues of knowledge inheritance. See Peter Vallentyne and Hillel Steiner, eds., *Left-Libertarianism and Its Critics: The Contemporary Debate* (London: Palgrave, 2004). See also the discussion in Cohen, *Self-Ownership, Freedom, and Equality*, pp. 102–11. Two other contributions related to the general position here presented are Robin Hahnel, "Economic Justice," *Review of Radical Political Economics* 37, no. 2 (Fall 2004), pp. 131–54; and Robin Hahnel, "Exploitation: A Modern Approach," *Review of Radical Political Economics* 38, no. 2 (Fall 2006), pp. 175–92.

INDEX